THE KINGSLEYS

Other works in the series

BELLOC
by Herbert van Thal

LANDOR
by Herbert van Thal
(*in preparation*)

THE KINGSLEYS

A Biographical Anthology

COMPILED BY
ELSPETH HUXLEY

London
GEORGE ALLEN & UNWIN LTD
RUSKIN HOUSE   MUSEUM STREET

14040
———
920

Printed in Great Britain
in 11 pt Plantin, 1 pt leaded
by W & J Mackay Limited, Chatham

PREFACE

Now and again a hitherto obscure family, for no apparent reason, erupts into fame, only to subside within a generation or two into its normal mediocrity. Such a one was the family of Charles Kingsley, born of sound old landed Cheshire stock. After taking his degree at Cambridge in 1816, Charles found the inheritance of a younger son insufficient to support a family and took refuge, like so many of his kind, in the Church, where he was assured of social esteem, good sport, ample leisure, a small stipend and a large rectory in which to rear a God-fearing family. The lineage of his wife, Mary Lucas, daughter of a judge in Barbados, appears to have been as solid and respectable as his own, but no more remarkable. Of their six children, comfortably reared in rectories in Lincolnshire, Devon and Chelsea, no less than four took to the pen. The eldest, Charles, made the deepest impression on his generation as a preacher, novelist, social reformer and poet. Had he lived a century later he would no doubt have become a famous radio and television personality, called upon to take part in every controversial discussion on the issues of the day. His death was treated almost as a national disaster, and Westminster Abbey was ready to receive his remains.

The youngest brother, Henry, launched himself as a novelist with two or three best-sellers and published nearly twenty books, but their sales steadily declined. In between came George, the dilettante doctor, who travelled incessantly, shot enormous quantities of animals and enjoyed a reputation as contributor to magazines, conversationalist, ethnologist and scholar on the basis of a very slender *oeuvre*. The fourth writer was Charlotte, who married the Rev. Chantor and wrote two novels, both successful in their day. The remaining two sons died before they had a chance to show the direction in which their talents lay.

Two members of the following generation carried on the literary tradition: Charles' daughter Mary St Leger, born in 1852, who under the name of Lucas Malet published a number of romantic novels highly popular with subscribers to the circulating libraries; and Mary, born in 1862, until the age of thirty the slave and amanuensis of her selfish, erratic but brilliant father George. On her parents' death she set out alone to collect specimens of plants

7

and fish in that part of West Africa then called the White Man's Grave. Only two books resulted from her astonishing solitary travels among cannibals, savages and 'palm oil ruffians', but they were outstanding, and her death at thirty-eight while nursing Boer prisoners at the Cape was a tragedy. Judged by modern rather than Victorian standards she was, as a writer, perhaps the greatest Kingsley of them all.

The word great, however, is too strong an adjective to be applied to any of the writing Kingsleys. Of the three brothers represented in this anthology, Henry was the only professional in that his primary aim was to tell a story, and also he earned his living by his pen. He has no place among the giants, but was a competent teller of tales and brought to their telling the gusto and gaiety all the Kingsleys commanded. George was a writer of sketches rather than a maker of books. Charles was by far the most versatile, serious, influential and prolific of the three. Twenty-eight volumes were needed to encompass his *Collected Works*, written between 1848 and 1872 and published by Macmillan between 1880 and 1885.

These included sermons, scientific and historical essays, pamphlets on social reform, historical romances, contemporary novels, poems, and a great output of letters. His energies were prodigious, his passions strong, his powers of expression uninhibited, his sense of history vivid, his heart tender and always in the right place. From the Queen at Windsor to the rustic poachers of Hampshire everyone loved and respected Charles Kingsley—with the exception, perhaps, of the High Churchmen he persistently lambasted—although he was not taken altogether seriously by the scholars he loved to meet and correspond with.

About his achievements he was genuinely modest. He thought of himself as a scientist manqué—he adopted Darwinism enthusiastically from the first, and believed the primary task to which God had called him was to further social reform and his country's greatness. A true romantic, it might be said that he regarded his pen as a sword to be drawn in such knightly causes as slaying the dragons of social injustice which stalked the land, attacking the doctrine of celibacy, and celebrating the glories of his English blood and state in which he fervently believed. He was a deeply patriotic man.

The key both to his popularity during his lifetime, and to the position into which his reputation has settled since, lies perhaps in that he so perfectly expressed and epitomized the emotions, the trends, the prejudices and the aspirations of his times. Insofar as such a being could exist, he was the archetypal Victorian, who was not at all the stuffy and complacent sort of creature he has often been represented to be. Charles Kingsley was racked by doubts, torn by emotions, moved by visions, sustained by hopes and spurred on by all these impulses to bouts of creativity, linked by periods of hard slogging at his duties and chores. His domestic life was happy and serene, but what was then called the seamy side of life was only too familiar to him. He believed in the social order, but sought constantly to bring men to their duty of loving their neighbours, living up to their responsibilities and succouring the poor. He wrote sentimental ballads, venerated little children, rushed hotly into theological controversy and extolled the men of Devon—all the minor as well as the major Victorian traits were there. In many directions, such as the position of women, he was in advance of his time. He was no intellectual. It is as a social reformer, a spinner of yarns and an engaging and at times eccentric figure that he will be remembered, rather than as a poet or serious novelist. Probably this assessment would have contented him. 'Be good, sweet maid, and let who will be clever'—advice to grown men no less than to maidens, and advice which by and large he followed with a stout heart, a generous nature and a ready pen.

CONTENTS

CONTENTS

PART ONE

CHARLES KINGSLEY
1819-75

I

Charles Kingsley

The Kingsleys came from that class of landless, therefore impoverished, country gentry that in the nineteenth century supplied England's armed forces with the bulk of their officers and her country parishes with most of their clergy. Charles was born in 1819—the same year as Queen Victoria—at Holne in Devon where his father was the curate, one of a family of five sons and one daughter. It was Devon that nourished his imagination as a writer, and drew him back to calm his mind and rest his body when, as was so often to happen, he worked himself into a state of mental and physical exhaustion.

He was a shy, rather solitary child with a stutter, happiest when searching beaches for shells and hedgerows for wild flowers. While he was a pupil at Clifton preparatory school the Chartist riots of 1831 devastated the city of Bristol and impressed upon him a lasting dread of mob violence. In 1836 the family moved to Chelsea. Charles read classics at King's College and two years later went up to Magdalene College at Cambridge where he extended his studies to ornithology and magic, became a confirmed tobacco-addict, and suffered from religious doubts which imparted an 'unsatisfied hungering look' to his gaunt and craggy features. 'I was very idle—and very sinful' he confessed, 'in my first year.' But he recovered his faith, 'refused hunting and driving, and made a solemn vow against cards'. All his energies, he resolved, would now 'be devoted utterly, I hope, to the service of God'. Formidable, indeed, were these energies. 'I hardly find my ten miles a day sufficient exercise to keep me healthy, and very often get a walk in the evening afterwards' he wrote to his mother; and he once walked from London to Cambridge, fifty-two miles, in a day. Already he had embraced the cult of physical fitness. 'My panacea for stupidity and "over-mentation" is a day in a roaring Fen wind.' Far from neglecting his studies, he was reading for seven or eight hours a day, and graduated in 1841 with a first in classics and senior optime in mathematics.

Charles was just twenty, and in his second year at Cambridge when, on 6 July 1839, in a garden at Checkendon, he met a dark-haired girl six years his senior, and fell in love at first sight—'eye-wedlock' as he described it. Their love was to become the core of his life and to endure until death parted them after thirty-six years. Fanny Grenfell, one of eleven sisters, came of a well-to-do and well-connected family and had a lively intelligence. Her family opposed her marriage to this penniless, doubt-tormented and somewhat uncouth undergraduate so much younger than Fanny, and they had to wait five years, sustained by a copious correspondence, before their marriage in January 1844.

On leaving Cambridge, Charles was ordained and became curate of Eversley in Hampshire where he was to remain, apart from a short interlude in Dorset, for the rest of his life. Throughout that life, three loves sustained him: for God, for Fanny, and for nature. The beauties of the natural world moved his spirit, while its mysteries challenged his mind; in fact he often declared that he was at heart a scientist, and was never happier than when classifying the creatures of the seashore or collecting plants from mountain-tops. Eversley offered no such stimulants to his imagination but had its quieter rural joys.

Letter to Fanny from Eversley
July 1842

Today it is hotter than yesterday, if possible, so I wandered out into the fields, and have been passing the morning in a lonely woodland bath—a little stream that trickles off the moor—with the hum of bees, and the sleepy song of birds around me, and the feeling of the density of life in the myriads of insects and flowers strong upon me, drinking in all the forms of beauty which lie in the leaves and pebbles, and mossy nooks of damp tree roots, and all the lowly intricacies of nature which no one stoops to see; and while eye and ear were possessed with the feeling that all had a meaning—all was a type—a language—which we should know in heaven, the intellect was not dreaming asleep. . . . And over all, as the cool water trickled on, hovered the delicious sense of childhood, and simplicity, and purity, and peace, which every temporary return to nature gives. A woodland bath to me always brings thoughts of Paradise. I know not whether they are foretastes of the simple bliss that shall be in the renovated earth, or whether they are back glimpses into the former age when we wandered—do you remember—beside the ocean of eternal love!

The young curate lived a solitary and spartan life, and the beauties of nature did not always make up for intellectual starvation and the absence of friends.

Letter to Peter (later Canon) Wood from Eversley
October 1842

PETER! Whether in the glaring saloons of Almack's, or making love in the equestrian stateliness of the park; whether breakfasting at one, or going to bed at three, thou art still Peter, the beloved of my youth, the staff of my academic days, the regret of my parochial retirement! Peter—I am alone! Around me are the everlasting hills, the everlasting bores of the country! My parish is peculiar for nothing beyond the want of houses and abundance of peat bogs; my parishioners remarkable only for aversion to education, and a predilection for fat bacon. I am wasting my sweetness on the desert air—I say my sweetness, for I have given up smoking, and smell no more. Oh Peter, Peter, come down and see me! Oh that I could behold your head towering above the fir-trees that surround my lonely dwelling! Take pity on me! I am 'like a kitten in the wash-house copper with the lid on'! And, Peter, prevail upon some of your friends here to give me a day's trout fishing, for my hand is getting out of practice. But, Peter, I am, considering the oscillations and perplex circumgurgitations of this piecemeal world, an improved man. I am much more happy, much more comfortable, reading, thinking, doing my duty—much more than ever I did before in my life. Therefore I am not discontented with my situation, or regretful that I buried myself in a country curacy, like the girl who shut herself up in a box on her wedding night. And my lamentations are not general (for I do not want an inundation of the froth and tidewash of Babylon the Great) but particular, being solely excited by want of thee, oh Peter, who art very pleasant to me, and wouldst be more so if thou wouldst come and eat my mutton, and drink my wine, and admire my sermons, some Sunday at Eversley. Your faithful friend, Boanerges Roar-at-the Clods.

'You think too much!' he admonished his Fanny, in one of the many letters they exchanged during their long engagement when they seldom met. 'Never give way to reveries. Have always some employment in your hands . . .' He always had some in his. The best times were when they held a rod, for he had always been an ardent fisherman, and on moving to the curacy of Pimperne, in Dorset, was introduced to chalk streams.

Letter from Durweston, Dorset
March 1844

I spent a delightful day yesterday. Conceive my pleasure at finding myself in Bemerton, George Herbert's parish, and seeing his house and church, and fishing in the very meadows, where he, and Dr Donne, and Isaac Walton, may have fished before me. I killed several trout and a brace of grayling, about three-quarters of a pound each—a fish quite new to me, smelling just like cucumbers. The dazzling chalk-wolds sleeping in the sun, the clear river rushing and boiling down in one ever-sliding sheet of transparent silver, the birds bursting into song, the mating and toying in every hedgerow—everything stirred with the gleam of God's eyes, when 'he reneweth the face of the earth.' I had many happy thoughts; but I am very lonely . . . I never was before in a chalk forest. It is very peculiar, and most beautiful; I like it better than Devon and Welsh moorland—it is more simple, and yet not so severe—more tender in its soft greys and greens, yet quite as sublime in the vast unbroken curves and sweeps of the open downs. I cannot express myself. I should like to preach a sermon on chalk downs and another on chalk streams. They are so *purely* beautiful.

While still an undergraduate, Charles had embarked upon a life of St Elizabeth of Hungary intended as a wedding present to his future bride, who at that time had strong Tractarian leanings and was even flirting with the idea of taking the veil. A life-long detestation of celi-

18

bacy and of asceticism carried to extremes found expression in this tale exemplifying 'the struggle between healthy affection, and the Manichean contempt with which a celibate clergy would have all men regard the name of husband, wife, and parent'. He decided to reshape his work into a drama in blank verse, and it was not until January 1848, that The Saint's Tragedy, with a preface by his life-long friend Frederick Denison Maurice, and illustrations by himself, appeared under the imprint of John Parker.

The story is that of Elizabeth, daughter of the King of Hungary, who married Lewis, Landgrave of Thuringia, an amiable but weak character ruled by his bride. She in turn is ruled by Conrad of Marpurg, a stern Savonarola-like monk bent on exterminating heresies and mortifying the flesh of everyone in sight. Lewis dies while on the Fifth Crusade (1218–21) leaving Elizabeth with three young children, whom Conrad directs her to renounce. She gives everything to the poor until Conrad forbids her even the solace of dispensing charity; barefoot, ragged and hungry, she succours lepers and idiots until she dies of emaciation in a hovel, and the arrogant monk is torn to pieces by a mob revenging his puritanical excesses.

Charles thought that the forthright speech of his hungry medieval peasants and rough barons would shock his readers. By an irony which often overtakes writers, it was not for his social messages concerning the evils of poverty, privilege and celibacy that his drama became known, but for the sentimental little ballad 'O! That we two were Maying', which was set to music by Hullah and added to the repertoire of every well-bred young lady who brought her music to a genteel soirée.

The first extract is a short scene at the marriage feast of Lewis and Elizabeth: then follows Elizabeth's dedication of her newborn baby to God, and finally an exchange with Conrad after she has obeyed his command to renounce all carnal pleasures, including those of bringing up her own family.

From
The Saint's Tragedy

The bridal feast. Elizabeth, Lewis, Sophia and company seated at the dias table. Court Minstrel and Fool sitting at the dias steps.

Min.

How gaily smile the heavens,
The light winds whisper gay;
For royal birth and knightly worth
Are knit to one today.

Fool (Drowning
his voice)

So we'll flatter them up, and we'll cocker
    them up
Till we turn young brains;
And pamper the brach till we make her a
    wolf,
And get bit by the legs for our pains.

Monks
(Chanting without)

A fastu et superbia
   Domine libera nos.

Min.

'Neath sandal red and samite
Are knights and ladies set;
The henchmen tall stride through the hall,
The board with wine is wet.

Fool

Oh! merrily growls the starving hind,
At my full skin;
And merrily howl wolf, wind and owl,
While I lie warm within.

Monks

A luxu et avaritia
   Domine libera nos.

Min.

Hark! from the bridal bower
Rings out the bridesmaid's song;
''Tis the mystic hour of an untried power,
The bride she tarries long.'

For she's schooling herself and she's steeling
    herself
Against the dreary day
When she'll pine and sigh from her lattice
    high
For the knight that's far away.

Monks

A carnis illectamentis
   Domine libera nos.

20

CHARLES KINGSLEY

Min.	Blest maid! fresh roses o'er thee The careless years shall fling; While days and nights shall new delights To sense and fancy bring.
Fool	Satins and silks, and feathers and lace, Will gild life's pill; In jewels and gold folks cannot grow old, Fine ladies will never fall ill.
Monks	*A vanitatibus saeculi* *Domine libera nos.*

A rocky path leading to a mountain chapel. Elizabeth enters, meanly clad, carrying her newborn infant.

Deep in the warm vale the village is sleeping,
Sleeping the firs on the bleak rock above;
Nought wakes, save grateful hearts, silently creeping
Up to the Lord in the might of their love.

What Thou has given me, Lord, here I bring Thee,
Odour, and light, and the magic of gold;
Feet which must follow Thee, lips which must sing Thee,
Limbs which must ache for Thee ere they grow old.

What Thou has given me, Lord, here I tender,
Life of my own life, the fruit of my love;
Take him, yet leave him me, till I shall render
Count of the precious charge, kneeling above.

Elizabeth has resolved to take the veil and renounce her children. Laying her hand on the altar, she declaims:

Elizabeth: All wordly goods and wealth, which once I loved,
I do now count but dross; and my beloved,
The children of my womb, I now regard
As if they were another's. God is my witness.
My pride is to despise myself; my joy
All insults, sneers, and slanders of mankind;
No creature now I love, but God alone.
Oh! to be clear, clear, clear, of all but Him!

Lo, here I strip me of my earthly helps—
  (Tearing off her clothes)
Naked and barefoot through the world to follow
My naked Lord—And for my filthy self—
Conrad: Stop, Madam—
Elizabeth: Why so, sir?
Conrad: Upon thine oath!
Thy wealth is God's, not thine.—How darest renounce
The trust He lays on thee? I do command thee,
Being, as Aaron, in God's stead, to keep it
Inviolate, for the Church and thine needs.
Elizabeth: Be it so—I have no part nor lot in't—
There—I have spoken.
Abess: Oh, noble soul! Which neither gold, no love,
Nor scorn can bend!
Gerard: And think what pure devotions,
What holy prayers must they have been, whose guerdon
In such a flood of grace!

II

Poems from Germany
1851

Back at Eversley in the bosom of his family, consisting of Fanny and his two eldest children Rose and Maurice, life for Charles might hold less controversy but it was no less strenuous. In a letter to Tom Hughes he described a single day. 'Up at five to see a dying man . . . was from 5.30–6.30 with the most dreadful case of agony—insensible to me, but not to his pain. Came home, got a wash and a pipe, and away to him again at eight. . . . Fished all morning in a roaring N.E. gale, with the dreadful agonized face between me and the river, pondering on the mystery. Killed eight on March Brown. Came off the water at 3.30. Found my man alive and, thank God, quiet.' *Then an Archdeacon's meeting*—'speechifying and shop'—*and home at 10.30 to write letters.* 'So goes one's day. All manner of incongruous things to do, and the very incongruity keeps one beany and jolly.'

All the same he needed a rest and went to Germany with his parents and his brother Henry. Thackeray's daughter Anne, a travelling companion, found him 'a fine, honest, go-ahead fellow who charges a subject heartily' *and remarked on his brave, blue, honest eyes. The Rhineland enchanted him with its wild flowers and trees and especially its great variety of butterflies. He had started work on his next novel but he preferred writing poetry. To John Ludlow he explained:*

'There is no denying it, I do feel a different being when I get into metre—I feel like an otter in the water, instead of an otter ashore. He can run fast enough ashore, and keep the hounds at a tearing gallop, as my legs found this spring in Snowdonia, but when he takes water, then indeed he becomes beautiful, full of divine grace and freedom, and exuberance of power. When I have done Hypatia I will write no more novels. I will write poetry . . .'

As with his prose, he took great pains to get the details accurate and careful observation of nature always underlay his images and descriptions. Writing again to Ludlow, he quoted some lines from a poem he had just written—Santa Maura, *'the deepest and clearest thing I have yet done'*—*which described an osprey's strike.*

Stunning with terrible heel the life of the brain in the blind head. Mind the 'terrible heel'. That is right, a hawk strikes with his heel, and afterwards grips with his whole foot. A fish or duck killed by a hawk is always scored up the neck and hind head; sometimes ripped up right along the back. If you'll consider: striking his prey at immense speed from behind, he couldn't drive his front claws in. The 'dark-eyebrowed' is Homer's 'melanophrus', and is the thing that struck me as most significant in a large osprey which I came upon at Issthal. For the same reason, doubt not, 'the wind rattling in his pinions'. A falcon does not, as the herd think, rush silently down head-foremost, but drives himself noiselessly down heels foremost by a succession of preternatural flaps, the philosophy of which I could never make out. A gull does the same, though he strikes with his beak when he wants to force himself under water; anything atop he takes as an owl does, by sliding down—or not quite—for an owl's silent fall is more mysterious still. He catches with his beak, and then takes the mouse out of his beak with his hand, like a Christian . . .

From Germany a number of verses found their way back to Fanny, among them one he called A Thought From The Rhine

> I heard an eagle crying all alone
> Above the vineyards through the summer night,
> Among the skeletons of robber towers:
> Because the ancient eyrie of his race
> Was trenched and walled by busy-handed men;
> All his forest-chace and woodland wild,
> Wherefrom he fed his young with hare and roe,
> Were trim with grapes which swelled from hour to hour,
> And tossed their golden tendrils to the sun
> For joy at their own riches:—So, I thought,
> The great devourers of the earth shall sit,
> Idle and impotent, they know not why,
> Down-staring from their barren height of state
> On nations grown too wise to slay and slave,

POEMS FROM GERMANY

The puppets of the few; while peaceful lore
And fellow-help make glad the heart of earth,
With wonders which they fear and hate, as he,
The Eagle, hates the vineyard slopes below.

III

The Three Fishers
1851

*Charles at this time was much under the influence of F. D. Maurice,
later Professor of English Literature and Modern History at King's
College, who was filling Lincoln's Inn Chapel every Sunday with sermons in which he expounded the doctrines of Christian Socialism.
When, immediately after the Chartist debacle and together with the
parson-barrister John Ludlow, the scientist Charles Mansfield, and
others, Maurice launched a magazine called* Politics for the People,
*Charles became assistant editor and a regular contributor under the
name of Parson Lot. He incurred the further displeasure of the Establishment by announcing at a meeting of intellectual sympathizers with
the Chartists: 'My only quarrel with the Charter is, it does not go far
enough in reform.'* Politics for the People *lasted only from May until
July 1848, but won some notoriety for Charles.*

*In June 1851, he preached by invitation a fiery sermon at St John's
Church, Fitzroy Square, on 'the message of the Church to labouring
men'. It was, he said, the business of a Christian priest to preach
'liberty, equality, and brotherhood in the fullest, deepest, widest, sim-
plest meaning of these three terms'. He went on to attack the system of
accumulating property, especially land, in the hands of a few and the
reduction of many almost to the status of serfs. Before he could deliver
the blessing, the vicar of the church rose to his feet to repudiate his
guest's preaching. An uproar was avoided by Kingsley's calm and
dignified withdrawal, but he was far from calm within. Returning to
Eversley he paced the floor all night and took refuge in his two
anodynes—composing poetry and remembering Devon.*

The Three Fishers

Three fishers went sailing away to the West,
  Away to the West as the sun went down;
Each thought on the woman who loved him the best,
  And the children stood watching them out of the town;
  For men must work and women must weep,
  And there's little to earn, and many to keep,
    Though the harbour bar be moaning.

Three wives sat up in the lighthouse tower,
  And they trimmed the lamps as the sun went down;
They looked at the squall, and they looked at the shower,
  And the night-rack came rolling up ragged and brown;
  But men must work, and women must weep,
  Though storms be sudden, and waters deep,
    And the harbour bar be moaning.

Three corpses lay out on the shining sand,
  In the morning gleam as the tide went down,
And the women are weeping and wringing their hands
  For those who will never come home to the town;
  For men must work, and women must weep,
  And the sooner it's over, the sooner to sleep;
    And goodbye to the bar and its moaning.

IV

Yeast

1851

In 1844, the rector of Eversley absconded, and Sir John Cope, a fox-hunting landlord and five-bottle man, bestowed the living upon the former curate who, after his move to Pimperne, had married his Fanny. The young couple found their first living in a sorry state. The church was bare and dilapidated, the rectory damp, insanitary and leaking, and the parishioners either engaged in smuggling and poaching or sunk in the lethargy of the half-starved, ignorant and ignored. There was no school, no provision for the sick, and the housing was abominable.

Charles took to carrying an auger on his pastoral visits in order to bore holes in walls of stinking sick-rooms to let in a little fresh air. He tramped or rode about his parish which was 'like a dachshund', he wrote, 'all at the ends and very little in the middle', until he knew the occupants of every hovel. He helped farmers thresh their wheat, rounded up the children for instruction in a ten-foot-square shed, and organized a time-table for himself and Fanny starting with early prayers and ending, after their daylong labours, with reading and drawing 'to feed the intellect'. As companions there was Victor the dachshund, Puff the mare, a family of running toads in the garden, a pair of sand-wasps breeding in a window-sill and a 'favourite slow-worm' in the churchyard. One of Charles' more endearing traits was a firm belief in an after-life for animals.

The refusal of Sir John Cope, busy with his hounds, gaming and claret, to lay out a penny on rectory repairs stimulated both the young rector's urge to write, and his growing awareness of the shocking conditions in which nine out of ten of his fellow-countrymen, and supposedly fellow-Christians, had to pass their lives. He became anti-landlord, pro-Chartist and, in the eyes of the Establishment, a dangerous, hot-headed radical: a stigma which for twenty-five years blocked any form of preferment, and kept him forever from the bishopric for which his abilities, energy, eloquence and sincerity so clearly befitted him.

28

YEAST

As soon as The Saint's Tragedy *was published, he asked John Parker of* Fraser's Magazine *for hack-work to help pay the builders, and had several articles accepted. Then he set to work on* Yeast, *his first novel, in which Sir John Cope (somewhat softened) appeared as squire Lavington, himself as Lancelot Smith the rich young seeker-after-truth, his Fanny as Argemone, the squire's pure but argumentative daughter, and his downtrodden parishioners as themselves, with the saintly gamekeeper Paul Tregarva as their spokesman. It was frankly a propaganda novel, with the misery of the rural poor and the selfishness of landlords as its main theme. He also returned to his attack on celibacy, 'Mari-idolatory' and the perverted (in his view) practices of Rome.*

Yeast *was serialized anonymously in 1848, and offended so many readers of* Fraser's Magazine *that the editor implored the author to shorten it. In 1851 it appeared in book form and won praise from critics such as John Ludlow, one of the founders of Christian Socialism, who wrote to Charles 'it is easy for you to become the greatest novelist of the age'. On the whole, however, it was badly received. 'It was written with his heart's blood,' Fanny wrote; and, of his books, it remained her favourite; she wished a copy to be buried in her grave.*

The novel's didactic dough is leavened by descriptions of sport and the countryside which always brought out the best in Charles' writing. The first extract is from the opening chapter. A wounded officer reading it in hospital in Scutari was said to have vowed that, if he recovered, he would hear the clergyman-author preach; he lived to become a regular member of the Eversley congregation. The second extract is a ballad supposedly written by Tregarva which, when it came to the notice of squire Lavington, brought on a fit of apoplexy, and the gamekeeper's instant dismissal.

The weather that day, the first day Lancelot ever saw his beloved, was truly national. A silent, dim, distantless, steaming, rotting day in March. The last brown oak-leaf which had stood out the winter's frost, spun and quivered plump down, and then lay; as if ashamed to have broken for a moment the ghastly stillness, like an awkward guest at a great dumb dinner-party. A cold suck of wind just proved its existence, by toothaches on the north side of all faces. The spiders having been weather-bewitched the night before, had unanimously agreed to cover every brake and briar with gossamer-cradles, and never a fly to be caught in them; like Manchester cotton-spinners glutting the markets in the teeth of 'no-demand'. The steam drawled out of the dank turf, and reeked off the flanks and nostrils of the shivering horses, and clung with clammy paws to frosted hats and dripping boughs.—A soulless, skyless, catarrhal day, as if that bustling dowager, old mother Earth—what with match-making in spring, and *fêtes champêtres* in summer, and dinner-giving in autumn—was fairly worn out, and put to bed with the influenza, under wet blankets and the cold-water cure.

There sat Lancelot by the cover-side, his knees aching with cold and wet, thanking his stars that he was not one of the whippers-in who were lashing about in the dripping cover, laying up for themselves, in catering for the amusement of their betters, a probable old age of bed-ridden torture, in the form of rheumatic gout. Not that he was at all happy—indeed, he had no reason to be so; for, first, the hounds would not find; next, he had left half-finished at home a review article on the Silurian System, which he had solemnly promised an abject and beseeching editor to send to post that night; next, he was on the windward side of the cover, and dare not light a cigar; and lastly, his mucous membrane in general was not in the happiest condition, seeing that he had been dining the evening before with Mr Vaurien of Rottenpalings, a young gentleman of a convivial and melodious turn of mind, who sang—and played also —as singing men are wont—in more senses than one, and had 'ladies and gentlemen' down from town to stay with him; and they sang and played too; and so somehow between vingt-un and champagne-punch, Lancelot had not arrived home till seven o'clock that morning, and was in a fit state to appreciate the feelings of our grandfathers, when, after the third bottle of port, they used to put the black silk tights into their pockets, slip on the leathers and boots, and ride the crop-tailed hack thirty miles on a winter's night, to meet the hounds in the next county by ten in the morning. They are 'gone down to Hades, even many stalwart souls of heroes,' with John Warde of Squerries at their head—the fathers of the men who conquered at Waterloo; and we their degenerate grandsons are left instead, with puny arms, and polished leather boots, and a considerable taint of hereditary disease, to sit in club-houses, and celebrate the progress of the species.

Whether Lancelot or his horse, under these depressing circumstances, fell asleep; or whether thoughts pertaining to such a life, and its fitness for a clever and ardent young fellow in the nineteenth century, became gradually too painful, and had to be peremptorily shaken off, this deponent sayeth not; but certainly, after five-and-thirty minutes of idleness and shivering, Lancelot opened his eyes with a sudden start, and struck spurs into his hunter without due cause shown; whereat Shiver-the-timbers, who was no Griselda in temper—(Lancelot had bought him out of the Pytchley for half his value, as unrideably vicious, when he had killed a groom, and fallen backwards on a rough-rider, the first season he came up from Horn-castle)—responded by a furious kick or two, threw his head up, put his foot in a drain, pitching Lancelot unawares shamefully on the pommel of his saddle. A certain fatality, by-the-bye, had lately attended all Lancelot's efforts to shine; he never bought a new coat without tearing it mysteriously next day, or tried to make a joke without bursting out coughing in the middle . . . and now the whole field were looking on at his mishap; between disgust and the start he turned almost sick, and felt the blood rush into his cheeks and forehead as he heard a shout of coarse jovial laughter burst out close to him, and the old master of the hounds, Squire Lavington, roared aloud—

'A pretty sportsman you are, Mr Smith, to fall asleep by the cover-side and let your horse down—and your pockets, too! What's that book on the ground? Sapping and studying still? I let nobody come out with my hounds with their pocket full of learning. Hand it up here, Tom; we'll see what it is. French, as I am no scholar! Translate for us, Colonel Bracebridge!'

And, amid shouts of laughter, the gay Guardsman read out,—

'St Francis de Sales: *Introduction to a Devout Life.*'

Poor Lancelot! Wishing himself fathoms underground, ashamed of his book, still more ashamed of himself for his shame, he had to sit there ten physical seconds, or spiritual years, while the colonel solemnly returned him the book, complimenting him on the proofs of its purifying influence which he had given the night before, in helping to throw the turn-pike-gate into the river.

But 'all things do end' and so did this; and the silence of the hounds also; and a faint but knowing whimper drove St Francis out of all heads, and Lancelot began to stalk slowly with a dozen horsemen up the wood-ride, to a fitful accompaniment of wandering hound-music, where the choristers were as invisible as nightingales among the thick cover. And hark! just as the book was returned to his pocket, the sweet hubbub suddenly crashed out into one jubilant shriek, and then swept away fainter and fainter among the trees. The walk became a trot—then a canter. Then a faint melancholy shout at a distance, answered by a 'Stole away!' from the fields; a doleful 'toot' of the horn; the dull thunder of many horsehoofs rolling along the further woodside. Then red coats, flashing like sparks of fire across the grey gap of mist at the ride's-mouth; then a whipper in, bringing up a belated hound, burst into the pathway, smashing and plunging, with shut eyes, through ash-saplings and hassock grass; then a fat farmer, sedulously pounding through the mud, was overtaken and bespattered in spite of all his struggles;— until the line streamed out into the wide rushy pasture, starting up pewits and curlews, as horsemen poured in from every side, and cunning old farmers rode off at inexplicable angles to some well-known haunts of pug: and right ahead, chiming and jangling sweet madness, and dappled pack glanced and wavered through the veil of soft grey mist.

'What's the use of this hurry?' growled Lancelot. 'They will all be back again. I never have the luck to see a run.'

But no; on and on—down the wind and down the vale; and the canter became a gallop, and the gallop a long straining stride; and a hundred horse-hoofs crackled like flame among the stubbles, and thundered fetlock-deep along the heavy meadows; and every fence thinned the cavalcade, till the madness began to stir all bloods, and with grim earnest silent faces, the initiated few settled themselves to their work, and with the colonel and Lancelot at their head, 'took their pleasure sadly, after the manner of their nation', as old Froissart has it.

Thorough bush, thorough briar,
Thorough park, through pale;

till the rolling grasslands spread out into flat black open fallows, crossed with grassy baulks, and here and there a long melancholy line of tall elms, while before them the high chalk ridges gleamed above the mist like a vast wall of emerald enamelled with snow, and the winding river glittering at their feet.

'A polite fox!' observed the colonel. 'He's leading the squire straight home to Whitford, just in time for dinner.'

They crossed the stream, passed the Priory shrubberies, leapt the gate into the park, and then onward and upward, called by the unseen Ariel's music before them.—Up, into the hills; past white crumbling chalk-pits, fringed with feathered juniper and tottering ashes, their floors strewn with knolls of fallen soil and vegetation, like wooded islets in a sea of milk.—Up, between steep ridges of turf, crested with black fir-woods and silver beech, and here and there a huge yew standing out alone, the advanced sentry of the forest, with its luscious fret-work of green velvet, like a mountain of Gothic spires and pinnacles, all glittering and steaming as the sun drank up the dew-drops. The lark sprang upwards into song, and called merrily to the new-opened sunbeams, while the wreaths and flakes of mist lingered reluctantly about the hollows, and clung with dewy fingers to every knoll and belt of pine.—Up, into the labyrinthine bosom of the hills,—but who can describe them? Is not all nature indescribable? every leaf infinite and transcendental? How much more those mighty downs, with their enormous sheets of spotless turf, where the dizzy eye loses all standard of size and distance before the awful simplicity, the delicate vastness, of these grand curves and swells, soft as the outlines of a Greek Venus, as if the great goddess-mother Hertha had laid herself down among the hills to sleep, her Titan limbs wrapt in a thin veil of silvery green.

Up, to a vast amphitheatre of sward, whose walls banked out the narrow sky above. And here, in the focus of the huge ring, an object appeared which stirred strange melancholy in Lancelot,—a little chapel, ivy-grown, girded with a few yews, and elders, and grassy graves. A climbing rose over the porch, and iron railings round the churchyard, told of human care; and from the graveyard itself burst up one of those noble springs known as winterbournes in the chalk ranges, which, awakened in autumn from the abysses to which it had shrunk during the summer's drought, was hurrying down upon its six months course, a broad sheet of oily silver, over a temporary channel of smooth greensward.

The hounds had checked in the woods behind; now they poured down the hillside, so close together 'that you might have covered them with a sheet', straight for the little chapel.

A saddened tone of feeling spread itself through Lancelot's heart. Here were the everlasting hills around, even as they had grown for countless ages, beneath the still depths of the primeval chalk ocean, in the milky youth of this great English land. And here was he, the insect of a day, fox-hunting upon *them*! He felt ashamed, and more ashamed when the inner voice whispered,—'Fox-hunting is not the shame—thou art the shame. If thou art the insect of a day, it is thy sin that thou art one.'

And his sadness, foolish as it may seem, grew as he watched a brown speck fleet rapidly up the opposite hill, and heard a gay view-halloo burst from the colonel at his side. The chase lost its charm for him the moment the game was seen. Then vanished that mysterious delight of pursuing an invisible object, which gives to hunting and fishing their unutterable and almost spiritual charm; which made Shakespeare a mighty poacher; Davy and Chantrey the patriarchs of fly-fishing; by which the twelve-foot rod is trans-figured into an enchanter's wand, potent over the unseen wonders of the water-world, to 'call up spirits from the vasty deep', which will really 'come if you do call them'—at least, if the conjuration be orthodox—and they there. That spell was broken by the sight of poor wearied pug, his once gracefully-floating brush all draggled and drooping, as he toiled up the sheep-paths towards the open down above.

But Lancelot's sadness reached its crisis, as he met the hounds just outside the churchyard. Another moment—they had leaped the rails; and there they swept round under the grey wall, leaping and yelling, like Berseck fiends among the frowning tombstones, over the cradles of the quiet dead.

Lancelot shuddered—the thing was not wrong—'it was no one's fault'—but there was a ghastly discord in it. Peace and strife, time and eternity—the mad noisy flesh, and the silent immortal spirit— the frivolous game of life's outside show, and the terrible earnest of its inward abysses, jarred together without and within him. He pulled his horse up violently, and stood as if rooted to the place, gazing at he knew not what.

The hounds caught sight of the fox, burst into one frantic shriek of joy—and then a sudden and ghastly stillness, as, mute and breathless, they toiled up the hillside, gaining on their victim at every stride. The patter of the horsehoofs and the rattle of rolling flints died away above. Lancelot looked up, startled at the silence; laughed aloud, he knew not why, and sat, regardless of his pawing and straining horse, still staring at the chapel and the graves.

On a sudden the chapel-door opened, and a figure, timidly yet loftily, stepped out without observing him, and, suddenly turning round, met him full, face to face, and stood fixed with surprise as completely as Lancelot himself.

That face and figure, and the spirit which spoke through them, entered his heart at once, never again to leave it. Her features were aquiline and grand, without a shade of harshness; her eyes shone out like twin lakes of still azure, beneath a broad marble cliff of polished forehead; her rich chestnut hair rippled downward round the towering neck. With her perfect masque and queenly figure, and earnest upward gaze, she might have been the very model from which Raphael conceived his glorious St Catherine—the ideal of the highest womanly genius, softened into self-forgetfulness by girlish devotion. She was simply, almost coarsely dressed; but a glance told him that she was a lady, by the courtesy of man as well as by the will of God.

They gazed one moment more at each other—but what is time to spirits? With them, as with their Father, 'one day is as a thousand years'. But that eye-wedlock was cut short the next instant by the decided interference of the horse, who, thoroughly disgusted at his master's whole conduct, gave a significant shake of the head, and shamming frightened (as both women and horses will do when only cross), commenced a war-dance, which drove Argemone Lavington into the porch, and gave the bewildered Lancelot an excuse for dashing madly up the hill after his companions.

'What a horribly ugly face!' said Argemone to herself, 'but so clever, and so unhappy!'

A Rough Rhyme on a Rough Matter

The merry brown hares came leaping
    Over the crest of the hill,
Where the clover and corn lay sleeping
    Under the moonlight still.

Leaping late and early,
    Till under their bite and their tread
The swedes, and the wheat, and the barley
    Lay cankered, and trampled, and dead.

THE KINGSLEYS

A poacher's widow sat sighing
  On the side of the white chalk bank,
Where under the gloomy fir-woods
  One spot in the ley throve rank.

She watched a long tuft of clover,
  Where rabbit or hare never ran,
For its black sour haulm covered over
  The blood of a murdered man.

She thought of the dark plantation,
  And the hares and her husband's blood,
And the voice of her indignation
  Rose up to the throne of God.

'I am long past wailing and whining—
  I have wept too much in my life:
I've had twenty years of pining
  As an English labourer's wife.

'A labourer in Christian England,
  Where they cant of a Saviour's name,
And yet waste mens' lives like the vermin's
  For a few more brace of game.

'There's blood on your new foreign shrubs, squire;
  There's blood on your pointer's feet;
There's blood on the game you sell, squire,
  And there's blood on the game you eat!

'You have sold the labouring man, squire,
  Body and soul to shame,
To pay for your seat in the House, squire,
  And to pay for the feed for your game.

'You made him a poacher yourself, squire,
  When you'd give neither work nor meat;
And your barley-fed hares robbed the garden
  At our starving childrens' feet;

36

YEAST

When packed in one reeking chamber
  Man, maid, mother and little ones lay;
While the rain pattered in on the rotting bride-bed,
  And the walls let in the day;

When we lay in the burning fever
  On the mud of the cold clay floor,
Till you parted us all for three months, squire,
  At the cursed work-house door.

We quarrelled like brutes, and who wonders?
  What self-respect could we keep?
Worse housed than your hacks and your pointers,
  Worse fed than your hogs and your sheep?

'Our daughters and base-born babies
  Have wandered away in their shame;
If your misses had slept, squire, where they did,
  Your misses might do the same.

'Can your lady patch hearts that are breaking
  With handfulls of coal and rice,
Or by dealing out flannel and sheeting
  A little below cost price?

'You may tire of the gaol and the work-house,
  And take to allotments and schools,
But you've run up a debt that will never
  Be repaid us by penny-club rules.

'In the season of shame and sadness,
  In the dark and dreary day,
When scrofula, gout, and madness
  Are eating your race away;

'When to kennels and liveried varlets
  You have cast your daughters' bread;
And worn out with liquor and harlots,
  Your heir at your feet lies dead;

37

THE KINGSLEYS

'When your youngest, the mealy-mouthed rector,
  Lets your soul rot asleep to the grave,
You will find in your God the protector
  Of the freeman you fancied your slave.'

She looked at the tuft of clover,
  And wept till her heart grew light;
And at last, when her passion was over,
  Went wandering into the night.

But the merry brown hares came leaping
  Over the uplands still,
Where the clover and corn lay sleeping
  On the side of the white chalk hill.

V

Alton Locke
1850

The publication of Alton Locke *established Charles as a leading novelist in the school of what would now be called social realism. The model for its central character, the eponymous young apprentice tailor, was the working-class poet Thomas Cooper whose poetic testament,* The Purgatory of Suicides, *was written in Stafford gaol and published in 1845. Like Cooper, Alton Locke pulled himself out of slum and sweat-shop by means of his poetic talent, helped by a pawky old Scots bookseller said to have been based on Thomas Carlyle. He rose only to fall, first by trimming his verse of its revolutionary content to catch the winds of patronage, and then by serving a prison sentence for his part, albeit an innocent one, in a Chartist riot.*

The young parson's indignation had been kindled by the sufferings of his own parishioners; later, largely through his acquaintance with Maurice, Ludlow and other founders of Christian Socialism, he realized that the sufferings of the London poor were even worse. Following up John Ludlow's investigations into the lives of sweated tailors, he wrote for Fraser's Magazine *a fervid article* Cheap Clothes and Nasty *which formed the germ of his novel. This Carlyle called 'a salvo of red-hot shot against the Devil's Dungheap', but most of Charles' contemporaries were shocked by, or at least disapproving of, its outspoken descriptions of slum conditions and its support for the Chartist demands, which in 1848 seemed to the orthodox as subversive and immoral as the Thoughts of Mao were to seem to their successors rather more than a century later.*

The tale, its author wrote, 'revealed itself to me so rapidly and methodically that I feel it comes down to me from above—and that only my folly can spoil it—which I pray against daily'. He was now thirty-one, struggling to support a wife and two children on a miserable stipend which he augmented by taking in pupils, and by journalism, mainly in his standby Fraser's Magazine. *He made time for his writing by getting up, like Trollope, at five in the morning.* Alton Locke *was refused by the editor, John Parker, as being too dangerous, and published by Chapman & Hall.*

The tale reaches its climax with the monster Chartist rally held on Kennington Common on April 10, 1848. England was thought to be on the brink of revolution. The Duke of Wellington was put in command of the military forces, 150,000 special constables were called up, buildings fortified and the Queen removed for safety to the Isle of Wight. In the event rain damped the ardour of the crowd that was to have marched with a great petition to the Houses of Parliament; instead, the document went with a few delegates in three cabs and, while it carried two million signatures, many of them turned out to be bogus. The rally fizzled out. In the novel a broken-hearted Alton Locke sees 'the People's Cause lost—the Charter a laughing stock'. Striding homewards in despair he reaches the river.

From Chapter 35

I looked out over the bridge into the desolate night. Below me the dark moaning river-eddies hurried downward. The wildest west-wind howled past me, and leapt over the parapet downward. The huge reflection of St Paul's, the great tap-roots of light from lamp and window that shone upon the lurid stream, pointed down-down- down. A black wherry shot through the arch beneath me, still and smoothly downward. My brain began to whirl madly—I sprang upon the step. A man rushed past me, clambered on the parapet, and threw up his arms wildly. A moment more, and he would have leapt into the stream. The sight recalled me to my senses—say, rather, it reawoke in me the spirit of manhood. I seized him by the arm, tore him down under the pavement, and held him, in spite of his frantic struggles. It was Jemmy Downes! Gaunt, ragged, sodden, blear-eyed, drivelling, the worn-out gin-drinker stood, his momentary paroxysm of strength gone, trembling and staggering.

'Why won't you let a cove die? Why won't you let a cove die? They're all dead—drunk and poisoned and dead! What is there left?'—he burst out suddenly in his old ranting style—'what is there left on earth to live for? The prayers of liberty are answered by the laughter of tyrants; her sun is sunk beneath the ocean wave, and her pipe put out by the raging billows of aristocracy! Those starving millions of Kennington Common—where are they? Where? I axes you,' he cried fiercely, raising his voice to a woman-ish scream—'where are they?'

'Gone home to bed, like sensible people; and you had better go too.'

'Bed! I sold ours a month ago; but we'll go. Come along, and I'll show you my wife and family; and we'll have a teaparty. Jacob's Island tea. Come along!

Flea, flea, unfortunate flea!

Bereft of his wife and his small family!'

He clutched my arm, and dragging me off towards the Surrey side, turned down Stamford Street.

I followed half perforce; and the man seemed quite demented—whether with gin or sorrow I could not tell. As he strode along the pavement, he kept continually looking back, with a perplexed terrified air, as if expecting some fearful object.

'The rats!—the rats! don't you see 'em coming out of the gulley-holes, atween the area railings—dozens and dozens?'

'No; I saw none.'

'You lie; I hear their tails whisking; there's their shiny hats a-glistening, and every one of 'em with peelers' staves! Quick! quick! or they'll have me to the station-house.'

'Nonsense!' I said; 'we are free men! What are the policemen to us?'

'You lie!' cried he, with a fearful oath, and a wrench at my arm which almost threw me down. 'Do you call a sweater's man a free man?'

'You a sweater's man?'

'Ay!' with another oath. 'My men ran away—folks said I drank, too; but here I am; and I, that sweated others, I'm sweated myself—and I'm a slave! I'm a slave—a negro slave, I am, you aristocratic villain!'

'Mind me, Downes; if you will go quietly, I will go with you; but if you do not let go of my arm, I will give you in charge to the first policeman I meet.'

'Oh, don't, don't!' whined the miserable wretch, as he almost fell on his knees, gin-drinkers' tears running down his face, 'or I shall be too late. And then the rats'll get in at the roof, and up through the floor, and eat 'em all up, and my work too—the grand new three-pound coat that I've been stitching at this ten days, for the sum of one half-crown sterling—and don't I wish I may see the money? Come on, quick; there are the rats, close behind!' And he dashed across the broad roaring thoroughfare of Bridge Street, and hurrying almost at a run down Tooley Street, plunged into the wilderness of Bermondsey.

He stopped at the end of a miserable blind alley, where a dirty gas-lamp just served to make darkness visible, and show the patched windows and rickety doorways of the crazy houses, whose upper stories were lost in a brooding cloud of fog; and the pools of stagnant water at our feet; and the huge heap of cinders which filled up the waste end of the alley—a dreary black, formless mound, on which two or three spectral dogs prowled up and down after the offal, appearing and vanishing like dark imps in and out of the black misty chaos beyond.

The neighbourhood was undergoing, as it seemed, 'improvements' of that peculiar metropolitan species which consists of pull-down the dwellings of the poor, and building up rich men's houses instead; and great buildings, within high temporary palings, had already eaten up half the little houses; as the great fish, and the great estates, and the great shopkeepers eat up the little ones of their species—by the law of competition; lately discovered to be the true creator and preserver of the universe. There they loomed up, the tall bullies, against the dreary sky, looking down with their grim, proud, stony visages, on the misery which they were driving out of one corner, only to accumulate and intensify it in another.

The house at which we stopped was the last in the row; all its companions had been pulled down; and there it stood, leaning out with one naked ugly side into the gap, and stretching out long props, like feeble arms and crutches, to resist the work of demolition.

A group of slatternly people were in the entry, talking loudly, and as Downes pushed by them, a woman seized him by the arm.

'Oh! you unnatural villain! To go away after your drink, and leave all them poor dear dead corpses locked up, without even letting a body go in and stretch them out!'

'And breeding the fever, too, to poison the whole house!' growled one.

'The relieving officer's been here, my cove,' said another, 'and he's gone for a peeler and a search warrant to break open the door, I can tell you!'

But Downes pushed past unheeding, unlocked a door at the end of the passage, thrust me in, locked it again, and then rushed across the room in chase of two or three rats, who vanished into cracks and holes.

And what a room! A low lean-to with wooden walls, without a single article of furniture; and through the broad chinks of the floor shone up as it were ugly glaring eyes, staring at us. They were the reflections of the rushlight in the sewer below. The stench was frightful—the air heavy with pestilence. The first breath I drew made my heart sink, and my stomach turn. But I forgot everything in the object which lay before me, as Downes tore a half-finished coat off three corpses laid side by side on the bare floor.

There was his little Irish wife—dead—and naked; the wasted white limbs gleamed in the lurid light; the unclosed eyes stared, as if reproachfully, at the husband whose drunkenness had brought her there to kill her with the pestilence; and on each side of her a little, shrivelled, impish child-corpse—the wretched man had laid their arms round the dead mother's neck—and there they slept, their hungering and wailing over at last for ever; the rats had been busy already with them—but what matter to them now?

'Look!' he cried; 'I watched 'em dying! Day after day I saw the devils come up through the cracks, like little maggots and beetles, and all manner of ugly things, creeping down their throats; and I asked 'em, and they said they were the fever devils.'

It was too true; the poisonous exhalations had killed them. The wretched man's delirium tremens had given that horrible substantiality to the poisonous fever gases.

Suddenly Downes turned on me, almost menacingly. 'Money! money! I want some gin!'

I was thoroughly terrified—and there was no shame in feeling fear, locked up with a madman far my superior in size and strength, in so ghastly a place. But the shame, and the folly, too, would have been in giving way to my fear; and with a boldness half assumed, half the real fruit of excitement and indignation at the horrors I beheld, I answered—

'If I had money, I would give you none. What do you want with gin ? Look at the fruits of your accursed tippling. If you had taken my advice, my poor fellow,' I went on, gaining courage as I spoke, 'and become a water-drinker, like me—'

'Curse you and your water-drinking! If you had had no water to drink or wash with for two years but that—that,' pointing to the foul ditch below—'if you had emptied the slops in there with one hand, and filled your kettle with the other—'

'Do you actually mean that that sewer is your only drinking water ?'

'Where else can we get any ? Everybody drinks it; and you shall, too—you shall!' he cried, with a fearful oath, 'and then see if you don't run off to the gin-shop, to take the taste of it out of your mouth. Drink ? and who can help drinking, with his stomach turned with such hell-broth as that—or such a hell's blast as this air is here, ready to vomit from morning till night with the smells ? I'll show you. You shall drink a bucketful of it, as sure as you live, you shall.'

And he ran out of the back door, upon a little balcony, which hung over the ditch.

I tried the door, but the key was gone, and the handle too. I beat furiously on it, and called for help. Two gruff authoritative voices were heard in the passage.

'Let us in; I'm the policeman!'

'Let me out, or mischief will happen!'

The policeman made a vigorous thrust at the crazy door; and just as it burst open, and the light of his lantern streamed into the horrible den, a heavy splash was heard outside.

'He has fallen into the ditch!'

'He'll be drowned, then, as sure as he's a born man,' shouted one of the crowd behind.

We rushed out on the balcony. The light of the policeman's lantern glared over the ghastly scene—along the double row of miserable housebacks, which lined the sides of the open tidal ditch—over strange rambling jetties, and balconies, and sleeping-sheds, which hung on rotting piles over the black waters, with phosphorescent scraps of rotten fish gleaming and twinkling out of the dark hollows, like devilish grave-lights—over bubbles of poisoned gas, and bloated carcasses of dogs, and lumps of offal, floating on the stagnant olive-green hell-broth—over the slow sullen rows of oily ripple which were dying away into the darkness far beyond, sending up, as they stirred, hot breaths of miasma—the only sign that a spark of humanity, after years of foul life, had quenched itself at last in that foul death. I almost fancied that I could see the haggard face staring up at me through the slimy water; but no, it was as opaque as stone.

I shuddered and went in again, to see slatternly, gin-smelling women stripping off their clothes—true women even there—to cover the poor naked corpses; and pointing to the bruises which told a tale of long tyranny and cruelty; and mingling their lamentations with stories of shrieks and beating, and children locked up for hours to starve; and the men looked on sullenly, as if they too were guilty, or rushed out to relieve themselves by helping to find the drowned body. Ugh! it was the very mouth of hell, that room. And in the midst of all the rout, the relieving officer stood impassive, jotting down scraps of information, and warning us to appear the next day, to state what we knew before the magistrates. Needless hypocrisy of law! Too careless to save the women and children from brutal tyranny, nakedness, starvation! Too superstitious to offend its idol of vested interests, by protecting the poor man against his tyrants, the house-owning shopkeepers under whose greed the dwellings of the poor become nests of filth and pestilence, drunkenness and degradation. Careless, superstitious, imbecile law!—leaving the victims to die unhelped, and then, when the fever and the tyranny has done its work, in thy sanctimonious prudishness, drugging thy respectable conscience by a 'searching inquiry' as to how it all happened—lest forsooth, there should have been 'foul play'! Is the knife or the bludgeon, then, the only foul play, and not the cesspool and the curse of Rabshakeh? Go through Bermondsey or Spitalfields, St Giles's or Lambeth, and see if there is not foul play enough already—to be tried hereafter at a more awful coroner's inquest than thou thinkest of!

Charles Kingsley formed the habit of working into his novels verses which express the mood and feeling of his characters and, as it were, concentrate his meaning into rhythmic form. Two of the verses from Alton Locke *follow. Like the lyric in* The Saint's Tragedy, *one of these,* The Sands of Dee, *was set to music and joined the repertoire of innumerable young ladies.*

THE KINGSLEYS

The Sands of Dee

Oh Mary, go and call the cattle home,
    And call the cattle home,
      And call the cattle home,
Across the sands o' Dee;
The western wind was wild and dank wi' foam,
    And all alone went she.

The creeping tide came up along the sand,
    And o'er and o'er the sand,
      And round and round the sand,
As far as eye could see;
The blinding mist came down and hid the land—
    And never home came she.

'Oh, is it weed, or fish, or floating hair—
    A tress o' golden hair,
      O' drowned maiden's hair,
Above the nets at sea?
Was never salmon yet that shone so fair,
    Among the stakes on Dee.'

They rowed her across in the rolling foam,
    The cruel crawling foam,
      The cruel hungry foam,
To her grave beside the sea;
But still the boatmen hear her call the cattle home,
    Across the sands o' Dee.

*The second set of verses comprise Alton Locke's valedictory, found
with the ink not yet dry in the cabin where, broken in health and spirit
by his experiences, he expires when in sight of the New World.*

My Last Word

Weep, weep, weep, and weep,
    For pauper, dolt and slave;

ALTON LOCKE

Hark! from wasted moor and fen,
Feverous alley, workhouse den,
Swells the wail of Englishmen:
'Work! or the grave!'

Down, down, down and down,
With idler, knave and tyrant:
Why for sluggards stint and moil?
He that will not live by toil
Has no right on English soil:
God's word's our warrant!

Up, up, up, and up,
Face your game, and play it!
The night is past—behold the sun—
The cup is full, the web is spun,
The Judge is set, the doom begun;
Who shall stay it?

VI

Hypatia
1852-53

'*This little sketch*', *as Charles described his long, excited, panoramic historical novel had, like all his novels, a moral purpose—several moral purposes in fact. He intended to 'set forth Christianity as the only real Democratic creed'. His picture of democracy in action in fifth century Alexandria among a mob of unruly, bigoted and often hysterical monks, who tore in pieces the beautiful philosopher Hypatia on the steps of an altar as the climax of the book, appears unlikely to have made many converts to the creed. Indeed the author himself, while an ardent democrat in theory, seems in practice to have taken a Shakespearean view of the masses; his crowd scenes in* Hypatia, *as in* Alton Locke, *reflect the mingled dread and fascination which memories of the Bristol riots of 1831 had imprinted on his mind.*

In Chapter 1 the handsome, innocent young monk Philammon leaves his desert community to see the world and convert its people; in Chapter 30 he returns, stripped of his illusions, to find a saintly peace in prayer and solitude. In between lies Alexandria during, as Charles put it, 'a very hideous, though very great, age', where Philammon defects from his order to become the enraptured, though pure, pupil of Hypatia. Turbulent, dangerous, corrupt and cruel, Charles sees Alexandria as a city of extremes: abject poverty confronts ostentatious riches and, in the shadow of the greatest library on earth, monks are flogged to death, slaves bought and sold, Jews despoiled, and captive desert tribesmen put to the sword by gladiators and devoured by wild beasts.

Charles Kingsley revelled in it all. With a fertility of imagination and disregard for probability that would have been the envy of a Hollywood script-writer in the heyday of Cecil B. de Mille, he devised for his pilgrim monk a series of fantastic adventures in which historical persons such as the patriarch Cyril, the Roman governor Orestes, Augustine of Hippo and the lovely neo-platonist philosopher herself

48

mingle with fictional Teutonic heroes (Charles was always in thrall to the Nordic myth), subtle Jews, quick-witted Greeks and voluptuous Romans—a fruity pudding whose characters are twice as large as life and ten times more voluble. He took the greatest pains to verify his background, and Hypatia *cost him more labour and research than any of his books. Perhaps for this reason, he rated it high among his* oeuvre. *Always modest about his work, he wrote to Maurice: 'I can never be a great poet. And what matter? I will do what I can; but I believe you are quite right in saying that my poetry is all of me which will last. Except, perhaps,* Hypatia.'

The Queen let it be known that this was her favourite among his novels. Serialized in Fraser's Magazine *in 1852–3, it was praised also by Froude, by his admirer The Chevalier de Bunsen, and by Mary Russell Mitford, who remarked that the author 'puts life into the very sands of the desert', but added a caution: 'there are some strange things, and I half dread what the Bishops may say'. Her fears were justified. Kingsley's outspokenness about feminine feet and legs, his charitable view of Pelagia, courtesan and mistress of the Goth's chieftain (she turned out to be Philammon's sister), and perhaps above all his uncharitable view of the monks' indiscipline, intrigue, greed and cruelty, by no means pleased some at least of the Bishops. In 1863 the Prince of Wales put forward his former tutor's name for an honorary degree of D.C.L. at Oxford. Despite this royal backing, and the eloquence of Charles' friends, the award was opposed by Dr Pusey on the ground that* Hypatia *was an immoral book and its author unworthy. Pusey's threat to call out* non placet *in the theatre in the presence of the Prince and Princess settled the matter, Charles himself agreeing that 'a fracas before the Prince's face had to be avoided at all risks'. So* Hypatia *cost him his scarlet gown.*

From Chapter 32

In Alexandria Philammon, released from prison, makes his way to the theatre where games are to be held under the auspices of the Roman governor Orestes, whose betrothal to Hypatia has been proclaimed.

As fate would have it, the passage by which he had entered opened close to the Prefect's chair of state, where sat Orestes, gorgeous in his robes of office, and by him—to Philammon's surprise and horror—Hypatia herself.

More beautiful than ever, her forehead sparkling, like Juno's own, with a lofty tiara of jewels, her white Ionic robe half hidden by a crimson shawl, there sat the vestal, the philosopher. What did she there? But the boy's eager eyes, accustomed but too well to note every light and shade of feeling which crossed that face, saw in a moment how wan and haggard was its expression. She wore a look of constraint, of half-terrified self-resolve, as of a martyr; and yet not an undoubting martyr; for as Orestes turned his head at the stir of Philammon's intrusion, and flashing with anger at the sight, motioned him fiercely back, Hypatia turned too, and as her eyes met her pupil's, she blushed crimson, and started, and seemed in act to motion him back also; and then, recollecting herself, whispered something to Orestes which quieted his wrath, and composed herself, or rather sunk into her place again, as one who was determined to abide the worst.

A knot of gay young gentlemen, Philammon's fellow-students, pulled him down among them, with welcome and laughter; and before he could collect his thoughts, the curtain in front of the stage had fallen, and the sport began.

The scene represented a background of desert mountains, and on the stage itself, before a group of temporary huts, stood huddling together the black Libyan prisoners, some fifty men, women and children, bedizened with gaudy feathers and girdles of tasselled leather, brandishing their spears and targets, and glaring out with white eyes on the strange scene before them, in childish awe and wonder.

Along the front of the stage a wattled battlement had been erected, while below, the hyposcenium had been painted to represent rocks, thus completing the rough imitation of a village among the Libyan hills.

Amid breathless silence, a herald advanced, and proclaimed that these were prisoners taken in arms against the Roman senate and people, and therefore worthy of immediate death: but that the Prefect, in his exceeding clemency toward them, and especial anxiety to afford the greatest possible amusement to the obedient and loyal citizens of Alexandria, had determined, instead of giving them at once to the beasts, to allow them to fight for their lives, promising to the survivors a free pardon if they acquitted themselves valiantly.

The poor wretches on the stage, when this proclamation was translated to them, set up a barbaric yell of joy, and brandished their spears and targets more fiercely than ever.

But their joy was short. The trumpets sounded the attack; a body of gladiators, equal in number to the savages, marched out from one of the two great side-passages, made their obeisance to the applauding spectators, and planting their scaling-ladders against the front of the stage, mounted to the attack.

The Libyans fought like tigers; yet from the first Hypatia, and Philammon also, could see that their promised chance of life was a mere mockery. Their light darts and naked limbs were no match for the heavy swords and complete armour of their brutal assailants, who endured carelessly a storm of blows and thrusts on head and faces protected by visored helmets: yet so fierce was the valour of the Libyans, that even they recoiled twice, and twice the scaling-ladders were hurled down again, while more than one gladiator lay below, rolling in the death-agony.

And then burst forth the sleeping devil in the hearts of that great brutalized multitude. Yell upon yell of savage triumph, and still more savage disappointment, rang from every tier of that vast ring of seats, at each blow and parry, onslaught and repulse; and Philammon saw with horror and surprise that luxury, refinement, philosophic culture itself, were no safeguards against the infection of bloodthirstyness. Gay and delicate ladies, whom he had seen three days before simpering with delight at Hypatia's heavenward aspirations, and some, too, whom he seemed to recollect in Christian churches, sprang from their seats, waved their hands and handkerchiefs, and clapped and shouted to the gladiators. For, alas! there was no doubt as to which side the favour of the spectators inclined. With taunts, jeers, applause, entreaties, the hired ruffians were urged on to their work of blood. The poor wretches heard no voice raised in their favour; nothing but contempt, hatred, eager lust of blood, glared from those thousands of pitiless eyes; and, broken-hearted, despairing, they flagged and drew back one by one. A shout of triumph greeted the gladiators as they climbed over the battlement, and gained a footing on the stage. The wretched blacks broke up, and fled wildly from corner to corner, looking vainly for an outlet . . .

And then began a butchery. . . . Some fifty men, women, and children were cooped together in that narrow space. . . . And yet Hypatia's countenance did not falter. Why should it? What were their numbers, beside the thousands who had perished year by year for centuries, by that and far worse deaths, in the amphitheatres of that empire, for that faith which she was vowed to re-establish? It was part of the great system; and she must endure it.

Not that she did not feel; for she, too, was a woman; and her heart, raised far above the brutal excitement of the multitude, lay calmly open to the most poignant stings of pity. Again and again she was in the act to entreat mercy for some shrieking woman or struggling child; but before her lips could shape the words, the blow had fallen, or the wretch was whirled away from her sight in the dense undistinguishable mass of slayers and slain. Yes, she had begun, and must follow to the end. . . . And, after all, what were the lives of those few semi-brutes, returning thus a few years earlier to the clay from which they sprang, compared with the regeneration of a world? . . . And it would be over in a few minutes more, and that black writhing heap be still forever, and the curtain fall. . . . And then for Venus Anadyomene, and art, and joy, and peace, and the graceful wisdom and beauty of the old Greek art, calming and civilizing all hearts, and softening them into pure devotion for the immortal myths, the immortal deities, who had inspired their forefathers in the glorious days of old. . . . But still the black heap writhed; and she looked away, up, down, and round, everywhere, to avoid the sickening sight; and her eye caught Philammon's gazing at her with looks of horror and disgust. . . . A thrill of shame rushed through her heart, and blushing scarlet, she sank her head, and whispered to Orestes—

'Have mercy! Spare the rest!'

'Nay, fairest vestal! The mob has tasted blood, and they must have their fill of it, or they will turn on us for aught I know. Nothing so dangerous as to check a brute, whether he be horse, dog or man, when once his spirit is up. Ha! There is a fugitive! How well the little rascal runs!'

As he spoke, a boy, the only survivor, leaped from the stage, and rushed across the orchestra toward them, followed by a rough cur-dog.

'You shall have this youth, if he reaches us.'

Hypatia watched breathless. The boy had just arrived at the altar in the centre of the orchestra, when he saw a gladiator close upon him. The ruffian's arm was raised to strike, when, to the astonishment of the whole theatre, boy and dog turned valiantly to bay, and leaping on the gladiator, dragged him between them to the ground. The triumph was momentary. The uplifted hands, the shout of 'Spare him!' came too late. The man, as he lay, buried his sword in the slender body of the child, and then rising, walked coolly back to the side passages, while the poor cur stood over the little corpse, licking its hands and face, and making the whole building ring with his doleful cries. The attendants entered, and striking their hooks into corpse after corpse, dragged them out of sight, marking their path by long red furrows in the sand; while the dog followed, until his inauspicious howlings died away down distant passages.

Philammon felt sick and giddy, and half rose to escape. But Pelagia! . . . No, he must sit it out, and see the worst, if worse than this was possible. He looked round. The people were coolly sipping wine and eating cakes, while they chatted admiringly about the beauty of the great curtain, which had fallen and hidden the stage, and represented, on a ground of deep-sea blue, Europa carried by a bull across the Bosphorus, while Nereids and Tritons played around.

A single flute within the curtain began to send forth luscious strains, deadened and distant, as if through far-off glens and woodlands; and from the side-passages issued three Graces, led by Peitho, the goddess of persuasion, bearing a herald's staff in her hand. She advanced to the altar in the centre of the orchestra, and informed the spectators that, during the absence of Ares in aid of a certain great military expedition, which was shortly to decide the diadem of Rome, and the liberty, prosperity, and supremacy of Egypt and Alexandria, Aphrodite had returned to her lawful allegiance, and submitted for the time being to the commands of her husband, Hephaestus; that he, as the deity of artificers, felt a peculiar interest in the welfare of the city of Alexandria, the workshop of the world, and had, as a sign of his especial favour, prevailed upon his fair spouse to exhibit, for this once, her beauties to the assembled populace, and, in the outspoken poetry of motion, to represent to them the emotions with which, as she arose new-born from the sea, she first surveyed that fair expanse of heaven and earth of which she now reigned undisputed queen.

A shout of rapturous applause greeted this announcement, and forthwith limped from the opposite slip the lame deity himself, hammer and pincers on shoulder, followed by a train of gigantic Cyclops, who bore on their shoulders various pieces of gilded metal work.

Hephaestus, who was intended to supply the comic element in the vast pantomimic pageant, shambled forth with studied uncouthness, amid roars of laughter; surveyed the altar with ludicrous contempt; raised his mighty hammer, shivered it to pieces with a single blow, and beckoned to his attendants to carry off the fragments, and replace it with something more fitting for his august spouse.

With wonderful quickness the metal open-work was put in its place, and fitted together, forming a frame of coral branches intermingled with dolphins, Nereids, and Tritons. Four gigantic Cyclops then approached, staggering under the weight of a circular slab of green marble, polished to a perfect mirror, which they placed on the framework. The Graces wreathed its circumference with garlands of seaweed, shells, and corallines, and the mimic sea was complete.

Peitho and the Graces retired a few steps, and grouped themselves with the Cyclops, whose grimed and brawny limbs, and hideous one-eyed masks, threw out in striking contrast the delicate hue and grace of the beautiful maiden figures; while Hephaestus turned toward the curtain, and seemed to await impatiently the forthcoming of the goddess.

Every lip was breathless with expectation as the flutes welled louder and nearer; horns and cymbals took up the harmony; and, to a triumphant burst of music, the curtain rose, and a simultaneous shout of delight burst from ten thousand voices.

The scene behind represented a magnificent temple, half hidden in an artificial wood of tropic trees and shrubs, which filled the stage. Fauns and Dryads peeped laughing from among their stems, and gorgeous birds, tethered by unseen threads, fluttered and sang among their branches. In the centre an over-arching avenue of palms led from the temple doors to the front of the stage; and had been replaced, in those few moments, by a broad slope of greensward, leading down into the orchestra, and fringed with myrtles, roses, apple-trees, poppies, and crimson hyacinths, stained with the life-blood of Adonis.

The folding doors of the temple opened slowly; the crash of instruments resounded from within; and, preceded by the musicians, came forth the triumph of Aphrodite, and passed down the slope, and down the outer ring of the orchestra.

A splendid car, drawn by white oxen, bore the rarest and gaudiest of foreign flowers and fruits, which young girls, dressed as Hours and Seasons, strewed in front of the procession and among the spectators.

A long line of beautiful maidens and youths, crowned with garlands, and robed in scarves of purple gauze, followed by two and two. Each pair carried or led a pair of wild animals, captives of the conquering might of Beauty.

Foremost were borne, on the wrists of the actors, the birds especially sacred to the goddess—doves and sparrows, wrynecks and swallows; and a pair of gigantic Indian tortoises, each ridden by a lovely nymph, showed that Orestes had not forgotten one wish, at least, of his intended bride.

Then followed strange birds from India, parakeets, peacocks, pheasants silver and golden; bustards and ostriches; the latter bestridden each by a tiny cupid, were led in on golden leashes, followed by antelopes and oryxes, elks from beyond the Danube, four-horned rams from the Isles of the Hyperborean Ocean, and the strange hybrid of the Libyan hills, believed by all spectators to be half-bull half-horse. And then a murmur of delighted awe ran through the theatre as bears and leopards, lions and tigers, fettered in heavy chains of gold, and made gentle for the occasion by narcotics, paced sedately down the slope, obedient to their beautiful guides; while behind them, the unwieldy bulk of two double-horned rhinoceroses, from the far south, was over-topped by the long slender necks and large soft eyes of a pair of giraffes, such as had not been seen in Alexandria for more than fifty years.

A cry arose of 'Orestes! Orestes! Health to the illustrious Prefect! Thanks for his bounty!' And a hired voice or two among the crowd cried, 'Hail to Orestes! Hail, Emperor of Africa!' . . . But there was no response.

'The rose is still in the bud,' simpered Orestes to Hypatia. He rose, beckened and bowed the crowd into silence; and then, after a short pantomimic exhibition of rapturous gratitude and humility, pointed triumphantly to the palm avenue, among the shadows of which appeared the wonder of the day—the huge tusks and trunk of the white elephant himself.

There it was at last! Not a doubt of it! A real elephant, and yet as white as snow. Sight never before seen in Alexandria—never to be seen again! 'Oh, thrice blest men of Macedonia!' shouted some worthy on high, 'the gods are bountiful to you this day!' And all the mouths and eyes confirmed the opinion, as they opened wider and yet wider to drink in the inexhaustible joy and glory.

On he paced solemnly, while the whole theatre resounded to his heavy tread, and the Fauns and Dryads fled in terror. A choir of nymphs swung round him hand in hand, and sang, as they danced along, the conquering might of Beauty, the tamer of beasts and men and deities. Skirmishing parties of little winged cupids spread themselves over the orchestra, from left to right, and pelted the spectators with perfumed comfits, shot among them from their tiny bows of fragrant sandal wood, or swung smoking censers, which loaded the air with intoxicating odours.

The procession came on down the slope, and the elephant approached the spectators; his tusks were wreathed with roses and myrtles; his ears were pierced with splendid ear-rings, a jewelled frontlet hung between his eyes; Eros himself, a lovely winged boy, sat on his neck, and guided him with the point of a golden arrow. But what precious things was it which that shell-formed car upon his back contained? The goddess! Pelagia Aphrodite herself?

Yes; whiter than the snow-white elephant—more rosy than the pink-tipped shell in which she lay, among crimson cushions and silver gauze, there shone the goddess, thrilling all hearts with those delicious smiles, and glances of the bashful playful eyes, and grateful wavings of her tiny hand, as the whole theatre rose with one accord, and ten thousand eyes were concentrated on the unequalled loveliness beneath them.

Twice the procession passed round the whole circumference of the orchestra, and then returning from the foot of the slope towards the central group around Hephaestus, deployed right and left in front of the stage. The lions and tigers were led away into the side passages; the youths and maidens combined themselves with the gentler animals into groups lessening gradually from the centre to the wings, and stood expectant, while the elephant came forward, and knelt behind the platform destined for the goddess.

The valves of the shell closed. The Graces unloosed the fastenings of the car. The elephant turned his trunk over his back, and guided by the hands of the girls, grasped the shell, and lifting it high in the air, deposited it on the steps at the back of the platform.

Hephaestus limped forward, and with his most uncouth gestures, signified the delight which he had in bestowing such a sight upon his faithful artisans of Alexandria, and the unspeakable enjoyment which they were to expect from the mystic dance of the goddess; and then retired, leaving the Graces to advance in front of the platform, and with their arms twined round each other, begin Hypatia's song of invocation.

As the first strophe died away, the valves of the shell re-opened, and discovered Aphrodite crouching on one knee within. She raised her head, and gazed around the vast circle of seats. A mild surprise was on her countenance, which quickened into a delightful wonder, and bashfulness struggling with the sense of new enjoyment and new powers. She glanced downward at herself; and smiled, astonished at her own loveliness; then upward at the sky; and seemed ready, with an awful joy, to spring up into the boundless void. Her whole figure dilated; she seemed to drink in strength from every object which met her in the great universe around; and slowly, from among the shells and seaweeds, she rose to her full height, the mystic cestus glittering round her waist, in deep festoons of emeralds and pearls, and stepped forward upon the marble sea-floor, wringing the dripping perfume from her locks, as Aphrodite rose of old.

For the first minute the crowd was too breathless with pleasure to think of applause. But the goddess seemed to require due homage; and when she folded her arms across her bosom, and stood motionless for an instant, as if to demand the worship of the universe, every tongue was loosed, and a thunderclap of 'Aphrodite!' rung out across the roofs of Alexandria, and startled Cyril in his chamber at the Serapeium, and weary muleteers on distant sand-hills, and dozing mariners far out at sea.

And then began a miracle of art, such as was only possible among a people of the free and exquisite physical training, and the delicate aesthetic perception of those old Greeks, even in their most fallen days. A dance, in which every motion was a word, and rest as eloquent as motion; in which every attitude was a fresh motive for a sculptor of the purest school, and the highest physical activity was manifested, not as in the coarser comic pantomimes, in fantastic bounds and unnatural distortions, but in perpetual delicate modulations of a stately and self-restraining grace. The artist was for the moment transformed into the goddess. The theatre, and Alexandria, and the gorgeous pageant beyond, had vanished from her imagination, and therefore from the imagination of the spectators, under the constraining inspiration of her art, and they and she alike saw nothing but the lonely sea around Cythera, and the goddess hovering above its emerald mirror, raying forth on sea, and air, and shore, beauty, and joy, and love . . .

Philammon's eyes were bursting from his head with shame and horror; and yet he could not hate her; not even despise her. He would have done so, had there been the faintest trace of human feeling in her countenance to prove that some germ of moral sense lingered within; but even the faint blush and the downcast eye with which she had entered the theatre, were gone; and the only expression on her face was that of intense enjoyment of her own activity and skill, and satisfied vanity, as of a petted child. . . . Was she accountable? A reasonable soul, capable of right or wrong at all? He hoped not. . . . He would trust not. . . . And still Pelagia danced on; and for a whole age of agony, he could see nothing in heaven or earth but the bewildering maze of those white feet, as they twinkled over their white image in the marble mirror. . . . At last it was over. Every limb suddenly collapsed, and she stood drooping in soft self-satisfied fatigue, awaiting the burst of applause which rang through Philammon's ears, proclaiming to heaven and earth, as with a mighty trumpet-blast, his sister's shame.

The elephant rose, and moved forward to the side of the slabs. His back was covered with crimson cushions, on which it seemed Aphrodite was to return without her shell. She folded her arms across her bosom, and stood smiling, as the elephant gently wreathed his trunk around her waist, and lifted her slowly from the slab, in act to place her on his back. . . .

The little feet, clinging half fearfully together, had just risen from the marble—The elephant started, dropped his delicate burden heavily on the slab, looked down, raised his forefoot, and throwing his trunk into the air, gave a shrill scream of terror and disgust . . .

The foot was red with blood—the young boy's blood—which was soaking and bubbling up through the fresh sand where the elephant had trodden, in a round, dark, purple spot . . .

Philammon could bear no more. Another moment and he had hurled down through the dense mass of spectators, clearing rank after rank of seats by sheer strength of madness, leaped the balustrade into the orchestra below, and rushed across the space to the foot of the platform.

'Pelagia! Sister! My sister! Have mercy on me! on yourself! I will hide you! save you! and we will flee together out of this infernal place! this world of devils! I am your brother! Come!'

She looked at him one moment with wide, wild eyes—The truth flashed on her—

'Brother!'

And she sprang from the platform into his arms. . . . A vision of a lofty window in Athens, looking out over far olive-yards and gardens, and the bright roofs and basins of the Piraeus, and the broad blue sea, with the purple peaks of Aegina beyond all, . . . And a dark-eyed boy, with his arm around her neck, pointed laughing to the twinkling masts in the far harbour, and called her sister. . . . The dead soul woke within her; and with a wild cry she recoiled from him in an agony of shame, and covering her face with both her hands, sank down among the blood-stained sand.

A yell, as of all hell broke loose, rang along that vast circle—

'Down with him!' 'Away with him!' 'Crucify the slave!' 'Give the barbarian to the beasts!' 'To the beasts with him, noble Prefect!' A crowd of attendants rushed upon him, and many of the spectators sprang from their seats, and were on the point of leaping down into the orchestra.

Philammon turned upon them like a lion at bay; and clear and loud his voice rose through the roar of the multitude.

'Ay! Murder me as the Romans murdered Saint Telemachus! Slaves as besotted and accursed as your besotted and accurst tyrants! Lower than the beasts whom you employ as your butchers! Murder and lust go fitly hand in hand, and the throne of my sister's shame is well built on the blood of innocents! Let my death end the devil's sacrifice, and fill up the cup of your iniquity!'

59

'To the beasts! Make the elephant trample him to powder!'

And the huge brute, goaded on by the attendants, rushed on the youth, while Eros leaped from his neck, and fled weeping up the slope.

He caught Philammon on his trunk and raised him high in the air. For an instant the great bellowing ocean of heads spun round and round. He tried to breathe one prayer, and shut his eyes—Pelagia's voice rang sweet and clear, even in the shrillness of intense agony—

'Spare him! He is my brother! Forgive him, men of Macedonia! For Pelagia's sake—Your Pelagia! One boon—only this one!'

And she stretched her arms imploringly toward the spectators, and then clasping the huge knees of the elephant, called madly to it in terms of passionate entreaty and endearment.

The men wavered. The brute did not. Quietly he lowered his trunk, and set down Philammon on his feet. The monk was saved. Breathless and dizzy, he found himself hurried away by the attendants, dragged through dark passages, and hurled out into the street, with curses, warnings, and congratulations, which fell on an unheeding ear.

But Pelagia kept her face still hidden in her hands, and rising, walked slowly back, crushed by the weight of some tremendous awe, across the orchestra, and up the slope; and vanished among the palms and oleanders, regardless of the applause and entreaties, and jeers, and threats, and curses, of that great multitude of sinful slaves.

VII

Westward Ho!
1856

While the Kingsleys were recuperating from overwork at Torquay, Charles' brother-in-law, the historian Anthony Froude (also a Devon man), lent him a copy of Hakluyt's Voyages. *His imagination was immediately fired by these tales of brave deeds and bold expeditions by English sailors and explorers in the days of Good Queen Bess. Early in 1854, in a ferment of excitement occasioned partly by creative activity and partly by the outbreak of the Crimean war, he began to write his first best-seller. He completed it at North Devon House, in Bideford where much of the novel is set.*

'A most ruthless, bloodthirsty book it is—just what the times want, I think.' What he thought the times wanted was a re-kindling of England's fighting spirit to warm her soldiers' hearts in the Crimea. There was no need to kindle his own, which was brought to incandescence by the war. To Tom Hughes he wrote that he was going rabbit-shooting, but 'Would that the rabbits were Russians, tin-pot on head and musket in hand! Oh! for one hour's skirmishing in those Inkerman ravines and five minutes with butt and bayonet as a bonne bouche *to finish off with! But every man has his calling, and the novel is mine, because I am fit for nothing better.'*

Even the critical acclaim with which the novel was received did not still his self-doubts. 'I have been living in those Elizabethan books, among such grand, beautiful, silent men, that I am learning to be sure of what I all along suspected, that I am a poor, queasy, hysterical, half-baked sort of fellow . . .' In Amyas Leigh he created the quintessential Muscular Christian, transparently honest, brave, strong, chivalrous, none too bright (the sinister implications of the word 'clever' would never tarnish him), but resourceful in emergencies, chaste, loyal to God, Queen, Devon and his mother, and an implacable foe of Spaniards and Jesuits.

An obsessive hatred of Papists runs through this rambling, vivid, ingenuous adventure story, written as much to rally Englishmen to militant Protestantism as to the Colours in the Crimean peninsular. 'Eustace Leigh vanishes henceforth from these pages'—thus he disposes of his principal villain—'This book is the history of men . . . and Eustace is a man no longer; he is become a thing, a tool, a Jesuit . . .'

The tropics always fascinated Charles, and jungle scenes call forth some of his most highly-coloured prose. Amyas' adventures take him to the Amazon, equipped with lovely maidens as well as with brilliant-plumaged birds and lush vegetation; equipped also with temptations, as the first extract shows.

From Chapter 24

So forth Amyas went, with Ayacanora as guide, some five miles upward along the forest slopes, till the girl whispered 'There they are;' and Amyas, pushing himself gently through a thicket of bamboo, beheld a scene which, in spite of his wrath, kept him silent, and perhaps softened, for a minute.

On the farther side of a little lawn, the stream leapt through a chasm beneath over-arching vines, and then sank foaming into a clear rock-basin, a bath for Dian's self. On its farther side, the crag rose some twenty feet in height, bank upon bank of feathered ferns and cushioned moss, over the rich green beds of which dropped a thousand orchids, scarlet, white and orange, and made the still pool gorgeous with the reflection of their gorgeousness. At its more quiet outfall, it was half-hidden in huge fantastic leaves and tall flowering stems; but near the waterfall the grassy bank sloped down toward the stream, and there, on palm-leaves strewed upon the turf, beneath the shadow of the crags, lay the two men whom Amyas sought, and whom, now he had found them, he had hardly heart to awake from their delicious dream.

For what a nest it was which they had found! The air was heavy with the scent of flowers, and quivering with the murmur of the stream, the humming of colibris and insects, the cheerful song of birds, the gentle cooing of a hundred doves; while now and then, from far away, the musical wail of the sloth, or the deep toil of the bell-bird, came softly to the ear. What was there not which eye or ear could need? And what which palate could need either? For on the rock above, some strange trees, leaning forward, dropped every now and then a luscious apple upon the grass below, and huge wild plantains bent beneath their load of fruit.

There, on the stream bank, lay the two renegades from civilized life. They had cast away their clothes, and painted themselves, like the Indians, with arnotto and indigo. One lay lazily picking up the fruit which fell close to his side; the other sat, his back against a cushion of soft moss, his hands folded languidly upon his lap, giving himself up to the soft influence of the narcotic coco-juice, with half-shut dreamy eyes fixed on the everlasting sparkle of the waterfall—

> While beauty, born of murmuring sound,
> Did pass into his face.

Somewhat apart crouched their two dusky brides, crowned with fragrant flowers, but working busily, like true women, for the lords whom they delighted to honour. One sat plaiting palm fibres into a basket; the other was boring the stem of a huge milk-tree, which rose like some mighty column on the right hand of the lawn, its broad canopy of leaves unseen through the dense underwood of laurel and bamboo, and betokened only by the rustle far aloft, and by the mellow shade in which it bathed the whole delicious scene.

Amyas stood silent for a while, partly from noble shame at seeing two Christian men thus fallen of their own self-will; partly because —and he could not but confess that—a solemn calm brooded above that glorious place, to break through which seemed sacrilege even while he felt it a duty. Such, he thought, was Paradise of old; such our first parents' bridal bower! Ah! If man had not fallen, he too might have dwelt forever in such a home—with whom? He started, and shaking off the spell, advanced sword in hand.

The women saw him, and springing to their feet, caught up their long pocunas, and leapt like deer each in front of her beloved. There they stood, the deadly tubes pressed to their lips, eyeing him like tigresses who protect their young, while every slender limb quivered, not with terror, but with rage.

Amyas paused, half in admiration, half in prudence; for one rash step was death. But rushing through the canes, Ayacanora sprang to the front, and shrieked to them in Indian. At the sight of the prophetess the women wavered, and Amyas, putting on as gentle a face as he could, stepped forward, assuring them in his best Indian that he would harm no one.

'Ebsworthy! Parracombe! Are you grown such savages already, that you have forgotten your captain? Stand up, men, and salute!'

Ebsworthy sprang to his feet, obeyed mechanically, and then slipped behind his bride again, as if in shame. The dreamer turned his head languidly, raised his hand to his forehead, and then returned to his contemplation.

Amyas rested the point of his sword on the ground, and his hands upon the hilt, and looked sadly and solemnly upon the pair. Ebsworthy broke the silence, half reproachfully, half trying to bluster away the coming storm.

'Well, noble captain, so you've hunted out us poor fellows; and want to drag us back again in a halter, I suppose?'

'I came to look for Christians, and I find heathens; for men, and I find swine. I shall leave the heathens to their wilderness, and the swine to their trough. Parracombe!'

'He's too happy to answer you, sir. And why not? What do you want of us? Our two years' vow is out, and we are free men now.'

'Free to become like the beasts that perish? You are the Queen's servants still, and in her name I charge you——'

'Free to be happy,' interrupted the man. 'With the best of wives, the best of food, a warmer bed than a duke's, and a finer garden than an emperor's. As for clothes, why the plague should a man wear them where he don't need them? As for gold, what's the use of it where Heaven sends everything ready-made to your hands? Hearken, Captain Leigh. You've been a good captain to me, and I'll repay you with a bit of sound advice. Give up your gold-hunting, and toiling and moiling after honour and glory, and copy us. Take that fair maid behind you there to wife, pitch here with us; and see if you are not happier here in one day than ever you were in all your life before.'

'You are drunk, sirrah! William Parracombe! Will you speak to me, or shall I heave you into the stream to sober you?'

'Who calls William Parracombe?' answered a sleepy voice.

'I, fool—your captain!'

'I am not William Parracombe. He is dead long ago of hunger, and labour, and heavy sorrow, and will never see Bideford town any more. He is turned into an Indian now; and he is to sleep, sleep, sleep for a hundred years, till he gets his strength again, poor fellow—'

'Awake, then, thou that sleepest, and arise from the dead, and Christ shall give thee light! A christened Englishman, and living thus the life of a beast!'

'Christ shall give thee light?' answered the same unnatural abstracted voice. 'Yes; so the parsons say. And they say too, that He is lord of heaven and earth. I should have thought His light was as near us here as anywhere, and nearer too, by the look of the place. Look round!' said he, waving a lazy hand, 'and see the works of God, and the place of Paradise, whither poor weary souls go home and rest, after their masters in the wicked world have used them up, with labour, and sorrow, and made them wade knee-deep in blood—I'm tired of blood, and tired of gold. I'll march no more; I'll fight no more; I'll hunger no more after vanity and vexation of spirit. What shall I get by it? Maybe I shall leave my bones in the wilderness. I can but do that here. Maybe I shall get home with a few pezos, to die an old cripple in some stinking hovel, that a monkey would scorn to lodge in here. You may go on; it'll pay you. You may be a rich man, and a knight, and live in a fine house, and drink good wine, and go to Court, and torment your soul with trying to get more, when you've got too much already; plotting and planning to scramble upon your neighbour's shoulders, as they all did—Sir Richard, and Mr Raleigh, and Chichester, and poor dear old Sir Warham, and all of them that I used to watch when I lived before. They were no happier than I was then; I'll warrant they are no happier now. Go your ways, captain; climb to glory upon some other backs than ours, and leave us here in peace, alone with God and God's woods, and the good wives that God has given us, to play a little like school children. It's long since I've had play-hours; and now I'll be a little child once more, with the flowers, and the singing birds, and the silver fishes in the stream, that are at peace, and think no harm, and want neither clothes, nor money, nor knighthood, nor peerage, but just take what comes; and their heavenly Father feedeth them, and Solomon in all his glory was not arrayed like one of these—and will not he much more feed us, that are of more value than many sparrows?'

'And will you live here, shut out from all Christian ordinances?'

'Christian ordinances? Adam and Eve had no parsons in Paradise. The Lord was their priest, and the Lord was their shepherd, and He'll be ours too. But go your ways, sir, and send up Sir John Brimblecombe, and let him marry us here in Church fashion (though we have sworn troth to each other before God already), and let him give us the Holy Sacrament once and for all, and then read the funeral service over us, and go his ways, and count us for dead, sir—for dead we are to the wicked worthless world we came out of three years ago. And when the Lord chooses to call us, the little birds will cover us with leaves, as they did the babies in the wood, and fresher flowers will grown out of our graves, sir, than out of yours in that bare Northam churchyard there beyond the weary, weary, weary sea.'

His voice died away to a murmur, and his head sank on his breast.

Amyas stood spell-bound. The effect of the narcotic was all but miraculous in his eyes. The sustained eloquence, the novel richness of diction in one seemingly drowned in sensual sloth, were, in his eyes, the possession of some evil spirit. And yet he could not answer the Evil One. His English heart, full of the divine instinct of duty and public spirit, told him that it must be a lie; but how to prove it a lie? And he stood for full ten minutes searching for an answer, which seemed to fly further and further off the more he sought it.

His eye glanced upon Ayacanora. The two girls were whispering to her smilingly. He saw one of them glance a look toward him, and then say something, which raised a beautiful blush in the maiden's face. With a playful blow at the speaker, she turned away. Amyas knew instinctively that they were giving her the same advice as Ebsworthy had given to him. Oh, how beautiful she was! Might not the renegades have some reason on their side after all?

He shuddered at the thought: but could not shake it off. It glided in like some gaudy snake, and wreathed its coils round his heart and brain. He drew back to the other side of the lawn, and thought and thought—

Should he ever get home? If he did, might he not get home a beggar? Beggar or no, he would still have to face his mother, to go through that meeting, to tell that tale, perhaps, to hear those reproaches, the forecast of which had weighed on him like a dark thunder-cloud for two weary years; to wipe out which by some desperate deed of glory he had wandered the wilderness, and wandered in vain.

Could he not settle here? He need not be a savage. He and his might Christianize, civilize, teach equal law, mercy in war, chivalry to women; found a community which might be hereafter as strong a barrier against encroachments of the Spaniard, as Manoa itself would have been. Who knew the wealth of the surrounding forests? Even if there were no gold, there were boundless vegetable treasures. What might he not export down the rivers? This might be the nucleus of a great commercial settlement—

And yet, was even that worth while? To settle here only to torment his soul with fresh schemes, fresh ambitions; not to rest, but only to change one labour for another? Was not your dreamer right? Did they not all need rest? What if they each sat down among the flowers, beside an Indian bride? They might live like Christians, while they lived like the birds of heaven—

What a dead silence! He looked up and round; the birds had ceased to chirp; the parraquets were hiding behind the leaves; the monkeys were clustered motionless upon the highest twigs; only out of the far depths of the forest, the campanero gave its solemn toll, once, twice, thrice, like a great death-knell rolling down from far cathedral towers. Was it an omen? He looked up hastily at Ayacanora. She was watching him earnestly. Heavens! was she waiting for his decision? Both dropped their eyes. The decision was not to come from them.

A rustle! a roar! a shriek! and Amyas lifted his eyes in time to see a huge dark bar shoot from the crag above the dreamer's head, among the group of girls.

A dull crash, as the group flew asunder; and in the midst, upon the ground, the tawny limbs of one were writhing beneath the fangs of a black jaguar, the rarest and most terrible of the forest kings. Of one? But of which? Was it Ayacanora? And sword in hand, Amyas rushed madly forward; before he reached the spot those tortured limbs were still.

It was not Ayacanora; for with a shriek which ran through the woods, the wretched dreamer, wakened thus at last, sprang up and felt for his sword. Fool! he had left it in his hammock! Screaming the name of his dead bride, he rushed on the jaguar, as it crouched above its prey, and seizing its head with teeth and nails, worried it, in the ferocity of his madness, like a mastiff-dog.

The brute wrenched its head from his grasp, and raised its dreadful paw. Another moment and the husband's corpse would have lain by the wife's.

But high in air gleamed Amyas' blade; down with all the weight of his huge body and strong arm, fell that most trusty steel; the head of the jaguar dropped grinning on its victim's corpse;

> And all stood still, who saw him fall,
> While men might count a score.

'O Lord Jesus,' said Amyas to himself, 'Thou has answered the devil for me! And this is the selfish rest for which I would have bartered the rest which comes by working where Thou has put me!'

They bore away the lithe corpse into the forest, and buried it under soft moss and virgin mould; and so the fair clay was transfigured into fairer flowers, and the poor, gentle, untaught spirit returned to God who gave it.

The story's climax comes with the defeat of the Armada for which Charles drew on Camden's Annales, Hakluyt's Voyages *and Raleigh's* History of the World. '*The boy who reads it will have a fair picture of the externals at least of the great battle, and he, and the most supercilious of modern readers, will be swept off his feet again and again by the narrative rush,' is the assessment of one of Charles' biographers, Margaret Thorp. Critics compared the novel favourably with those of Scott and Thackeray; Macmillan published it, and for the first time Charles had to pay income tax.*

After the victory, Amyas Leigh in his vessel Vengeance *pursued a personal vendetta against the Spaniard Don Guzman in the* Santa Catherina, *which he hunted round the north of Scotland and down the coast of Wales, to lose sight of her in the Bristol Channel.*

From Chapter 32

Slowly and wearily broke the dawn, on such a day as often follows heavy thunder; a sunless, drizzly day, roofed with low dingy cloud, barred and netted, and festooned with black, a sign that the storm is only taking breath awhile before it bursts again; while all the narrow horizon is dim and spongy with vapour drifting before a chilly breeze. As the day went on, the breeze died down, and the sea fell to a long glassy foam-flecked roll, while overhead brooded the inky sky, and round them the leaden mist shut out alike the shore and the chase.

Amyas paced the sloppy deck fretfully and fiercely. He knew that the Spaniard could not escape; but he grudged every moment which lingered between him and that one great revenge which blackened all his soul. The men sat sulkily about the deck, and whistled for a wind; the sails flapped idly against the masts; and the ship rolled in the long troughs of the sea, till her yard-arms almost dipped right and left.

'Take care of those guns. You will have something loose next,' growled Amyas.

'We will take care of the guns, if the Lord will take care of the wind,' said Yeo.

'We shall have plenty before night,' said Cary, 'and thunder too.'

'So much the better,' said Amyas. 'It may roar till it splits the heavens, if it does but get my work done.'

'He's not far off, I warrant,' said Cary. 'One lift of the cloud, and we should see him.'

'To windward of us, likely as not,' said Amyas. 'The devil fights for him, I believe. To have been on his heels sixteen days, and not sent this through him yet!' And he shook his sword impatiently.

So the morning wore away, without a sign of living thing, not even a passing gull; and the black melancholy of the heaven reflected itself in the black melancholy of Amyas. Was he to lose his prey after all? The thought made him shudder with rage and disappointment. It was intolerable. Anything but that.

'No, God!' he cried, 'let me but once feel this in his accursed heart, and then—strike me dead, if Thou wilt.'

'The Lord have mercy on us!' cried John Brimblecombe. 'What have you said?'

'What is that to you, sir? There, they are piping to dinner. Go down. I shall not come.'

And Jack went down, and talked in a half-terrified whisper of Amyas' ominous words.

All thought they portended some bad luck, except old Yeo.

'Well, Sir John,' said he, 'and why not? What better can the Lord do for a man, than take him home when he has done his work? Our captain is wilful and spiteful, and must kill needs his man himself; while for me, I don't care how the Don goes, provided he does go. I owe him no grudge, nor any man. May the Lord give him repentance, and forgive him all his sins; but if I could see him once safe ashore, as he may be ere nightfall on the Mortestone or the back of Lundy, I would say, "Lord, now lettest Thou thy servant depart in peace", even if it were the lightening that was sent to fetch me.'

'But, master Yeo, a sudden death?'

'And why not a sudden death, Sir John? Even fools long for a short life and a merry one, and shall not the Lord's people pray for a short life and a merry one? Let it come as it will to old Yeo. Hark! There's the captain's voice!'

'Here she is!' thundered Amyas from the deck; and in an instant all were scrambling up the hatchway as fast as the frantic rolling of the ship would let them.

Yes. There she was. The cloud had lifted suddenly, and to the south a ragged bore of blue sky let a long stream of sunshine down on her tall masts and stately hull, as she lay rolling some four or five miles to the eastward: but as for land, none was to be seen.

'There she is: and here we are,' said Cary; 'but where is here? and where is there? How is the tide, master?'

'Running up the channel by this time, sir.'

'What matters the tide?' said Amyas, devouring the ship with terrible and cold blue eyes. 'Can't we get at her?'

'Not unless someone jumps out and shoves behind,' said Cary. 'I shall go down again and finish that mackerel, if this roll has not chucked it to the cockroaches under the table.'

'Don't jest, Will! I can't stand it!' said Amyas, in a voice which quivered so much that Cary looked at him. His whole frame was trembling like an aspen. Cary took his arm, and drew him aside.

'Dear old lad,' said he, as they leaned over the bulwarks, 'what is this? You are not yourself, and have not been these four days.'

'No. I am not Amyas Leigh. I am my brother's avenger. Do not reason with me, Will: when it is over I shall be merry old Amyas again,' and he passed his head over his brow.

'Do you believe,' said he, after a moment, 'that men can be possessed by devils?'

'The Bible says so.'

'If my cause were not a just one, I should fancy I had a devil in me. My throat and heart are hot as the pit. Would to God it were done, for done it must be. Now go.'

Carey went away with a shudder. As he passed down the hatchway he looked back. Amyas had got the hone out of his pocket, and was whetting away again on his sword-edge, as if there was some dreadful doom on him, to whet, and whet forever.

The weary day wore on. The strip of blue sky was curtained over again, and all was dismal as before, though it grew sultrier every moment; and now and then a distant mutter shook the air to westward. Nothing could be done to lessen the distance between the ships, for the Vengeance had had all her boats carried away but one, and that was much too small to tow her; and while the men went down again to finish their dinner, Amyas worked on again at his sword, looking up every now and then suddenly at the Spaniard, as if to satisfy himself that it was not a vision that had vanished.

About two Yeo came up to him.

'He is ours safely now, sir. The tide has been running to the eastward these two hours.'

'Safe as a fox in a trap. Satan himself cannot take him from us!'

'But God may,' said Brimblecombe simply.

'Who spoke to you, sir? If I thought that He—There comes the thunder at last!'

As he spoke an angry growl from the westward heavens seemed to answer his wild words, and rolled and loudened nearer and nearer, till right over their heads it crashed against some cloud-cliff far above, and all was still.

Each man looked in the other's face: but Amyas was unmoved.

'The storm is coming,' said he, 'and the wind in it. It will be Eastward-ho now, for once, my merry men all!'

'Eastward-ho never brought us luck,' said Jack in an undertone

71

to Cary. But by this time all eyes were turned to the north-west, where a black line along the horizon began to define the boundary of sea and air, till now all dim in mist.

'There comes the breeze.'

'And there the storm too.'

And with that strangely accelerating pace which some storms seem to possess, the thunder, which had been growling slow and seldom far away, now rang peal on peal along the cloudy floor above their heads.

'Here comes the breeze. Round with the yards, or we shall be taken aback.'

The yards creaked round; the sea grew crisp around them; the hot air swept their cheeks, tightened every rope, filled every sail, bent her over. A cheer burst from the men as the helm went up, and they staggered away before the wind, right down upon the Spaniard, who lay still becalmed.

'And there is more behind, Amyas,' said Cary. 'Shall we not shorten sail a little?'

'No. Hold on every stitch,' said Amyas. 'Give me the helm, man. Boatswain, pipe away to clear for fight.'

It was done, and in ten minutes the men were all at quarters, while the thunder rolled louder and louder overhead, and the breeze freshened fast.

'The dog has it now. There he goes!' said Cary.

'Right before the wind. He has no liking to face us.'

'He is running into the jaws of destruction,' said Yeo. 'An hour more will send him right up the Channel, or smack on shore somewhere.'

'There! he has put his helm down. I wonder if he sees land?'

'He is like a march hare beat out of his country,' said Cary, 'and don't know whither to run next.'

Cary was right. In ten minutes more the Spaniard fell off again, and went away dead down wind, while the Vengeance gained on him fast. After two hours more, the four miles had diminished to one, while the lightning flashed nearer and nearer as the storm came up; and from the vast mouth of a black cloud-arch poured so fierce a breeze that Amyas yielded unwillingly to hints which were growing into open murmurs, and bade shorten sail.

On they rushed with scarcely lessened speed, the black arch following fast, curtained by one flat grey sheet of pouring rain, before which the water was boiling in a long white line; while every moment behind the watery veil, a keen blue spark leapt down into the sea, or darted zigzag through the rain.

'We shall have it now, and with a vengeance; this will try your tackle, master,' said Cary.

The functionary answered with a shrug, and turned up the collar of his rough frock, as the first drops flew stinging round his ears. Another minute and the squall burst full upon them, in rain, which cut like hail—hail which lashed the sea into froth, and wind which whirled off the heads of the surges, and swept the waters into one white seething waste. And above them, and behind them, and before them, the lightning leapt and ran, dazzling and blinding, while the deep roar of the thunder was changed to sharp ear-piercing cracks.

'Get the arms and ammunition under cover, and then below with you all,' shouted Amyas from the helm.

'And heat the pokers in the galley fire,' said Yeo, 'to be ready if the rain pits our linstocks out. I hope you'll let me stay on deck, sir, in case—'

'I must have someone, and who better than you? Can you see the chase?'

No; she was wrapped in the grey whirlwind. She might be within half a mile of them, for aught they could have seen of her.

And now Amyas and his old liegeman were alone. Neither spoke; each knew the other's thoughts, and knew that they were his own. The squall blew fiercer and fiercer, the rain poured heavier and heavier. Where was the Spaniard?

'If he has laid-to, we may overshoot him, sir!'

'If he has tried to lay to, he will not have a sail left in the bolt-ropes, or perhaps a mast on deck. I know the stiff-neckedness of those Spanish tubs. Hurrah! There he is, right on our larboard bow!'

There she was indeed, two musket-shots' off, staggering away with canvas split and flying.

'He has been trying to hull, sir, and caught a buffet,' said Yeo, rubbing his hands. 'What shall we do now?'

'Range alongside, if it blow live imps and witches, and try our luck once more. Pah! How this lightning dazzles!'

On they swept, gaining fast on the Spaniard.

'Call the men up, and to quarters; the rain will be over in ten minutes.'

Yeo ran forward to the gangway; and sprang back again, with a face white and wild—

'Land right ahead! Port your helm, sir! For the love of God, port your helm!'

Amyas, with the strength of a bull, jammed the helm down, while Yeo shouted to the men below.

She swung round. The masts bent like whips; crack went the fore-sail like a cannon. What matter? Within two hundred yards of them was the Spaniard; in front of her, and above her, a huge dark bank rose through the dense hail, and mingled with the clouds; and at its foot, plainer every moment, pillars and spouts of leaping foam.

'What is it, Morte? Hartland?'

It might be anything for thirty miles.

'Lundy!' said Yeo. 'The south end! I see the head of the Shutter in the breakers! Hard a-port yet, and get her close-hauled as you can, and the Lord have mercy on us still! Look at the Spaniard!'

Yes, look at the Spaniard!

On their left hand, as they broached-to, the wall of granite sloped down from the clouds towards an isolated peak of rock, some two hundred feet in height. Then a hundred yards of roaring breaker upon a sunken shelf, across which the race of the tide poured like a cataract; then, amid a column of salt smoke, the Shutter, like a huge black fang, rose waiting for its prey; and between the Shutter and the land, the great galleon loomed dimly through the storm.

He, too, has seen his danger, and tried to broach-to. But his clumsy mass refused to obey the helm; he struggled a moment, half hid in foam; fell away again, and rushed upon his doom.

'Lost! lost! lost!' cried Amyas madly, and throwing up his hands, let go the tiller. Yeo caught it just in time.

'Sir! Sir! What are you at? We shall clear the rock yet.'

'Yes!' shouted Amyas in his frenzy; 'but he will not!'

Another minute. The galleon gave a sudden jar, and stopped. Then one long heave and bound, as if to free herself. And then her bows lighted clean upon the Shutter.

An awful silence fell on every English soul. They heard not the roaring of the wind and surge; they saw not the blinding flashes of the lightning; but they heard one long ear-piercing wail to every saint in heaven rise from five hundred human throats; they saw the mighty ship heel over from the wind, and sweep headlong down the cataract of the race, plunging her yards into the foam, and showing her whole black side even to her keel, till she rolled clean over, and vanished for ever and ever.

'Shame!' cried Amyas, hurling his sword far into the sea, 'to lose my right, my right! when it was in my very grasp! Unmerciful!'

A crack which rent the sky, and made the granite ring and quiver; a bright world of flame, and then a blank of utter darkness, against which stood out, glowing red-hot, every mast, and sail, and rock, and Salvation Yeo as he stood just in front of Amyas, the tiller in his hand. All red-hot, transfigured into fire; and behind, the black, black night.

VIII

Brave Words for Brave Soldiers and Sailors

1855

Even the writing of Westward Ho!, *completed in seven months, did not get out of Charles' system the patriotic fervour aroused by the Crimean war. All he could do to express it was to succour those in the forefront of the battle by proclaiming the justness of their cause. He wrote anonymously, and Macmillan published, a reassuring pamphlet and thousands of copies were distributed to troops in the field. The following is an extract:*

I think some of you will fancy this is almost too good news to be true, and yet the very news which you want to hear. I think some of you have been saying as you read this, 'All this is blessed and comforting news for the poor fellows lying wounded in a hospital, or fretting their souls away about the wives and children they have left behind; but we want something more than that even. We have to fight and to kill; we want to be sure that God's blessing is on our fighting and our killing; we have to go into battle; and we want to know that there, too, we are doing God's work, and to be sure that God is on our side.'

Well, my brave men, *Be sure of it then!* Be sure that God's blessing is as much upon you; be sure that you are doing God's work, as much when you are handling a musket or laying a gun in your country's battles, as when you are bearing frost and hunger in the trenches, and pain and weakness of a sickbed.

For the Lord Jesus Christ is not only the *Prince of Peace*; He is the *Prince of War* too. He is the Lord of Hosts, the God of armies; and whosoever fights in a just war, against tyrants and oppressors, he is fighting on Christ's side, and Christ is fighting on his side; Christ is his Captain and his Leader, and he can be in no better

76

service. Be sure of it: for the Bible tells you so. The old wars of Abraham against the robber-kings; of Joshua against the Canaanites; of David against the Philistines; of Hezekiah against the Assyrians; of the Maccabees against the Greeks—all tell the soldier the same brave news, that he is doing God's work, and that God's blessing is on him when he fights in a just cause. And you are fighting in a just cause, if you are fighting for freedom and law. If to you God gives the noble work of fighting for the liberty of Europe, God will reward you according as you do that work like men. You will be fighting in that everlasting war against all injustice and wrong, the Captain and Leader whereof is the Lord Jesus Christ Himself. Believe that—for the Bible tells it you. You must think of the Lord Jesus Christ not merely as a sufferer, but as a warrior; not merely as the Man of Sorrows (blessed as that thought is) but as the Lord of Hosts—the God of armies—the King who executes justice and judgment in the earth, who has sworn vengeance against all unrighteousness and wrong, and will destroy the wicked with the breath of His mouth. You must think of Him as the God of the fatherless and the widow; but you must think of Him, too, as the God of the sailor and the soldier, the God of Duty, the God of justice, the God of vengeance, the God to whom *your colours were solemnly offered*, and *His blessing on them prayed for*, when they were given to your regiment.

I know that you would follow those colours to the mouth of the pit, and that you would die twice over sooner than let them be taken. Good! but remember, too, that those colours are a sign to you that Christ is with you, ready to give you courage, coolness, and right judgment, in the charge and in the death-grapple, just as much as He is with those ministering angels who will nurse and tend your wounds in hospital. God's blessing is on them; but do you never forget that your colours are a sign to you that Christ's blessing is on *you*. If they do not mean that to you, what was the use of blessing them with prayer? It must have been a lie and a sham. But it is no lie, brave men, and no sham; it is a glorious truth, of which these noble rags, inscribed with noble names of victory, should remind you every day and every hour, that he who fights for Queen and country in a just cause, is fighting not only in the Queen's army, but in Christ's army, and that he shall in no wise lose his reward.

IX

Letters and Verses
1852–7

The issues and events of the day always stirred Charles' feelings to the depths. Some aroused his passionate partisanship, as in the case of Rajah Brooke, who got into trouble for his measures against head-hunting Dyaks and to whom Charles dedicated Westward Ho! *To John Ludlow he wrote:*

'I say at once I think he (Brooke) has been utterly right and righteous. If I had been in his place I would have done the same. If it is to do again I hope he will have the courage to do it again. The truest benevolence is occasional severity. It *is* expedient that one man die for the people. One tribe exterminated, if need be, to save a whole continent. Sacrifice of human life? Prove that it *is* human life. It is *beast* life. These Dyaks have put on the image of the beast and must take the consequences. "Value of life"? Oh Ludlow read history; look at the world and see whether God values mere physical existence. . . . Physical death is no evil. It may be a blessing to the survivors. Else why pestilence, famine, Cromwell and Perrot in Ireland, Charlemagne hanging 4,000 Saxons over the Weser bridge; did not God bless these terribly righteous judgements? Do you believe in the Old Testament? Surely then say what does destruction of the Canaanites mean? If it was right, Rajah Brooke was right. If he be wrong then Moses, Joshua, David were wrong. No! I say. Because Christ's kingdom is a kingdom of peace; because the meek alone shall inherit the earth, therefore you Malays and Dyaks of Sarawak, you also are enemies of peace . . . you are beasts, all the more dangerous because you have a semi-human cunning. . . . Honour to a man who dares act manfully on the broad sense of right as Rajah Brooke is doing.'

The bellicose cleric did not apply these stern principles to his own

78

domestic life. Despite his belief that 'the truest benevolence is occasional severity', and in an age convinced of the beneficial effects on children of frequent caning, he opposed corporal punishment and would not inflict it on his own children or allow others to do so. Nor would he lay down petty family rules. 'It is difficult enough to keep the Ten Commandments,' he wrote, 'without making an eleventh in every direction.'

Nor did he expect of children the moral rectitude proper to God-fearing adults. 'More than half the lying of children is, I believe, the result of fear, and the fear of punishment.' Parents who could not put up with children's noisiness should not bring them into the world. In other domestic matters his views were equally unorthodox. 'We are shocked to hear of Mrs Hughes's sorrows and we both entreat her to keep to the sofa, and do, do put her stays into the fire! . . . My Fanny, thanks to no stays goes on getting better and better.' As to his views on the status of women, they were at least a century ahead of his time. 'Woman is a part of and equal to man,' he wrote to Lady Hardwicke, 'and not his inferior, his puppet and his slave, as he in his brute force has always tried to make her.'

In 1855, the effort of writing Westward Ho!—*a quarter of a million words in seven months and all in a white-hot ferment of mind—exhausted its author, and reaction set in. There was another side to the fighting in the Crimea besides glory, heroism and* bonnes bouches *with bayonets. The doubts that had beset him at Cambridge had been buried deep but not quite deep enough to suffocate forever. As usual he found relief in pouring out his feelings to F. D. Maurice.*

Letter to F. D. Maurice, 1855

I am losing a zest for work. Everything seems to me not worth working at—except the simple business of telling poor people, Don't fret, God cares for you, and Christ understands you—and that I can't tell fully, because I daren't say what I think, I daren't preach my own creed, which seems to me as different from what I hear preached and find believed, everywhere, as modern creeds are from Popery, of from St Paul. And St Paul—horrible thought! seems to me at moments away from the plain simple words of our Lord. I *don't* believe he *does* differ from our Lord, but the dread will arise, and torment me. And when my trust in the Bible as a whole seems to be falling to pieces it is—you must feel it is—a terrible work for a poor soul to know where the destructive process must stop; and one feels alone in the universe, at least alone among mankind, on a cliff which is crumbling beneath one, and falling peicemeal into the dark sea.

And it is this, in that book which makes me tremble. The denial of Christ as the ideal and perfect man. If I lose that, I lose all. . . . Did He die to deliver the world from sin?—Oh my God, is the world delivered from sin? Do I not hate history because it is the record of brutality, stupidity, cruelty, murder—to bring on *thus far*, to a nineteenth century in which one can look with complacency on no nation, no form of belief, from pole to pole, in which one looks at one's own nation, really the most righteous of all, with the dreadful feeling that God's face is turned from it, that perhaps He has given it over to strong delusion, that it should believe a lie, and fall in the snare of its own pride? I cannot escape that wretched fear of a national catastrophe, which haunts me night and day. I live in dark nameless dissatisfaction and dread . . . and I try to forget it in amusement, for in study, I cannot. And then I cry—'It is the devil's voice slandering my countrymen to me, slandering priests, statesmen, rich and poor, and I am a devil myself, who is sinning against the Holy Ghost, and calling good men's works evil. The nation is going right, and the Bishops are right in not denouncing the Governors who allow Crimean tragedies; everyone is right in leaving well alone—even in leaving ill alone, where it is inextricably mixed up with good that you cannot root up the tares without rooting up the wheat also.' Is that God's voice, or the Devil's?

His spirits were revived in 1857 when a British fleet bombarded Canton because the Chinese governor refused to apologize for seizing the crew of a pirate vessel flying the British flag. Controversy at home led to a general election and Lord Palmerston and his government swept back to office on a tide of imperialism which carried with it the rector of Eversley. In an exultant mood he composed an ode which in its tenor anticipated Kipling.

Ode to the North-East Wind

Welcome, wild North-easter!
  Shame it is to see
Ode to every zephyr;
  Ne'er a verse to thee.
Welcome, black North-easter!
  O'er the German foam;
O'er the Danish moorlands
  From thy frozen home.
Tired we are of summer,
  Tired of gaudy glare,
Showers soft and steaming,
  Hot and breathless air.
Tired of listless dreaming,
  Through the lazy day;
Jovial wind of winter
  Turns us out to play!
Sweep the golden reed-beds;
  Crisp the lazy dyke;
Hunger into madness
  Every plunging pike.
Fill the lake with wild-fowl;
  Fill the marsh with snipe;
While on dreary moorlands
  Lonely curlew pipe.
Through the black fir-forest
  Thunder harsh and dry
Shattering down the snowflakes
  Off the curdled sky.
Hark! The brave North-easter!
  Breast-high lies the scent,
On by holt and headland
  Over heath and bent.
Chime, ye dappled darlings,
  Through the sleep and snow.
Who can over-ride you?
  Let the horses go!

THE KINGSLEYS

Chime, ye dappled darlings
  Down the roaring blast;
You shall see a fox die
  Ere an hour be past.
Go! and rest tomorrow,
  Hunting in your dreams,
While our skates are ringing
  O'er the frozen streams.
Let the luscious south-wind
  Breathe in lovers' sighs,
While the lazy gallants
  Bask in ladies' eyes.
What does he but soften
  Heart alike and pen?
'Tis the hard grey English weather
  Breeds hard Englishmen.
What's the soft South-wester?
  'Tis the ladies' breeze,
Bringing home their true-loves
  Out of all the seas.
But the black North-easter
  Through the snowstorm hurled
Drives our English hearts of oak
  Seaward round the world.
Come, as came our fathers,
  Heralded by thee,
Conquering from the eastward,
  Lords by land and sea.
Come: and strong within us
  Stir the Vikings' blood;
Bracing brain and sinew;
  Blow, thou wind of God!

Then came the Indian Mutiny and Charles could not sustain his mood of confidence in Britain's destiny and in divine omniscience. To F. D. Maurice he wrote:

I can think of nothing but these Indian massacres. The moral problems they involve make me half wild. Night and day the heavens seem black to me, though I was never so prosperous and blessed in my life as I am now. I can hardly bear to look at a woman or child—even my own sometimes. They raise such horrible images, from which I can't escape. What does it all mean? Christ is king, nevertheless! I tell my people so. I should do—I dare not think what—if I did not believe so. But I want someone sorely to tell me that he believes it too. Do write to me and give me a clue out of this valley of the shadow of death . . .

X

Glaucus
1853-5

After 1852 or thereabouts, Charles' interest in social reform had appeared to wane, although throughout his life certain aspects, notably sanitation, remained a burning cause. His parish, his family and his writing fully occupied his energies; and perhaps he was growing tired of attacks from fellow-clerics and reviewers; and he was even ostracized, as happened when, in the winter of 1852–3, the family sought refuge in Torquay from the ill-health that always dogged them at Eversley with its damp and dark rectory. The clergy of Torquay banned the notorious rector of Eversley from their pulpits and even kept the Kingsleys at arms' length socially. This gave Charles all the more time to do what he really enjoyed—prospecting on the foreshore, cliffs and caves for marine life. He had made friends with the Plymouth Brother Philip Gosse, also an amateur naturalist, who was then living in London, and despatched to him regularly hampers of wicker-covered jars containing everything from seaweeds and polyps to crabs and shells.

'Those who fancy me as a "sentimentalist" and a "fanatic" little know how thoroughly my own bent is for physical sciences,' he wrote to Thomas Cooper. 'How I am happier now in classifying a new polype, or solving a new geognostic problem of strata, or any other bit of hard Baconian induction, than in writing all the novels in the world.' Unlike many of his fellow clerics, Darwin's theory of evolution presented him with no theological problems. 'Darwin is conquering everywhere, and rushing in like a flood,' he wrote in 1863 to Maurice, 'by mere force of truth and fact.' In natural selection the hand of God could be seen at work guiding primitive forms of life towards their highest development in the shape of Man. 'What can the theologian have to say, save that God's works are even more wonderful than he always believed them to be?' In a sense he even anticipated the formulation of the evolutionary theory in a strange dream-sequence inter-

polated into Alton Locke, *in which the protagonist imagined himself
to exist first 'at the lowest point of created life: a madrepore rooted to
the rock', and thence up the evolutionary ladder becoming in turn a
soft crab, a remora, a mylodon in South American forests and an ape
in Borneo.*

*The fruit of Charles' explorations of the sea-coast of Devon was a
series of sketches published first in the* North British Review *and
subsequently collected in a small book,* Glaucus: Or Wonders of the
Sea Shore, *which appeared in 1855. It was written mainly with the
object of passing on to his children his almost passionate involvement
in marine biology, and in a manner calmer, more objective, more sym-
pathetic than that of his political salvos against the evils of the day.*

*The first of these two extracts describes how the long black sea-
worm entraps its dinner; the second, an encounter with madrepores
under the ruins of a pier.*

Next, what are those bright little buds, like salmon-coloured Bank-
sia roses half expanded, sitting closely on the stone? Touch them;
the soft part is retracted, and the orange flower of flesh is transformed into a pale pink flower of stone. That is the Madrepore,
Caryophyllia smithii; one of our south coast rarities; and see, on the
lip of the last one, which we have carefully scooped off with the
chisel, two little pink towers of stone, delicately striated; drop them
into this small bottle of sea-water, and from the top of each tower
issues every half-second—what shall we call it?—a hand or net of
finest hairs, clutching at something invisible to our grosser sense.
That is the Pyrgoma, parasitic only (so far as we know) on the lip
of this same Madrepore; a little 'cirrhipod', the cousin of those tiny
barnacles which roughen every rock, and one of those larger ones
also who burrow in the thick hide of the whale, and, borne about
upon his mighty sides, throw out their tiny casting nets, as this
Pyrgoma does, to catch every passing animalcule, and sweep them
into the jaws concealed within its shell. And this creature, rooted
to one spot through life and death, was in its infancy a free swimming animal, hovering from place to place upon delicate ciliae,
till, having sown its wild oats, it settled down in life, built itself a
good stone house, and became a landowner, or rather a glebe
adscriptus, for ever and a day. Mysterious destiny!—yet not so
mysterious as that of the free medusoid young of every polyp and

coral, which ends as a rooted tree of horn or stone, and seems to the eye of sensuous fancy to have literally degenerated into a vegetable . . .

There are a few other true cellepore corals round the coast. The largest of all, Cervicornis, may be dredged a few miles outside on the Exmouth bank, with a few more Tubulipores: but all tiny things, the lingering and, as it were, expiring remnants of the great coral-world which, through the abysmal depths of past ages, formed here in Britain our limestone hills, storing up for generations yet unborn the materials of agriculture and architecture. Inexpressibly interesting, even solemn, to those who will think, is the sight of those puny parasites which, as it were, connect the ages of the aeons: yet not so solemn and full of meaning as that tiny relic of an older world, the little pear-shaped Turbinolia (cousin of the Madrepores and Sea-anemones) found fossil in the Suffolk Crag, and yet still lingering here and there alive in the deep water of Scilly and the west coast of Ireland, possessor of a pedigree which dates, perhaps, from ages before the day in which it was said, 'Let us make man in our image, after our likeness.' To think that the whole human race, its joys and sorrows, its virtues and its sins, its aspirations and its failures, has been rushing out of eternity and into eternity again, as Arjoon in the Bhagavad Gita beheld the race of men issuing from Kreeshna's flaming mouth and swallowed up in it again 'as the crowds of insects swarm into the flame, as the homeless streams leap down into the ocean bed', in an everlasting heartpulse whose blood is living souls—and all that while, and ages before that mystery began, that humble coral, unnoticed on the dark seafloor, has been 'continuing as it was at the beginning' and fulfilling 'the law which cannot be broken', while races and dynasties and generations have been

'Playing such fantastic tricks before high heaven
As make the angels weep.'

XI

The Heroes
1856

Charles' biographer, Dame Una Pope-Hennessy, believes The Heroes
*to have been the 'first English childrens' book that was not written
primarily to inculcate good morals'. Nevertheless, children who read it
can hardly have failed to draw the moral that to do all and dare all is
the highest virtue of a hero, no less among ancient Greeks than among
Elizabethan sailors and soldiers in the Crimea. This 'little present of
old Greek fairy tales' was written for his three children Rose, Maurice
and Mary, and retells in simple language the legends of Perseus and
the Gorgon, Jason and the Golden Fleece and Theseus and the Mino-
taur. 'I love these old Heliens dearly', Charles wrote in the preface;
'they seem to me like brothers.' It was true that they were heathens, but
Zeus had been 'a dim remembrance of the blessed true God', and the
Hellenes had observed six out of the ten commandments.*

*In these tales Charles wrote plainly and rhythmically and without
the hyperbole and over-painting of the scene which sometimes impeded
the flow of his novels. The following extract describes Theseus' encounter with Procrustes.*

And as he was skirting the Vale of Cephisus, along the foot of lofty
Parnes, a very tall and strong man came down to meet him, dressed
in rich garments. On his arms were golden bracelets, and round his
neck a collar of jewels; and he came forward, bowing courteously,
and held out both his hands, and spoke—

'Welcome, fair youth, to these mountains; happy am I to have
met you! For what greater pleasure to a good man, than to entertain
strangers? But I see that you are weary. Come up to my castle and
rest yourself awhile.'

'I give you thanks,' said Theseus: 'but I am in haste to go up the
valley, and to reach Aphidnai in the Vale of Cephisus.'

'Alas! you have wandered far from the right way, and you cannot reach Aphidnai tonight, for there are many miles of mountain between you and it, and steep passes, and cliffs dangerous after nightfall. It is well for you that I met you, for my whole joy is to find strangers, and to feast them at my castle, and hear tales from them of foreign lands. Come up with me, and eat the best of venison, and drink the rich red wine, and sleep upon my famous bed, of which all travellers say that they never saw the like. For whatsoever the stature of my guest, however tall or short, that bed fits him to a hair, and he sleeps on it as he never slept before.' And he laid hold on Theseus' hands, and would not let him go.

Theseus wished to go forwards: but he was ashamed to seem churlish to so hospitable a man; and he was curious to see that wondrous bed; and beside, he was hungry and weary: yet he shrank from the man, he knew not why; for, though his voice was gentle and fawning, it was dry and husky like a toad's; and though his eyes were gentle, they were dull and cold like stones. But he consented, and went with the man up a glen which led from the road toward the peaks of Parnes, under the dark shadow of the cliffs.

And as they went up, the glen grew narrower, and the cliffs higher and darker, and beneath them a torrent roared, half seen between bare limestone crags. And around them was neither tree nor bush, while from the white peaks of Parnes the snow-blasts swept down the glen, cutting and chilling, till a horror fell on Theseus as he looked round at that doleful place. And he asked at last, 'Your castle stands, it seems, in a dreary region.'

'Yes; but once within it, hospitality makes all things cheerful. But who are these?' and he looked back, and Theseus also; and far below, along the road which they had left, came a string of laden asses, and merchants walking by them, watching their ware.

'Ah, poor souls!' said the stranger. 'Well for them that I looked back and saw them! And well for me too, for I shall have the more guests at my feast. Wait awhile till I go down and call them, and we will eat and drink together the livelong night. Happy am I, to whom Heaven sends so many guests at once!'

And he ran back down the hill waving his hand and shouting to the merchants, while Theseus went slowly up the steep pass.

But as he went up he met an aged man, who had been gathering driftwood in the torrent-bed. He had laid down his faggot in the road, and was trying to lift it again to his shoulder. And when he saw Theseus, he called to him, and said—

'O fair youth, help me up with my burden, for my limbs are stiff and weak with years.'

Then Theseus lifted the burden on his back. And the old man blest him, and then looked earnestly upon him, and said—

'Who are you, fair youth, and wherefore travel you this doleful road?'

'Who I am my parents know; but I travel this doleful road because I have been invited by a hospitable man, who promises to feast me, and to make me sleep upon I know not what wondrous bed.'

Then the old man clapped his hands together and cried—

'O house of Hades, man-devouring! will thy maw never be full? Know, fair youth, that you are going to torment and to death, for he who met you (I will requite your kindness by another) is a robber and a murderer of men. Whatsoever stranger he meets he entices him hither to death; and as for this bed of which he speaks, truly it fits all comers, yet none ever rose alive off it save me.'

'Why?' asked Theseus, astonished.

'Because, if a man be too tall for it, he lops his limbs till they be short enough, and if he be too short, he stretches his limbs till they be long enough; but me only he spared, seven weary years agone; for I alone of all fitted his bed exactly, so he spared me, and made me his slave. And once I was a wealthy merchant, and dwelt in brazen-gated Thebes; but now I hew wood and draw water for him, the torment of all mortal men.'

Then Theseus said nothing; but he ground his teeth together.

'Escape, then,' said the old man, 'for he will have no pity on thy youth. But yesterday he brought up hither a young man and a maiden, and fitted them upon his bed; and the young man's hands and feet he cut off, but the maiden's limbs he stretched until she died, and so both perished miserably—but I am tired of weeping over the slain. And therefore he is called Procrustes the stretcher, though his father called him Damastes. Flee from him: yet whither will you flee? The cliffs are steep, and who can climb them? and there is no other road.'

But Theseus laid his hand upon the old man's mouth, and said, 'There is no need to flee;' and he turned to go down the pass.

89

THE KINGSLEYS

'Do not tell him that I have warned you, or he will kill me by some evil death;' and the old man screamed after him down the glen; but Theseus strode on in his wrath.

And he said to himself, 'This is an ill-ruled land; when shall I have done ridding it of monsters?' And as he spoke, Procrustes came up the hill, and all the merchants with him, smiling and talking gaily. And when he saw Theseus, he cried, 'Ah, fair young guest, have I kept you too long waiting?'

But Theseus answered, 'The man who stretches his guests upon a bed and hews off their hands and feet, what shall be done to him, when right is done throughout the land?'

Then Procrustes' countenance changed, and his cheeks grew as green as a lizard, and he felt for his sword in haste; but Theseus leapt on him, and cried—

'Is this true, my host, or is it false?' and he clasped Procrustes round waist and elbow, so that he could not draw his sword.

'Is this true, my host, or is it false?' But Procrustes answered never a word.

Then Theseus flung him from him, and lifted up his dreadful club; and before Procrustes could strike him he had struck, and felled him to the ground.

And once again he struck him; and his evil soul fled forth, and went down to Hades squeaking, like a bat into the darkness of a cave.

Then Theseus stript him of his gold ornaments, and went up to his house, and found there great wealth and treasure, which he had stolen from the passers-by. And he called the people of the country, whom Procrustes had spoiled a long time, and parted the spoil among them, and went down the mountains, and away.

XII

Two Years Ago
1857

At the end of 1855 the Kingsleys returned to Eversley but not to the unwholesome rectory; they rented a house on higher ground called Farley Court. Charles resumed his parochial duties and began a new novel. 'Two years ago,' he wrote in his preface, 'was the time for work; for men to do with all their might, whatsoever their hands found to do. But now the storm has lulled once more', and people could recollect in tranquillity 'the wonders of that sudden strange and sad' period.

Two Years Ago is a rag-bag of a book with all sorts of recollections bundled in—a shipwreck seen in childhood off Clovelly (Aberalva in the novel); the cholera epidemic; a holiday in Germany; a storm on the Glyder Fawr;—many hares started but none caught. The cheerful, devil-may-care, foot-loose young doctor, Tom Thurnall, is a portrait of the author's brother George and an embodiment, with one serious flaw, of Charles' ideal of the manly, self-reliant, fearless young Englishman, chivalrous to women and concealing a heart of gold beneath a mask of cynical realism. (And sharing his creator's devotion to marine biology.)

Tom turns up in Aberalva as the sole survivor of the wreck, plucked from a tumultuous ocean by the beautiful but excessively pious school-teacher, Grace Harvey. In the course of the rescue, a belt strapped to his waist and containing £1500 in gold coins, intended for the succour of his blind old father, disappears. Can that angel of mercy Grace, selflessly devoted to prayer, little children and her mother, have stolen it?

On the slender thread of Tom's suspicion hangs this tale, which offers an airing to such favourite Kingsley topics as absentee landlords, effeminate poets, popish practices, dissenting narrowness, slavery in North America and the nature of women. (He is more realistic about this than one might expect, putting into Tom's mouth the remark that you will always find two women to every man at public hangings— 'quaint—that appetite for horrors the sweet creatures have'.) Eventually

THE KINGSLEYS

Tom, after quelling the cholera, disappears to the Crimean war to
escape the conflict between his love for Grace and his distrust of her
honesty. Grace follows, having retrieved the belt which had been stolen
by her mother. Failing to find him, she instals herself as ministering
angel to his blind old father. On Christmas Eve (snow on the way) Dr
Thurnall senior is listening 'with a triumphant smile to wonders which
he will never behold with mortal eyes'—an account of a recent photo-
graphic exhibition—when in walks Tom, lean and ragged but cheerful
as ever, and with the basic flaw at last removed from his character:
restored not only to the arms of Grace, but to faith in his Eternal Father.

The novel, published by Macmillan in 1857, was a best-seller,
earning a £1000 advance. Charles described it, rather strangely, as
'another side-stroke at the Tartarus doctrine, which is never out of my
mind'. Tartarus—the nethermost region of hell—was like the public's
bad tooth, he wrote; people would endure anything, rather than have
it out. Too compassionate a man fully to accept his Church's doctrine
of eternal damnation, he felt that death could not obliterate all hope
of redemption for sinners; but this 'must be carefully taught, as other-
wise people might mistake it for the Romish doctrine of purgatory'.

In the chosen extract Elsley Vavasour, a posturing poet, has taken
to the crags of Snowdon in a half-demented attempt to escape from
the torments caused by his belief (a false one) that his wife has been
unfaithful.

Elsley left the door of Pen-y-gwryd, careless whither he went, if
he went only far enough.

In front of him rose the Glyder Vawr, its head shrouded in soft
mist, through which the moonlight gleamed upon the chequered
quarries of that enormous desolation, the dead bones of the eldest-
born of time. A wild longing seized him; he would escape up
thither; up into those clouds, up anywhere to be alone—alone
with his miserable self. That was dreadful enough; but less dreadful than having a companion—ay, even a stone by him—which
could remind him of the scene which he had left; even remind him
that there was another human being on earth besides himself. Yes
—to put that cliff between him and all the world! Away he plunged
from the high road, splashing over the boggy uplands, scrambling
among scattered boulders, across a stormy torrent bed, and then
across another and another:—when would he reach that dark

marbled wall, which rose into the infinite blank, looking within a stone-throw of him, and yet no nearer after he had walked a mile?

He reached it at last, and rushed up the talus of boulders, springing from stone to stone; till his breath failed him, and he was forced to settle into a less frantic pace. But upward he would go, and upward he went, with a strength which he had never felt before. Strong? How should he not be strong, while every vein felt filled with molten lead; and while some unseen power seemed not so much to attract him upwards, as to drive him by magical repulsion from all that he had left below?

So upward and upward ever, driven on by the terrible gadfly, like Io of old he went; stumbling upwards along torrent beds of slippery slate, writhing himself upward through crannies where the waterfall plashed cold upon his chest and face, yet could not cool the inward fire; climbing, hand and knee, up cliffs of sharp-edged rock; striding over downs where huge rocks lay crouched in the grass, like fossil monsters of some ancient world, and seemed to stare at him with still and angry brows. Upward still, to black terraces of lava, standing out hard and black against the gray cloud, gleaming, like iron in the moonlight, stair above stair, like those over which Vathek and the princess climbed up to the halls of Eblis. Over their crumbling steps, up through their cracks and crannies, out upon a dreary slope of broken stones, and then—before he dives upward into the cloud ten yards above his head—one breathless look back upon the world.

The horizontal curtain of mist; gauzy below, fringed with white tufts and streamers, deepening above into the blackness of utter night. Below it a long gulf of soft yellow haze, in which, as in a bath of gold, lie delicate bars of far-off western cloud; and the faint glimmer of the western sea, above long knotted spurs of hill, in deepest shades, like a bunch of purple grapes flecked here and there from behind with gleams of golden light; and beneath them again, the dark woods sleeping over Gwynnant, and their dark double sleeping in the bright lake below.

On the right hand Snowdon rises. Vast sheets of utter blackness —vast sheets of shining light. He can see every crag that juts from the green walls of Galt-y-Wennalt; and far past it into the Great Valley of Cwm Dyli; and then the red peak, now black as night, shuts out the world with its huge mist-topped cone. But on the left

hand all is deepest shade. From the highest saw-edges where Moel
Meirch cuts the golden sky, down to the very depths of the abyss,
all is lustrous darkness, sooty, and yet golden still. Let the darkness
lie upon it forever! Hidden by those woods where she stood an hour
ago! Hidden that road down which, even now, they may be pacing
together!—Curse the thought! He covers his face in his hands and
shudders in every limb.

He lifts his hands from his face at last:—what has befallen?

Before the golden haze a white veil is falling fast. Sea, mountain,
lake are vanishing, fading as in a dream. Soon he can see nothing
but the twinkle of a light in Pen-y-gwyrd, a thousand feet below;
happy children are nestling there in innocent sleep. Jovial voices
are chatting round the fire. What has he to do with youth, and
health, and joy? Lower, lower, ye clouds! Shut out that insolent
and intruding spark, till nothing be seen but the silver sheet of Cwm
Fynnon, and the silver zig-zag lines which wander into it among
black morass, while down the mountain side go, softly sliding,
troops of white mist-angels. Softly they slide, swift and yet motionless, as if by some inner will, which needs no force of limbs; gliding
gently round the crags, diving gently off into the abyss, their long
white robes trailing about their feet in upward-floating folds. 'Let
us go hence' they seem to whisper to the God-forsaken, as legends
say they whispered when they left their doomed shrine in old
Jerusalem. Let the white fringe fall between him and the last of that
fair troop; let the grey curtain follow, the black pall above descend;
till he is alone in darkness that may be felt, and in the shadow of
death.

Now he is safe at last; hidden from all living things—hidden, it
may be, from God; for at least God is hidden from him. He has
desired to be alone; and he is alone: the centre of the universe, if
universe there be. All created things, suns and planets, seem to
revolve round him, and he a point of darkness, not of light. He
seems to float self-poised in the centre of the boundless nothing,
upon an ell-broad slab of stone—and yet not even on that; for the
very ground on which he stands he does not feel. He does not feel
the mist which wets his cheek, the blood which throbs within his
veins. He only is; and there is none besides.

Horrible thought! Permitted but to few, and to them—thank
God!—but rarely. For two minutes of that absolute self-isolation

would bring madness; if, indeed, it be not the very essence of madness itself.

There he stood; he knew not for how long; without motion, without thought, without even rage or hate, now—in one blank paralysis of his whole nature; conscious only of his whole nature; conscious only of self, and of a dull, inward fire, as if his soul were a dark vault, lighted with lurid smoke.

What was that? He started; shuddered—as well he might. Had he seen heaven opened? or another place? So momentary was the vision, that he scarce knew what he saw—

There it was again! Lasting but for a moment: but long enough to let him see the whole western heaven transfigured into one sheet of pale blue gauze, and before it Snowdon towering black as ink, with every saw and crest cut out hard and terrible against the lightning-glare: and then the blank of darkness.

Again! The awful black giant, towering high in air, before the gates of that blue abyss of flame: but a black crown of cloud has settled upon his head; and out of it the lightning sparks leap to and fro, ringing his brows with a coronet of fire.

Another moment, and the roar of that great battle between earth and heaven crashed full on Elsley's ears.

He heard it leap from Snowdon, sharp and rattling, across the gulf toward him, till it crashed full upon the Glyder overhead, and rolled and flapped from crag to crag, and died away along the dreary downs. No! There it boomed out again, thundering full against Siabod on the left; and Siabod tossed it on to Moel Meirch, who answered from all her clefts and peaks with a long confused battle-growl, and then tossed it across to Aran; and Aran, with one dull, bluff report from her flat cliff, to nearer Lliwedd; till, worn out with the long buffetings of that giant ring, it sank and died on Gwynnant far below—but ere it died, another and another thunder-crash burst, sharper and nearer every time, to hurry round the hills after the one which roared before it.

Another minute, and the blue glare filled the sky once more: but no black Titan towered before it now. The storm had leapt Llanberris pass, and all round Elsley was one howling chaos of cloud, and rain, and blinding flame. He turned and fled again.

By the sensation of his feet, he knew that he was going up-hill;

and if he but went upward, he cared not whither he went. The rain gushed through, where the lightning pierced the cloud, in drops like musket balls. He was drenched to the skin in a moment; dazzled and giddy from the flashes; stunned by the everlasting roar, peel over-rushing peel, echo out-shouting echo, till rocks and air quivered alike beneath the continuous battle-cannonade. 'What matter? What fitter guide for such a path of mine than the blue lightning-flashes?'

Poor wretch! He had gone out of his way for many a year, to give himself up, a willing captive, to the melodramatic view of nature, and had let sights and sounds, not principles and duties, mould his feelings for him: and now, in his utter need and utter weakness, he had met her in a mood which was too awful for one such as he was to resist. The Nemesis had come; and swept away helplessly, without faith and hope, by those outward impressions of things on which he had feasted his soul so long, he was the puppet of his own eyes and ears; the slave of glare and noise.

Breathless, but still untired, he toiled up a steep incline, where he could feel beneath him neither moss nor herb. Now and then his feet brushed through a soft tuft of parsley fern: but soon even that sign of vegetation ceased; his feet only rasped over rough bare rock, and he was along in a desert of stone.

What was that sudden apparition above him, seen for a moment dim and gigantic through the mist, hid the next in darkness? The next flash showed him a line of obelisks, like giants crouching side by side, staring down on him from the clouds. Another five minutes, and he was at their feet, and past them; to see above them again another line of awful watchers through the storms and rains of many a thousand years, waiting, grim and silent, like those doomed senators in the Capitol of Rome, till their own turn should come, and the last lightning stroke hurl them down, to lie forever by their fallen brothers, whose mighty bones bestrewed the screes below.

He groped his way between them; saw some fifty yards beyond a higher peak; gained it by fierce struggles and many falls; saw another beyond that; and, rushing down and up two slopes of moss, reached a region where the upright lava-ledges had been split asunder into chasms, crushed together again into caves, toppled over each other, hurled up into spires, in such chaotic confusion that progress seemed impossible.

A flash of lightning revealed a lofty cairn above his head. There was yet, then, a higher point! He would reach it, if he broke every limb in the attempt! and madly he hurried on, feeling his way from ledge to ledge, squeezing himself through crannies, crawling on hands and knees along the sharp chines of the rocks, till he reached the foot of the cairn; climbed it, and threw himself at full length on the summit of Glyder Vawr.

An awful place it always is; and Elsley saw it at an awful time, as the glare unveiled below him a sea of rock-waves, all sharp on edge, pointing toward him on every side; or rather one wave-crest of a sea; for twenty yards beyond, all sloped away into the abysmal dark.

Terrible were those rocks below; and ten times more terrible as seen through the lurid glow of his distempered brain. All the weird peaks and slabs seemed pointing up at him; sharp-toothed jaws gaped upward—tongues hissed upward—arms pointed upward—hounds leaped upward—monstrous snake-heads peered upward out of cracks and caves. Did he not see them move, writhe? or was it the ever-shifting light of the flashes? Did he not hear them howl, yell at him? or was it but the wind, tortured in their labyrinthine caverns?

The next moment, and all was dark again; but the images which had been called up remained, and fastened on his brain, and grew there; and when, in the light of the next flash, the scene returned, he could see the red lips of the phantom hounds, the bright eyes of the phantom snakes; the tongues wagged in mockery; the hands brandished great stones to hurl at him; the mountain-top was instinct with fiendish life—a very Blocksberg of all hideous shapes and sins.

And yet he did not shrink. Horrible it was; he was going mad before it. And yet he took a strange and fierce delight in making it more horrible; in maddening himself yet more and more; in clothing those fantastic stones with every fancy which could inspire another man with dread. But he had no dread. Perfect rage, like perfect love, casts out fear. He rejoiced in his own misery, in his own danger. His life hung on a thread; any instant might hurl him from that cairn, a blackened corpse.

What better end? Let it come! He was Prometheus on the peak of Caucasus, hurling defiance at the unjust Jove! His hopes, his love, his very honour—curse it!—ruined! Let the lightning stroke come! He were a coward to shrink from it. Let him face the worst, unprotected, bare-handed, naked, and do battle, himself, and nothing but himself, against the universe! And, as men at such moments will do, in the mad desire to free the self-tortured spirit from some unseen and choking bond, he began wildly tearing off his clothes.

But merciful nature brought relief, and stopped him in his mad efforts, or he had been a frozen corpse long ere the dawn. His hand, stiff with cold, refused to obey him: as he delayed he was saved. After the paroxysm came the collapse; he sank upon the top of the cairn half senseless. He felt himself falling over its edge; and the animal instinct of self-preservation, unconsciously to him, made him slide down gently, till he sank into a crack between two rocks, sheltered somewhat, as it befell happily, from the lashing of the rain.

Another minute, and he slept a dreamless sleep.

But there are two men upon that mountain, whom neither rock nor rain, storm nor thunder, have conquered, because they are simply brave honest men; and who are, perhaps, far more 'poetic' characters at this moment than Elsley Vavasour, or any dozen of mere verse-writers, because they are hazarding their lives on an errand of mercy; and all the while have so little notion that they are hazarding their lives, or doing anything dangerous or heroic, that, instead of being touched for a moment by nature's melodrama, they are jesting at each other's troubles, greeting each interval of darkness with mock shouts of misery and despair, likening the crags to various fogies of their acquaintance, male and female, and only pulling the cutty pipes out of their mouths to chant snatches of jovial songs. They are Wynd and Naylor, the two Cambridge boating-men, in bedrabbled flannel trousers, and shooting-jackets pocketful of water; who are both fully agreed that hunting a mad poet over the mountains in a thunderstorm is, on the whole, 'the jolliest lark they ever had in their lives'.

'He must have gone up here somewhere. I saw the poor beggar against the sky as plain as I see you—which I don't—' for darkness cut the speech short.

'Where be you, William? says the keeper.'

'Here I be, sir, says the beater, with my 'eels above my 'ead.'

'Wery well, William; when you get your 'ead above your 'eels, gae on.'

'But I'm stuck fast between two stones! Hang the stones!' And
Naylor bursts into an old seventeenth century ditty, of the days of
'three-man glees'.

> They stoans, they stoans, they stoans, they stoans—
> They stoans that built George Riddler's oven,
> O they was fetched from Blackeney quarr';
> And George he was a jolly old man,
> And his head did grow above his har'.

> One thing in George Riddler I must commend,
> And I hold it for a valiant thing;
> With any three brothers in Gloucestershire
> He swore that his three sons should sing.

> There was Dick the tribble, and Tom the mane,
> Let every man sing in his own place;
> And William he was the eldest brother,
> And therefore he should sing the base—

I'm down again! This is my thirteenth fall.'
'So am I! I shall just lie and light a pipe!'
'Come on, now, and look round the lee side of this crag. We shall
find him bundled up under the lee of one of them.'
'He don't know the lee from the windward, I dare say.'
'He'll soon find out the difference by his skin; if it's half as wet,
at least, as mine is.'
'I'll tell you what, Naylor, if the poor fellow has crossed the
ridge, and tried to go down the Twll du, he's a dead man by this
time.'
'He'll have funked it, when he comes to the edge, and sees nothing but mist below. But if he has wandered on to the cliffs above
Trifaen, he's a dead man then, at all events. Get out of the way of
that flash! A close shave that! I believe my whiskers are singed.'
"Pon my honour, Wynd, we ought to be saying our prayers
rather than joking in this way.'
'We may do both, and be none the worse. As for coming to grief,
old boy, we're on a good errand, I suppose, and the devil himself
can't harm us. Still, shame to him who's ashamed to saying his
prayers, as Arnold used to say.'

And all the while, these two brave lads have been thrusting their lanthorn into every nook and cranny, and beating round every crag careful and cunningly, till long past two in the morning.

'Here's the ordnance cairn at last; and—here am I astride of a carving-knife, I think! Come and help me off, or I shall be split to the chin!'

'I'm coming! What's this soft under my feet? Who-o-o-oop! Run him to earth at last!'

And diving down into a crack, Wynd drags out by the collar the unconscious Elsley.

'What a swab! Like a piece of wet blotting-paper. Lucky he's not made of salt.'

'He's dead!' says Naylor.

'Not a bit. I can feel his heart. There's life in the old dog yet.'

And they begin, under the lee of a rock, chafing him, wrapping him in their plaids, and pouring whisky down his throat.

It was some time before Vavasour recovered his consciousness. The first use which he made of it was to bid his preservers leave him; querulously at first; and then fiercely, when he found out who they were.

'Leave me, I say! Cannot I be alone if I choose? What right have you to dog me in this way?'

'My dear sir, we have as much right here as any one else; and if we find a man dying here of cold and fatigue—'

'What business of yours, if I choose to die?'

'There is no harm in your dying, sir,' says Naylor. 'The harm is in our letting you die; I assure you it is entirely to satisfy our own consciences we are troubling you thus;' and he begins pressing him to take food.

'No, sir, nothing from you! You have shown me impertinence enough in the last few weeks, without pressing on me benefits for which I do not wish. Let me go! If you will not leave me, I shall leave you!'

And he tried to rise; but, stiffened with cold, sank back again upon the rock.

In vain they tried to reason with him; begged his pardon for all past jests: he made effort after effort to get up; and at last, his limbs, regaining strength by the fierceness of his passion, supported him; and he struggled onward toward the northern slope of the mountain.

'You must not go down till it is light; it is as much as your life is worth.'

'I am going to Bangor, sir; and go I will!'

'I tell you there are fifteen hundred feet of slippery screes below you.'

'As steep as a house-roof, with every tile on it loose. You will roll from top to bottom before you have gone a hundred yards.'

'What care I? Let me go, I say! Curse you, sir! Do you mean to use force?'

'I do,' said Wynd quietly, as he took his arms and body, and set him down on the rock like a child.

'You have assaulted me, sir! The law shall avenge this insult, if there be law in England!'

'I know nothing about law: but I suppose it will justify me in saving any man's life who is rushing to certain death.'

'Look here, sir!' said Naylor. 'Go down, if you will, when it grows light; but from this place you do not stir yet. Whatever you may think of our conduct tonight, you will thank us for it tomorrow morning, when you see where you are.'

The unhappy man stamped with rage. The red glare of the lanthorn showed him his two powerful warders, standing right and left. He felt that there was no escape from them, but in darkness; and suddenly he dashed at the lanthorn, and tried to tear it out of Wynd's hands.

'Steady, sir!' said Wynd, springing back, and parrying his outstretched hand. 'If you wish us to consider you in your senses, you will be quiet.'

'And if you don't choose to appear sane,' said Naylor, 'you must not be surprised if we treat you as men are treated who—you understand me.'

Elsley was silent awhile; his rage finding itself impotent, subsided into dark cunning. 'Really, gentlemen,' he said at length, 'I believe you are right; I have been very foolish, and you very kind; but you would excuse my absurdities if you knew their provocation.'

'My dear sir,' said Naylor, 'we are bound to believe that you have good cause enough for what you are doing. We have no wish to interfere impertinently. Only wait till daylight, and wrap yourself in one of our plaids, as the only possible method of carrying out your own intentions; for dead men can't go to Bangor, whithersoever else they may go.'

'You really are too kind; but I believe I must accept your offer, under penalty of being called mad;' and Elsley laughed a hollow laugh; for he was by no means sure he was not mad. He took the proffered wrapper, lay down, and seemed to sleep.

Wynd and Naylor, congratulating themselves on his better mind, lay down also beneath the other plaid, intending to watch him. But worn out with fatigue, they were both fast asleep ere ten minutes had passed.

Elsley had determined to keep himself awake at all risks; and he paid a bitter penalty for so doing; for now that the fury had passed away, his brain began to work freely again, and inflicted torture so exquisite, that he looked back with regret at the unreasoning madness of last night, as a less fearful hell than that of thought; of deliberate, acute recollections, suspicions, trains of argument, which he tried to thrust from him, and yet could not. Who has not known in the still, sleepless hours of night, how dark thoughts will possess the mind with terrors, which seem logical, irrefutable, inevitable?

So it was then with the wretched Elsley; within his mind a whole train of devil's advocates seemed arguing, with triumphant subtlety, the certainty of Lucia's treason; and justifying to him his rage, his hatred, his flight, his desertion of his own children—if indeed (so far had the devil led him astray) they were his own. At last he could bear it no longer. He would escape to Bangor, then to London, cross to France, to Italy, and there bury himself amid the forests of the Appenines, or the sunny glens of Calabria. And for a moment the vision of a poet's life in that glorious land brightened his dark imagination. Yes! He would escape thither, and be at peace; and if the world heard of him again, it should be in such a thunder-voice as those which Shelley and Byron, from their southern seclusion, had shaken the ungrateful motherland which cast them out. He would escape; and now was the time to do it! For the rain had long since ceased; the dawn was approaching fast; the cloud was thinning from black to pearly gray. Now was his time— were it not for those two men! To be kept, guarded, stopped by them, or by any man! Shame! intolerable! He had fled hither to be free, and even here he found himself a prisoner. True, they had promised to let him go if he waited till daylight; but perhaps they were deceiving him, as he was deceiving them—why not? They thought him mad. It was a ruse, a stratagem to keep him quiet awhile, and then bring him back—'restore him to his afflicted friends.' His friends, truly! He would be too cunning for them yet. And even if they meant to let him go, would he accept liberty from them, or any man? No; he was free. He had a right to go; and go he would, that moment!

He raised himself cautiously. The lanthorn had burned to the socket; and he could not see the men, though they were not four yards off; but by their regular and heavy breathing he could tell that they both slept soundly. He slipped from under the plaid, drew his shoes off for fear of noise among the rocks, and rose. What if he did make a noise? What if they woke, chased him, and brought him back by force? Curse the thought! and gliding close to them, he listened again to their heavy breathing.

How could he prevent their following him?

A horrible, nameless temptation came over him. Every vein in his body throbbed fire; his brain seemed to swell to bursting; and ere he was aware, he found himself feeling about in the darkness for a loose stone.

He could not find one. Thank God that he could not find one! But after that dreadful thought had once crossed his mind, he must flee that place ere the brand of Cain be on his brow.

With a cunning and activity utterly new to him, he glided away like a snake; downward over crags and boulders, he knew not how long or how far; all he knew was, that he was going down, down, down into a dim abyss. There was just light enough to discern the upper surface of a rock within arm's length; beyond that all was blank. He seemed to be hours descending; to be going down mile after mile; and still he reached no level spot. The mountain-side was too steep for him to stand upright, except at moments. It seemed one uniform quarry of smooth broken slate, slipping down for ever beneath his feet. Whither? He grew giddy, and more giddy; and a horrible fantastic notion seized him, that he had lost his way; and somehow the precipices had no bottom, no end at all; that he was going down some infinite abyss, into the very depths of the earth, and the molten roots of the mountains, never to re-ascend. He stopped, trembling, only to slide down again; terrified, he tried to struggle upward, but the shale gave way beneath his feet, and go he must.

What was that noise above his head? A falling stone? Were his enemies in pursuit? Down to the depth of hell rather than that they should take him! He drove his heels into the slippery shale, and rushed forward blindly, springing, slipping, falling, rolling, till he stopped breathless on a jutting slab.

And lo! below him, through the thin pearly veil of cloud, a dim world of dark cliffs, blue lakes, gray mountains with their dark heads wrapped in cloud, and the straight vale of Nant Francon, magnified in mist, till it seemed to stretch for hundreds of leagues towards the rosy north-east dawning and the shining sea.

With a wild shout he hurried onward. In five minutes he was clear of the cloud. He reached the foot of that enormous slope, and hurried over rocky ways, till he stopped at the top of a precipice, full six hundred feet above the lonely tarn of Idwal.

Never mind. He knew where he was now; he knew that there was a passage somewhere, for he had once seen one from below. He found it, and almost ran along the boggy shore of Idwal, looking back every now and then at the black wall of the Twll du, in dread lest he should see two moving specks in hot pursuit.

And now he had gained the shore of Ogwen, and the broad coach-road; and down it he strode, running at times, past the roaring cataract, past the enormous cliffs of the Carnedds, past Tin-y-maes, where nothing was stirring but a barking dog; on through the sleeping streets of Bethseda, past the black stairs of the Penrhyn quarry. The huge clicking ant-heap was silent now, save for the roar of Ogwen, as he swirled and bubbled down, rich coffee-brown from last night's rain.

On, past rich woods, past trim cottages, gardens gay with flowers; past rhododendron shrubberies, broad fields of golden stubble, sweet clover, and gray swedes, with Ogwen making music far below. The sun is up at last, and Colonel Pennant's grim slate castle, towering above black woods glitters metallic in its rays, like Chaucer's house of fame. He stops, to look back once. Far up the vale, eight miles away, beneath a roof of cloud, the pass of Nant Francon gapes high in air between the great jaws of Carnedd and the Glyder, its cliffs marked with the upright white line of the waterfall. He is clear of the mountains, clear of that cursed place, and all its cursed thoughts! On, past Llandegai and all its rose-clad cottages; past yellow quarrymen walking out to their work; who

stare as they pass at his haggard face drenched clothes, and stream-
ing hair. He does not see them. One fixed thought is in his mind,
and that is, the railway station at Bangor.

He is striding through Bangor streets now, beside the summer
sea, from which fresh scents of shore-weed greet him. He had rather
smell the smoke and gas of the Strand.

The station is shut. He looks at the bill outside. There is no train
for full two hours; and he throws himself, worn-out with fatigue,
upon the doorstep.

Now a new terror seizes him. Has he money enough to reach
London? Has he his purse at all? Too dreadful to find himself
stopped short, on the very brink of deliverance! A cold perspiration
breaks from his forehead as he feels in every pocket. Yes, his purse
is there; but he turns sick as he opens it, and hardly dare look.
Hurrah! Five pounds, six—eight! That will take him as far as
Paris. He can walk, beg the rest of the way, if need be.

What will he do now? Wander over the town, and gaze vacantly
on one little object and another about the house fronts. One thing
he will not look at; and that is the bright summer sea, all golden in
the sun rays, flecked with gay white sails. From all which is bright and
calm, and cheerful, his soul shrinks as from an impertinence; he longs
for the lurid gas-light of London, and the roar of the Strand, and
the everlasting stream of faces, among whom he may wander free,
sure that no one will recognize him, the disgraced, the desperate.

The weary hours roll on. Too tired to stand longer, he sits down
on the shafts of a cart, and tries not to think. It is not difficult. Body
and mind are alike worn out, and his brain seems filled with uniform
dull mist.

A shop-door opens in front of him; a boy comes out. He sees
bottles inside, and shelves, the look of which he knows too well.

The bottle-boy, whistling, begins to take the shutters down. How
often, in Whitbury of old, had Elsley done the same! Half amused,
he watched the lad, and wondered how he spent his evenings, and
what works he read, and whether he ever thought of writing poetry.

And as he watched, all his past life rose up before him, ever since
he served out medicines fifteen years ago—his wild aspirations,
heavy labours, struggles, plans, brief triumphs, long disappoint-
ments; and here was what it had all come to—a failure—a miserable,
shameful failure! Not that he thought of it with repentance, with a

single wish that he had done otherwise; but only with disappointed rage. 'Yes!' he said bitterly to himself—

> We poets in our youth begin in gladness,
> But after some despondency and madness.

This is the way of the world with all who have nobler feelings in them than will fit into its cold rules. Curse the world! what on earth had I to do with mixing myself up in it, and marrying a fine lady? Fool that I was! I might have known from the first that she could not understand me; that she would go back to her own! Let her go! I will forget her, and the world, and everything—and I know how!'

And, springing up, he walked across to the druggist's shop.

Years before, Elsley had tried opium, and found, unhappily for him, that it fed his fancy without inflicting those tortures of indigestion which keep many, happily for them, from its magic snare. He had tried it more than once of late; but Lucia had had a hint of the fact from Thurnall: and in just terror had exacted from him a solemn promise never to touch opium again. Elsley was a man of honour, and the promise had been kept. But now—'I promised her, and therefore I will break my promise! She has broken hers, and I am free!'

And he went in and bought his opium. He took a little on the spot, to allay the cravings of hunger. He reserved a full dose for the railway-carriage. It would bridge over the weary gulf of time which lay between him and the town.

He took his second-class place at last; not without stares and whispers from those round at the wild figure which was starting for London without bag or baggage. But as the clerks agreed, 'If he was running away from his creditors, it was a shame to stop him. If he was running from the police, they would have the more sport the longer the run. At least, it was no business of theirs.'

There was one more thing to do, and he did it. He wrote to Campbell a short note.

'If, as I suppose, you expect from me "the satisfaction of a gentleman", you will find me at . . . Adelphi. I am not escaping from you, but from the whole world. If, by shooting me, you can quicken my escape, you will do me the first and last favour which I am likely to ask from you.'

He posted his letter, settled himself in a corner of the carriage, and took his second dose of opium. From that moment he recollected little more. A confused whirl of hedges and woods, rattling stations, screaming and flashing trains, great red towns, white chalk cuttings; while the everlasting roar and rattle of the carriages shaped themselves in his brain into a hundred snatches of old tunes, all full of a strange merriment, as if mocking at his misery, striving to keep him awake and conscious of who and what he was. He closed his eyes and shut out the hateful garish world; but that sound he could not shut out. Too tired to sleep, too tired even to think, he could do nothing but submit to the ridiculous torment; watching in spite of himself every note, as one jig-tune after another was fiddled by all the imps close to his ear, mile after mile, and county after county, which seemed full seven years long.

At Euston Square the porter called him several times ere he could rouse him. He could hear nothing for awhile but that same imps' melody, even though it had stopped. At last he got out, staring round him, shook himself awake by one strong effort, and hurried away, not knowing whither he went.

Wrapt up in self, he wandered on till dark, slept on a doorstep, and awoke, not knowing at first where he was. Gradually all the horror came back to him, and with the horror the craving for opium wherewith to forget it.

He looked round to see his whereabouts. Surely this must be Golden Square? A sudden thought struck him. He went to a chemist's shop, bought a fresh supply of his poison, and, taking only enough to allay the cravings of his stomach, hurried tottering in the direction of Drury Lane.

Be Good . . .
1857

Charles Kingsley's habit of inserting into his novels verses and ballads was followed in Two Years Ago. *It contains one of his best-known and widely-quoted quatrains.*

> Be good, sweet maid, and let who will be clever,
> Do noble things, not dream them, all day long,
> So making life, death, and the vast forever,
> One grand, sweet song.

XIII

Andromeda and other poems
1858

*Charles loved writing poetry and he loved Greek myths; the two com-
bined, in* Andromeda, *gave him the greatest pleasure to compose. This
poem was 'sometimes considered the best use of hexameters in English',
although Matthew Arnold thought its composer 'too coarse a workman
for poetry'. Certainly the hexameters flow with a rhythmic punch and
gusto across the pages, though not perhaps without an element of
monotony. The story is that of Cassiopea's beautiful daughter who was
chained to a sea-girt rock to appease a sea-monster ravaging the
country. She was rescued by Perseus who showed the monster the
Medusa's head. In the following extract, Perseus, 'golden-haired,
ivory-limbed, ambrosial', having alighted on Andromeda's rock and
fallen instantly in love, deals with the monster and wins his bride.*

    Then, lifting her neck, like a sea-bird
Peering up over the wave, from the foam-white swells of her bosom,
Blushing she kissed him: afar on the topmost Idalian summit
Laughed in the joy of her heart, far-seeing, the queen Aphrodite.
Loosing her arms from his waist he flew upward, awaiting the sea-
    beast.
Onward it came from the southward, as bulky and black as a galley,
Lazily coasting along, as the fish fled leaping before it;
Lazily breasting the ripple, and watching by sandbar and headland,
Listening for laughter of maidens at bleaching, or song of the fisher,
Children at play on the pebbles, or cattle that pawed on the sand-
    hills.
Rolling and dripping it came, where bedded in glistening purple
Cold on the sea-weeds lay the long white sides of the maiden,
Trembling, her face in her hands, and her tresses afloat in the water.
As when an osprey aloft, dark-eyebrowed, royally crested,

Flags on by creek and by cove, and in scorn of the anger of Nereus
Ranges, the king of the shore; if he see on a glittering shallow,
Chasing the bass and the mullet, the fin of a wallowing dolphin,
Halting, he wheels round slowly, in doubt at the weight of his
      quarry,
Whether to clutch it alive, or to fall on the wretch like a plummet,
Stunning with terrible talon the life of the brain in the hindhead:
Then rushes up with a scream, and stooping the war wrath of his
      eyebrows
Falls from the sky like a star, while the wind rattles hoarse in his
      pinions.
Over him closes the foam for a moment; then from the sandbed
Rolls up the great fish, dead, and his side gleams white in the
      sunshine.
Thus fell the boy on the beast, unveiling the face of the Gorgon;
Thus fell the boy on the beast; thus rolled up the beast in his
      horror,
Once, as the dead eyes glared into his; then his sides, death-
      sharpened,
Stiffened and stood, brown rocks, in the wash of the wandering
      water.

*Several poems from this collection have already been selected. Two
more follow, and then a light-hearted invitation (with omissions) to
his friend Tom Hughes to join him on a fishing expedition in North
Wales.*

The Night Bird

A floating, a floating
Across the sleeping sea,
All night I heard a singing bird
Upon the topmost tree.

'Oh came you off the isles of Greece
Or off the banks of Seine;
Or off some tree in forests free
Which fringe the western main?'

'I came not off the old world
Nor yet from off the new—
But I am one of the birds of God
Which sing the whole night through.'

'Oh sing, and wake the dawning—
Oh whistle for the wind;
The night is long, the current strong,
My boat it lags behind.'

'The current sweeps the old world,
The current sweeps the new;
The wind will blow, the dawn will glow
Ere thou hast sailed them through.'

The Watchman

'Watchman, what of the night?'
  'The stars are out in the sky;
And the merry round moon will be rising soon,
  For us to go sailing by.'

'Watchman, what of the night?'
  'The tide flows in from the sea;
There's water to float a little cockboat
  Will carry such fishers as we.'

'Watchman, what of the night?'
  'The night is a fruitful time;
When to many a pair are born children fair,
  To be christened at morning chime.'

Invitation to Tom Hughes

Come away with me, Tom,
Term and talk is done;
My poor lads are reaping
Busy everyone.

Curates mind the parish.
Sweepers mind the court,
We'll away to Snowdon
For our ten days sport,
Fish the August evening
Till the eve is past,
Whoop like boys at pounders
Fairly played and grassed . . .

* * * *

Down, and bathe at day-dawn,
Tramp from lake to lake,
Washing brain and heart clean
Every step we take.
Leave to Robert Browning
Beggars, fleas and vines;
Leave to mournful Ruskin
Popish Apennines,
Dirty Stones of Venice
And his gas-lamps Seven;
We've the stones of Snowdon
And the lamps of Heaven . . .

* * * *

See in every hedgerow
Marks of angels' feet,
Epics in each pebble
Underneath our feet;
Once a year, like schoolboys,
Robin-Hooding go,
Leaving fops and fogies
A thousand feet below.

XIV

The Roman and the Teuton
1860-1

At the age of forty, Charles said to his wife: 'I feel very old. How blessed it will be when all is over! What a long life I have lived!' He was going through one of his periodic collapses into nervous exhaustion and depression. On this occasion his spirits were restored by a Royal Command to preach in the Chapel of Buckingham Palace on Palm Sunday. The Queen, he was warned, liked her sermons short, so he kept his down to well under ten minutes. Much taken with the rector, the Queen appointed him as her Chaplain in Ordinary, with the duty of preaching one sermon a year at the Chapel Royal, St James's, at an annual salary of £30.

This Court connection brought him into contact with the Prince Consort, and the two men took an immediate liking to each other. ('I have fallen in love with that man,' Charles said.) Probably as a result of this, in May 1860, Lord Palmerston offered to the rector of Eversley the Regius Professorship of Modern History at Cambridge. The rector was scarcely less surprised than the historians, for nothing in his training or experience had fitted him for such academic distinction. His wife, however, had no such doubts, and he took up the position after a fishing expedition to Ireland where, to his intense excitement, he caught his first salmon. In November 1860, he delivered his inaugural address on 'The Limits of Exact Science as applied to History', and continued with a series examining the rise and fall of the Goths, whom he extolled, and their final destruction of the disintegrating Roman Empire. These were published under the title of The Roman and the Teuton *in 1864.*

Among the undergraduates, Kingsley was a great success. His lectures were crowded and applauded, and Professor Max Muller, who occupied the Chair of Modern European Languages at Oxford, remarked that they sent young men to 'ask for books which undergraduates had never asked for before at the University libraries'. But he admitted that 'historians by profession would naturally be incensed at some portions' of the lectures, and Justin McCarthy dismissed them as 'downright buffoonery', adding that the lecturer was 'grave as a church and earnest as an owl'. However much historians might look down their noses, the lectures met with favour at Windsor, and led to Charles' appointment as tutor to the Prince of Wales. Unfortunately, having specialized in early German history, he had to mug up English history from the reign of William III to the Battle of Waterloo. This opportunity to mould the royal undergraduate's mind and character was cut short by the death of the Prince Consort at the end of the Prince's first term.

In the following extract from 'The Monk as a Civilizer' Charles returns to his attack on monastic celibacy, and gives some of his reasons.

From Lecture IX: The Monk as a Civilizer
1864

For out of those monasteries sprang—what did not spring? They restored again and again sound law and just government, when the good old Teutonic laws, and the Roman law also, was trampled underfoot amid the lawless strife of ambition and fury. Under their shadow sprang up the towns with their corporate rights, their middle classes, their artizan classes. They were the physicians, the alms-givers, the relieving officers, the school-masters of the middle-age world. They first taught us the great principle of the division of labour, to which we owe, at this moment, that England is what she is, instead of being covered with a horde of peasants, each making and producing everything for himself, and starving each upon his rood of ground. They transcribed or composed all the books of the then world; many of them spent their lives in doing nothing but writing; and the number of books, even of those to be found in single monasteries, considering the tedious labour of copying, is altogether astonishing. They preserved to us the treasures of classical antiquity. They discovered for us the germs of all our modern inventions. They brought in from abroad arts and new knowledge; and while they taught men to know that they had a common humanity, a common Father in heaven taught them also to profit by each other's wisdom instead of remaining in isolated ignorance.

They, too, were the great witnesses against feudal caste. With them was neither high-born nor low-born, rich nor poor: worth was their only test; the meanest serf entering there might become the lord of knights and vassels, the counsellor of kings and princes. Men may talk of democracy—those old monasteries were the most democratic institutions the world had ever till then seen. 'A man's a man for 'a that', was not only talked of in them, but carried out in practice—only not in anarchy, and as a cloak for licentiousness: but under those safeguards of strict discipline, and almost military order, without which men may call themselves free, and yet be really only slaves to their own passions.

Yes, paradoxical as it may seem, in those monasteries was preserved the sacred fire of modern liberty, through those feudal centuries when all the outside world was doing its best to trample it out. Remember, as a single instance, that in the Abbot's lodging at Bury St Edmunds, the Magna Carta was drawn out, before being presented to John at Runnymede. I know what they became afterwards, better than most do here; too well to defile my lips, or your ears, with tales too true. They had done their work, and they went. Like all things born in time, they died; and decayed in time; and the old order changes, giving place to new; and God fulfilled himself in many ways. But in them, too, He fulfilled himself. They were the best things the world had seen; the only method of Christianizing and civilizing semi-barbarous Europe. Like all human plans and conceptions, they contained in themselves original sin: idolatry, celibacy, inhuman fanaticism; there were their three roots of bitterness; and when they bore the natural fruit of immorality, the monasteries fell with a great and just destruction.

But had not those monasteries been good at first, and noble at first; had not the men in them been better and more useful men than the men outside, do you think they would have endured for centuries? They would not even have established themselves at all. They would soon, in those stormy times, have burnt down. But men found that they were good. Their own plunderers found that they could not do without them; and repented, and humbled themselves, and built them up again, to be centres of justice and mercy and peace, amid the wild weltering sea of war and misery. For all things endure, even for a generation, only by virtue of the good which is in them. By the Spirit of God in them they live, as do all

THE ROMAN AND THE TEUTON

created things; and when He taketh away their breath they die, and return again to their dust.

And what was the original sin of them? We can hardly say that it was their superstitious and partially false creed: because that they held in common with all Europe. It was rather that they had identified themselves with, and tried to realize on earth, one of the worst falsehoods of that creed—celibacy. Not being founded on the true and only ground of all society, family life, they were merely artificial and self-willed arrangements of man's invention, which could not be developed to any higher form. And when the sanctity of marriage was revindicated at the Reformation, the monasteries, having identified themselves with celibacy, naturally fell. They could not partake in the Reformation movement, and rise with it into some higher form of life, as the laity outside did. I say, they were altogether artificial things. The Abbot might be called the Abba, Father, of his monks; but he was not their father—just as when young ladies now play at being nuns, they call their superior, Mother: but all the calling in the world will not make that sacred name a fact and a reality, as they too often find out.

And celibacy brought serious evils from the first. It induced an excited, hysterical tone of mind, which is most remarkable in the best men; violent, querulous, suspicious, irritable, credulous, visionary; at best more womanly then manly; alternately in tears and rapture. You never get in their writings anything of that manly calmness, which we so deservedly honour, and at which we all aim for ourselves. They are bombastic; excited; perpetually mistaking violence for strength, putting us in mind for ever of the allocutions of the Popes. Read the writings of one of the best of monks, and of men, who ever lived, the great St Bernard, and you will be painfully struck by this hysterical element. The fact is, that their rule of life, from the earliest to the latest,—from that of St Benedict of Casino, 'father of all monks', to that of Loyola the Jesuit, was pitched not too low, but too high. It was an ideal which, for good or evil, could only be carried out by new converts, by people in a state of high religious excitement, and therefore the history of the monastic orders is just that of the protestant sects.

We hear of continual fallings off from their first purity; of continual excitements, revivals, and startings of new orders, which hoped to realize the perfection which the old orders could not. You must bear this in mind, as you read medieval history. You will be puzzled to know why continual new rules and new orders sprang up. They were so many revivals, so many purist attempts at new sects. You will see this very clearly in the three great revivals which exercized such enormous influence on the history of the 13th, the 16th and the 17th centuries—I mean the rise first of the Franciscans and Dominicans, next of the Jesuits, and lastly of the Port Royalists. They each professed to restore monachism to what it had been at first; to realize the unnatural and impossible ideal.

Another serious fault of these monasteries may be traced to their artificial celibate system. I mean their avarice. Only one generation after St Sturmi, Charlemagne had to make indignant laws against Abbots who tried to get into their hands the property of everyone around them: but in vain. The Abbots became more and more the great landholders, till their power was intolerable. The reasons are simple enough. An abbey had no children between whom to divide its wealth, and therefore more land was always flowing in and concentrating, and never breaking up again; while almost every Abbot left his personalities, all his private savings and purchases, to his successors.

Then again, in an unhappy hour, they discovered that the easiest way of getting rich was by persuading sinners, and weak persons, to secure the safety of their souls by leaving land to the Church, in return for the prayers and masses of monks; and that shameful mine of wealth was worked by them for centuries, in spite of statures of mortmain, and other checks which the civil power laid on them— very often by the most detestable means. One is shocked to find good men lending themselves to such base tricks: but we must recollect that there has always been among men a public and a private conscience, and that these two, alas! have generally been very different. It is an old saying, that 'committees have no conciences:' and it is too true. A body of men acting in concert for a public purpose will do things which they would shrink from with disgust, if the same trick would merely put money into their private purses; and this is often the case when the public object is a good one. Then the end seems to sanctify the means, to almost any amount of chicanery.

XV

The Water-Babies
1862

The Heroes *was written for the three eldest Kingsley children and published when the fourth, Arthur Grenville, was not quite two. 'Rose, Maurice and Mary have got their book,' Fanny remarked one morning at breakfast, 'and baby must have his.' Charles 'made no answer, but got up at once and went to his study, locking the door. In half an hour hour he had returned with the story of little Tom. This was the first chapter of* The Water-Babies *written off without a correction.' It was published serially by Macmillan in 1862–3.*

In Chapter II Tom the chimney-sweep is drowned in a stream and becomes a water-baby less than four inches long, with gills like an eft's. The subsequent chapters relate his underwater adventures, at first in the stream and then when he gets carried out to sea and to regions beyond the furthest oceans where Mother Cary dwells. It is a highly moral tale, involving fairies with names like Mrs Bedonebyasyoudid and Mrs Doasyouwouldbedoneby, and eventually uniting a Tom purged of any taint of wickedness with Sir John Harthover's little daughter, by then a water-baby too. In this tale Charles' imagination was at its most creative, his writing free and playful in, for modern tastes, a somewhat ponderous way, and he allowed himself elbow-room for digs at bêtes noires *such as pompous professors given to scientific jargon, ignorant and self-important doctors, and salmon poachers; and for good words for favourites like Bewick, the anglers' art, madrepores and stag-hunting.*

Whenever he went on holiday, the rector used to take the works of Rabelais and he read some, at least, every year. 'Unspeakably filthy' as he was, Charles considered Rabelais also 'priceless in wisdom and often in true evangelic goodliness'. Dame Una Pope-Henessy has pointed out that he adopted several of Rabelais' tricks of style, notably the habit of stringing together long lists of nouns or adjectives, as when, in the giving chase to Tom, never was there heard such a 'noise, row,

*hubbub, babel, shindy, hullaballoo, stramash, charivari, and total con-
tempt of dignity, repose and order . . .'; The fantasy is full of other
examples.*

*Fanny's wifely devotion must have betrayed her into mis-reading
the clock, for even her husband's ferocious energies could hardly have
accomplished some 7000 words in half an hour. The opening chapter is
given here in full.*

From Chapter 1

Once upon a time there was a little chimney-sweep, and his name
was Tom. That is a short name, and you have heard it before, so
you will not have much trouble in remembering it. He lived in a
great town in the North country, where there were plenty of chimneys to sweep, and plenty of money for Tom to earn and for his
master to spend. He could not read nor write, and did not care to
do either; and he never washed himself, for there was no water up
the court where he lived. He had never been taught to say his
prayers. He had never heard of God, or of Christ, except in words
which you never have heard, and which it would have been well if
he had never heard. He cried half his time, and laughed the other
half. He cried when he had to climb the dark flues, rubbing his poor
knees and elbows raw; and when the soot got into his eyes, which
it did every day in the week; and when he had not enough to eat;
which happened every day in the week likewise. And he laughed
the other half of the day, when he was tossing halfpennies with the
other boys, or playing leap-frog over the posts, or bowling stones at
the horses' legs as they trotted by, which last was excellent fun,
when there was a wall at hand behind which to hide. As for the
chimney-sweeping, and being hungry, and being beaten, he took all
that for the way of the world, like the rain and snow and thunder,
and stood manfully with his back to it till it was over, as his old
donkey did to a hailstorm; and then shook his ears and was as jolly
as ever; and thought of the fine times coming when he would be a
man, and a master sweep, and sit in the public-house with a quart
of beer and a long pipe, and play cards for silver money, and wear
velveteens and ankle-jacks, and keep a white bulldog with one gray
ear, and carry her puppies in his pocket, just like a man. And he

would have apprentices, one, two, three, if he could. How he would bully them, and knock them about, just as his master did to him; and make them carry home the soot sacks, while he rode before them on his donkey, with a pipe in his mouth and a flower in his button-hole, like a king at the head of his army. Yes, there were good times coming; and, when his master let him have a pull at the leavings of his beer, Tom was the jolliest boy in the whole town.

One day a smart little groom rode into the court where Tom lived. Tom was just hiding behind a wall, to heave half a brick at his horse's legs, as is the custom of that country when they welcome strangers; but the groom saw him, and hailed him to know where Mr Grimes, the chimney-sweep, lived. Now, Mr Grimes was Tom's own master, and Tom was a good man of business, and always civil to customers, so he put the half-brick down quietly behind the wall, and proceeded to take orders.

Mr Grimes was to come up next morning to Sir John Harthover's, at the Place, for his old chimney-sweep was gone to prison, and the chimneys wanted sweeping. And so he rode away, not giving Tom time to ask what the sweep had gone to prison for, which was a matter of interest to Tom, as he had been in prison once or twice himself. Moreover, the groom looked so very neat and clean, with his drab gaiters, drab breeches, drab jacket, snow-white tie with a smart pin in it, and clean round ruddy face, that Tom was offended and disgusted at his appearance, and considered him a stuck-up fellow, who gave himself airs because he wore smart clothes, and other people paid for them; and went behind the wall to fetch the half-brick after all; but did not, remembering that he had come in the way of business, and was, as it were, under a flag of truce.

His master was so delighted at his new customer that he knocked Tom down out of hand, and drank more beer that night than he usually did in two, in order to be sure of getting up in time next morning; for the more a man's head aches when he wakes, the more glad he is to turn out, and have a breath of fresh air. And, when he did get up at four next morning, he knocked Tom down again, in order to teach him (as young gentlemen used to be taught at public schools) that he must be an extra good boy that day, as they were going to a very great house, and might make a very good thing of it, if they could but give satisfaction.

And Tom thought so likewise, and, indeed, would have done and behaved his best, even without being knocked down. For, of all places upon earth, Harthover Place (which he had never seen) was the most wonderful, and, of all men on earth, Sir John (whom he had seen, having been sent to jail by him twice) was the most awful.

Harthover Place was really a grand place, even for the rich North country; with a house so large that in the frame-breaking riots, which Tom could just remember, the Duke of Wellington, and ten thousand soldiers to match, were easily housed therein; at least, so Tom believed; with a park full of deer, which Tom believed to be monsters who were in the habit of eating children; with miles of game-preserves, in which Mr Grimes and the collier lads poached at times, on which occasions Tom saw pheasants, and wondered what they tasted like; with a noble salmon-river, in which Mr Grimes and his friends would have liked to poach; but then they must have got into cold water, and that they did not like at all. In short, Harthover was a grand place, and Sir John a grand old man, whom even Mr Grimes respected; for not only could he send Mr Grimes to prison when he deserved it, as he did once or twice a week; not only did he own all the land about for miles; not only was he a jolly, honest, sensible squire, as ever kept a pack of hounds, who would do what he thought right by his neighbours, as well as get what he thought right for himself; but, what was more, he weighed full fifteen stone, was nobody knew how many inches round the chest, and could have thrashed Mr Grimes himself in fair fight, which very few folk round here could do, and which, my dear little boy, would not have been right for him to do, as a great many things are not which one both can do, and would like very much to do. So Mr Grimes touched his hat to him when he rode through the town, and called him a 'buirdly awd chap', and his young ladies 'gradely lasses', which are two high compliments in the North country; and thought that that made up for his poaching Sir John's pheasants; whereby you may perceive that Mr Grimes had not been to a properly inspected Government National School.

Now, I daresay, you never got up at three o'clock on a midsummer morning. Some people get up then because they want to catch salmon; and some because they want to climb Alps; and a great many more because they must, like Tom. But, I assure you, that three o'clock on a midsummer morning is the pleasantest time of all the twenty-four hours, and all the next three hundred and sixty-five days; and why every one does not get up then, I never could tell, save that they are all determined to spoil their nerves and their complexions by doing all night what they might just as well do all day. But Tom, instead of going out to dinner at half-past eight at night, and to a ball at ten, and finishing off somewhere between twelve and four, went to bed at seven, when his master went to the public-house, and slept like a dead pig; for which reason he was as piert as a game-cock (who always get up early to wake the maids), and just ready to get up when the fine gentlemen and ladies were just ready to go to bed.

So he and his master set out; Grimes rode the donkey in front, and Tom and the brushes walked behind; out of the court, and up the street, past the closed window-shutters, and the winking weary policemen, and the roofs all shining gray in the gray dawn.

They passed through the pitmens' village, all shut up and silent now, and through the turnpike; and then they were out in the real country, and plodding along the black dusty road, between black slag walls, with no sound but the groaning and thumping of the pit-engine in the next field. But soon the road grew white, and the walls likewise; and at the wall's foot grew long grass and gay flowers, all drenched with dew; and instead of the groaning of the pit-engine, they heard the skylark saying his matins high up in the air, and the pit-bird warbling in the sedges, as he had warbled all night long.

All else was silent. For old Mrs Earth was still fast asleep; and, like many pretty people, she looked still prettier asleep than awake. The great elm-trees in the green-gold meadows were fast asleep above, and the cows fast asleep beneath them; nay, the few clouds which were about were fast asleep likewise, and so tired that they had lain down on the earth to rest, in long white flakes and bars, among the stems of the elm-trees, and along the tops of the alders by the stream, waiting for the sun to bid them rise and go about their day's business in the clear blue overhead.

On they went; and Tom looked, and looked, for he had never been so far into the country before; and longed to get over a gate, and pick buttercups, and look for birds' nests in the hedge; but Mr Grimes was a man of business, and would not have heard of that.

Soon they came up with a poor Irishwoman, trudging along with a bundle at her back. She had a gray shawl over her head, and a crimson madder petticoat; so you may be sure she came from Galway. She had neither shoes nor stockings, and limped along as if she were tired and footsore; but she was a very tall handsome woman, with bright gray eyes, and heavy black hair hanging about her cheeks. And she took Mr Grimes' fancy so much, that when he came up alongside he called out to her:

'This is a hard road for a gradely foot like that. Will ye up, lass, and ride behind me?'

But, perhaps, she did not admire Mr Grimes' look and voice; for she answered quietly:

'No, thank you, I'd sooner walk with your little lad here.'

'You may please yourself,' growled Grimes, and went on smoking.

So she walked beside Tom, and talked to him, and asked him where he lived, and what he knew, and all about himself, till Tom thought he had never met such a pleasant-spoken woman. And she asked him, at last, whether he ever said his prayers! and seemed sad when he told her that he knew no prayers to say.

Then he asked her where she lived, and she said far away by the sea. And Tom asked her about the sea; and she told him how it rolled and roared over the rocks in winter nights, and lay still in the bright summer days, for the children to bathe and play in it; and many a story more, till Tom longed to go and see the sea, and bathe in it likewise.

At last, at the bottom of a hill, they came to a spring; not such a spring as you see here, which soaks up out of a white gravel in the bog, among red fly-catchers, and pink bottle-heath, and sweet white orchis; nor such a one as you may see, too, here, which bubbles up under the warm sand-bank in the hollow lane, by the great tuft of lady ferns, and makes the sand dance reels at the bottom, day and night, all the year round; not such a spring as either of those; but a real North country limestone fountain, like one of those in Sicily or Greece, where the old heathen fancied the nymphs sat cooling themselves the hot summer's day, while shepherds peeped at them from behind the bushes. Out of a low cave of rock, at the foot of a limestone crag, the great fountain rose, quelling, and bubbling, and gurgling, so clear that you could not tell where the water ended and the air began; and ran away under the road, a stream large enough to turn a mill; among the blue geranium, and golden globe-flower, and wild raspberry, and the bird-cherry with its tassels of snow.

And there Grimes stopped, and looked; and Tom looked too. Tom was wondering whether anything lived in that dark cave, and came out at night to fly in the meadows. But Grimes was not wondering at all. Without a word, he got off his donkey, and clambered over a low road wall, and knelt down, and began dipping his ugly head into the spring—and very dirty he made it.

Tom was picking the flowers as fast as he could. The Irishwoman helped him, and showed him how to tie them up; and a very pretty nosegay they had made between them. But when he saw Grimes actually wash, he stopped, quite astonished; and when Grimes had finished, and began shaking his ears to dry them, he said:

'Why, master, I never saw you do that before.'

'Now will again, most likely. Twasn't for cleanliness I did it, but for coolness. I'd be ashamed to want washing every week or so, like any smutty collier lad.'

'I wish I might go and dip my head in,' said poor little Tom. 'It must be as good as putting it under the town-pump; and there is no beadle here to drive a chap away.'

'Thou come along,' said Grimes; 'what dost want with washing thyself? Thou did not drink half a gallon of beer last night, like me.'

'I don't care for you,' said naughty Tom, and ran down to the stream, and began washing his face.

Grimes was very sulky, because the woman preferred Tom's company to his; so he dashed at him with horrid words, and tore him up from his knees, and began beating him. But Tom was accustomed to that, and got his head safe between Mr Grimes' legs, and kicked his shins with all his might.

'Are you not ashamed of yourself, Thomas Grimes?' cried the Irishwoman over the wall.

Grimes looked up, startled at her knowing his name; but all he answered was, 'No, nor never was yet;' and went on beating Tom.

'True for you. If you had ever been ashamed of yourself, you would have gone over into Vendale long ago.'

'What do you know about Vendale?' shouted Grimes; but he left off beating Tom.

'I know about Vendale, and about you, too. I know, for instance, what happened in Aldermire Copse, by night, two years ago come Martinmas.'

'You do?' shouted Grimes; and leaving Tom, he climbed up over the wall, and faced the woman. Tom thought he was going to strike her; but she looked him too full and fierce in the face for that;

'Yes; I was there,' said the Irishwoman quietly.

'You are no Irishwoman, by your speech,' said Grimes, after many bad words.

'Never mind who I am. I saw what I saw; and if you strike that boy again, I can tell what I know.'

Grimes seemed quite cowed, and got on his donkey without another word.

'Stop!' said the Irishwoman. 'I have one more word for you both; for you will both see me again before all is over. Those that wish to be clean, clean they will be; and those that wish to be foul, foul they will be. Remember.'

And she turned away, and through a gate into the meadow. Grimes stood still a moment, like a man who had been stunned. Then he rushed after her, shouting, 'You come back.' But when he got into the meadow, the woman was not there.

Had she hidden away? There was no place to hide in. But Grimes looked about, and Tom also, for he was as puzzled as Grimes himself at her disappearing so suddenly; but look where they would, she was not there.

Grimes came back again, as silent as a post, for he was a little frightened; and, getting on his donkey, filled a fresh pipe, and smoked away, leaving Tom in peace.

And now they had gone three miles and more, and came to Sir John's lodge-gates.

Very grand lodges they were, with very grand iron gates and stone gate-posts, and on top of each a most dreadful bogy, all teeth, horns, and tail, which was the crest Sir John's ancestors wore in the Wars of the Roses; and very prudent men they were to wear it, for all their enemies must have run for their lives at the very first sight of them.

Grimes rang at the gate, and out came a keeper on the spot, and opened.

'I was told to expect thee,' he said. 'Now thou'lt be so good as to

THE WATER-BABIES

keep to the main avenue, and not let me find a hare or a rabbit on thee when thou comest back. I shall look sharp for one, I tell thee.'

'Not if it's in the bottom of the soot-bag,' quoth Grimes, and at that he laughed; and the keeper laughed and said:

'If that's thy sort, I might as well ride up with thee to the hall.'

'I think thou best had. It's thy business to see after thy game, man, and not mine.'

So the keeper went with them; and, to Tom's surprise, he and Grimes chatted together all the way quite pleasantly. He did not know that a keeper is only a poacher turned outside in, and a poacher a keeper turned inside out.

They walked up a great lime avenue, a full mile long, and between their stems Tom peeped trembling at the horns of the sleeping deer, which stood up among the ferns. Tom had never seen such enormous trees, and as he looked up he fancied that the blue sky rested on their backs. But he was puzzled very much by a strange murmuring noise, which followed them all the way. So much puzzled, that at last he took courage to ask the keeper what it was.

He spoke very civilly, and called him Sir, for he was horribly afraid of him, which pleased the keeper, and he told him that they were the bees about the lime flowers.

'What are bees?' asked Tom.

'What make honey.'

'What is honey?' asked Tom.

'Thou hold thy noise,' said Grimes.

'Let the boy be,' said the keeper. 'He's a civil young chap now, and that's more than he'll be long if he bides with thee.'

Grimes laughed, for he took that for a compliment.

'I wish I were a keeper,' said Tom, 'to live in such a beautiful place, and wear green velveteens, and have a real dog-whistle at my button, like you.'

The keeper laughed; he was a kind-hearted fellow enough.

'Let well alone, lad, and ill too at times. Thy life's safer than mine at all events, eh, Mr Grimes?'

And Grimes laughed again, and then the two men began talking quite low. Tom could hear, though, that it was about some poaching fight; and at last Grimes said surlily, 'Hast thou anything against me?'

'Not now.'

'Then don't ask me any questions till thou hast, for I am a man of honour.'

And at that they both laughed again, and thought it a very good joke.

And by this time they were come up to the great iron gates in front of the house; and Tom stared through them at the rhododendrons and azaleas, which were all in flower; and then at the house itself, and wondered how many chimneys there were in it, and how long ago it was built, and what was the man's name that built it, and whether he got much money for his job?

These last were very difficult questions to answer. For Harthover had been built at ninety different times, and in nineteen different styles, and looked as if somebody had built a whole street of houses of every imaginable shape, and then stirred them together with a spoon.

For the attics were Anglo-Saxon.

The third floor Norman.

The second Cinque-cento.

The first-floor Elizabethan.

The right wing Pure Doric.

The centre Early English, with a huge portico copied from the Parthenon.

The left wing pure Boeotian, which the country folk admired most of all, because it was just like the new barracks in the town, only three times as big.

The grand staircase was copied from the Catacombs at Rome.

The back staircase from the Tajmahal at Agra. This was built by Sir John's great-great-great-uncle, who won, in Lord Clive's Indian wars, plenty of money, plenty of wounds, and no more taste than his betters.

The cellars were copied from the caves of Elephanta.

The offices from the Pavilion at Brighton.

And the rest from nothing in heaven, or earth, or under the earth.

So that Harthover House was a great puzzle to antiquarians, and a thorough Naboth's Vineyard to critics, and architects and all persons who like meddling with other mens' business, and spending other mens' money. So they were all setting upon poor Sir John, year after year, and trying to talk him into spending a hundred thousand pounds or so, in building to please them and not himself. But he always put them off, like a canny North-countryman as he was. One wanted him to build a Gothic house, but he said he was no Goth; and another an Elizabethan, but he said he lived under good Queen Victoria, and not good Queen Bess; and another was bold enough to tell him his house was ugly, but he said he lived inside it, not outside; and another, that there was no unity in it, but he said that that was just why he liked the old place. For he liked to see how each Sir John, and Sir Hugh, and Sir Ralph, and Sir Randal, had left his mark upon the place, each after his own taste; and he had no more notion of disturbing his ancestors' work than of disturbing their graves. For now the house looked like a real live house, that had a history, and had grown and grown as the world grew; and that it was only an upstart fellow who did not know who his own grandfather was, who would change it for some spick and span new Gothic or Elizabethan thing, which looked as if it had been all spawned in a night, as mushrooms are. From which you may collect (if you have wit enough) that Sir John was a very sound-headed, sound-hearted squire, and just the man to keep the country-side in order, and show good sport with his hounds.

But Tom and his master did not go in through the great iron gates, as if they had been Dukes or Bishops, but round the back way, and a very long way round it was; and into a little back-door, where the ash-boy let them in, yawning horribly; and then in a passage the housekeeper met them, in such a flowered chintz dressing-gown that Tom mistook her for My Lady herself, and she gave Grimes solemn orders about 'You will take care of this, and take care of that,' as if he was going up the chimneys, and not Tom. And Grimes listened, and said every now and then, under his voice, 'You'll mind that, you little beggar?' and Tom did mind, all at least that he could. And then the housekeeper turned them into a grand room, all covered up in sheets of brown paper, and bade them begin, in a lofty and tremendous voice; and so after a whimper or two, and a kick from his master, into the grate Tom went, and up the chimney, while a housemaid stayed in the room to watch the furniture; to whom Mr Grimes paid many playful and chivalrous compliments, but met with very slight encouragement in return.

How many chimneys Tom swept I cannot say; but he swept so

many that he got quite tired, and puzzled too, for they were not like the town flues to which he was accustomed, but such as you would find—if you would only get up them and look, which perhaps you would not like to do—in old country-houses, large and crooked chimneys, which had been altered again and again, till they ran into one another, anastomosing (as Professor Owen would say) considerably. So Tom fairly lost his way in them; not that he cared much for that, though he was in pitchy darkness, for he was as much at home in a chimney as a mole is underground; but at last, coming down as he thought the right chimney, he came down the wrong one, and found himself standing on the hearthrug in a room the like of which he had never seen before.

Tom had never seen the like. He had never been in gentlefolks' rooms but when the carpets were all up, and the curtains down, and the furniture huddled together under a cloth, and the pictures covered with aprons and dusters; and he had often enough wondered what the rooms were like when they were all ready for the quality to sit in. And now he saw, and he thought the sight very pretty.

The room was all dressed in white—white window-curtains, white bed-curtains, white furniture, and white walls, with just a few lines of pink here and there. The carpet was all over gay little flowers; and the walls were hung with pictures in gilt frames, which amused Tom very much. There were pictures of ladies and gentlemen, and pictures of horses and dogs. The horses he liked; but the dogs he did not care for much, for there were no bulldogs among them, not even a terrier. But the two pictures which took his fancy most were, one a man in long garments, with little children and their mothers round him, who was laying his hand upon the childrens' heads. That was a very pretty picture, Tom thought, to hang in a lady's room. For he could see that it was a lady's room by the dresses which lay about.

The other picture was that of a man nailed to a cross, which surprised Tom much. He fancied that he had seen something like it in a shop window. But why was it there? 'Poor man,' thought Tom, 'and he looks so kind and quiet. But why should the lady have such a sad picture as that in her room? Perhaps it is some kinsman of hers, who had been murdered by the savages in foreign parts, and she kept it there for a remembrance.' And Tom felt sad, and awed, and turned to look at something else.

The next thing he saw, and that too puzzled him, was a washing-stand, with ewers and basins, and soap and brushes, and towels, and a large bath full of clean water—what a heap of things all for washing! 'She must be a very dirty lady,' thought Tom, 'by my master's rule, to want as much scrubbing as all that. But she must be very cunning to put the dirt out of the way so well afterwards, for I don't see a speck about the room, not even on the very towels.'

And then, looking toward the bed, he saw that dirty lady, and held his breath with astonishment.

Under the snow-white coverlet, upon the snow-white pillow, lay the most beautiful little girl that Tom had ever seen. Her cheeks were almost as white as the pillow, and her hair was like threads of gold spread all about over the bed. She might have been as old as Tom, or maybe a year or two older; but Tom did not think of that. He thought only of her delicate skin and golden hair, and wondered whether she was a real live person, or one of the wax dolls he had seen in the shops. But when he saw her breathe, he made up his mind that she was alive, and stood staring at her, as if she had been an angel out of heaven.

No. She cannot be dirty. She never could have been dirty, thought Tom to himself. And then he thought, 'Are all people like that when they are washed?' And he looked at his own wrist, and tried to rub the soot off, and wondered if it ever would come off. 'Certainly I should look much prettier then, if I grew at all like her.'

And looking round, he suddenly saw, standing close to him, a little ugly, black, ragged figure, with bleared eyes and grinning white teeth. He turned on it angrily. What did such a little black ape want in that sweet young lady's room? And behold, it was himself, reflected in a great mirror, the like of which Tom had never seen before.

And Tom, for the first time in his life, found out that he was dirty; and burst into tears with shame and anger; and turned to sneak up the chimney again and hide; and upset the fender and threw the fire-irons down, with a noise as of ten thousand tin kettles tied to ten thousand mad dogs' tails.

Up jumped the little white lady in her bed, and, seeing Tom, screamed as shrill as any peacock. In rushed a stout old nurse from the next room, and seeing Tom likewise, made up her mind he had come to rob, plunder, destroy and burn; and dashed at him, as he lay over the fender, so fast that she caught him by the jacket.

But she did not hold him. Tom had been in a policeman's hands many a time, and out of them too, what is more; and he would have been ashamed to face his friends for ever if he had been stupid enough to be caught by an old woman; so he doubled under the good lady's arm, across the room, and out of the window in a moment.

He did not need to drop out, though he would have done so bravely enough. Nor even to let himself down a spout, which would have been an old game to him; for once he got up by a spout to the church roof, he said to take jackdaws' eggs, but the policeman said to steal lead; and, when he was seen on high, sat there till the sun got too hot, and came down by another spout, leaving the policemen to go back to the stationhouse and eat their dinners.

But all under the window spread a tree, with great leaves and sweet white flowers, almost as big as his head. It was a magnolia, I suppose; but Tom knew nothing about that, and cared less; for down the tree he went, like a cat, and across the garden lawn, and over the iron railings, and up the park towards the wood, leaving the old nurse to scream murder and fire at the window.

The under gardener, mowing, saw Tom, and threw down his scythe; caught his leg in it, and cut his shin open, whereby he kept his bed for a week; but in his hurry he never knew it, and gave chase to poor Tom. The dairymaid heard the noise, got the churn between her knees, and tumbled over it, spilling all the cream; and yet she jumped up, and gave chase to Tom. A groom cleaning Sir John's hack at the stables let him go loose, whereby he kicked himself lame in five minutes; but he ran out and gave chase to Tom. Grimes upset the soot-sack in the new-gravelled yard, and spoilt it all utterly; but he ran out and gave chase to Tom. The old steward opened the park-gate in such a hurry, that he hung up his pony's chin upon the spikes, and, for aught I know, it hangs there still; but he jumped off, and gave chase to Tom. The ploughman left his horses at the headland, and one jumped over the fence, and pulled the other into the ditch, plough and all; but he ran on, and gave chase to Tom. The keeper, who was taking a stoat out of a trap, let the stoat go, and caught his own finger; but he jumped up, and ran after Tom; and considering what he said, and how he looked, I should have been sorry for Tom if he had caught him. Sir John looked out of his study window (for he was an early old gentleman) and up at the nurse, and a martin dropped mud in his eye, so he had at last to send for the doctor; and yet he ran out, and gave chase to Tom. The Irishwoman, too, was walking up to the house to beg—she must have got round by some by-way—but she threw away her bundle, and gave chase to Tom likewise. Only my Lady did not give chase; for when she had put her head out of the window, her night-wig fell into the garden, and she had to ring up her lady's-maid, and send her down for it privately, which quite put her out of the running, so that she came in nowhere, and is consequently not placed.

In a word, never was there heard at Hall Place—not even when the fox was killed in the conservatory, among acres of broken glass, and tons of smashed flower-pots—such a noise, row, hubbub, babel, shindy, hullabaloo, stramash, charivari, and total contempt of dignity, repose, and order, as that day, when Grimes, gardener, the groom, the dairymaid, Sir John, the steward, the ploughman, the keeper, and the Irishwoman, all ran up the park, shouting 'Stop thief' in the belief that Tom had at least a thousand pounds' worth of jewels in his empty pockets; and the very magpies and jays followed Tom up, screaking and screaming, as if he were a hunted fox, beginning to droop his brush.

And all the while poor Tom paddled up the park with his little bare feet, like a small black gorilla fleeing to the forest. Alas for him! there was no big father gorilla therein to take his part—to scratch out the gardener's inside with one paw, toss the dairymaid into a tree with another, and wrench off Sir John's head with a third, while he cracked the keeper's skull with his teeth as easily as if it had been a cocoa-nut or a paving-stone.

However, Tom did not remember ever having had a father; so he did not look for one, and expected to have to take care of himself; while as for running, he could keep up for a couple of miles with any stage-coach, if there was the chance of a copper or a cigar-end, and turn coach-wheels on his hands and feet ten times following, which is more than you can do. Wherefore his pursuers found it very difficult to catch him; and we will hope that they did not catch him at all.

Tom, of course, made for the woods. He had never been in a

wood in his life; but he was sharp enough to know that he might hide in a bush, or swarm up a tree, and, altogether, had more chance there than in the open. If he had not known that, he would have been foolisher than a mouse or a minnow.

But when he got into the wood, he found it a very different sort of place from what he had fancied. He pushed into a thick cover of rhododendrons, and found himself at once caught in a trap. The boughs laid hold of his legs and arms, poked him in his face and his stomach, made him shut his eyes tight (though that was no great loss, for he could not see at best a yard before his nose); and when he got through the rhododendrons, the hassock-grass and sedges tumbled him over, and cut his poor little fingers afterwards most spitefully; the birches birched him as soundly as if he had been a nobleman at Eton, and over the face too (which is not fair swishing, as all brave boys will agree); and the lawyers tripped him up, and tore his shins as if they had sharks' teeth—which lawyers are likely enough to have.

'I must get out of this,' thought Tom, 'or I shall stay here till somebody comes to help me—which is just what I don't want.'

But how to get out was the difficult matter. And indeed I don't think he would ever have got out at all, but have stayed there till the cock-robins covered him with leaves, if he had not suddenly run his head against a wall.

Now running your head against a wall is not pleasant, especially if it is a loose wall, with the stones all set on edge, and a sharp cornered one hits you between the eyes and makes you see all manner of beautiful stars. The stars are very beautiful, certainly; but unfortunately they go in the twenty-thousandth part of a split second, and the pain which comes after them does not. And so Tom hurt his head; but he was a brave boy, and did not mind that a penny. He guessed that over the wall the cover would end; and up it he went, and over like a squirrel.

And there he was, out on the great grouse-moors, which the country folk called Harthover Fell—heather and bog and rock, stretching away and up, up to the very sky.

Now, Tom was a cunning little fellow—as cunning as an old Exmoor stag. Why not? Though he was but ten years old, he had lived longer than most stags, and had more wits to start with into the bargain.

He knew as well as a stag that if he backed he might throw the hounds out. So the first thing he did when he was over the wall was to make the neatest double sharp to his right, and run along under the wall for nearly half a mile.

Whereby Sir John, and the keeper, and the steward, and the gardener, and the ploughman, and the dairymaid, and all the hue-and-cry together, went on ahead half a mile in the very opposite direction, and inside the wall, leaving him a mile off on the outside; while Tom heard their shouts die away in the woods and chuckled to himself merrily.

At last he came to a dip in the land, and went to the bottom of it, and then he turned bravely away from the wall and up the moor; for he knew that he had put a hill between him and his enemies, and could go on without their seeing him.

But the Irishwoman, alone of them all, had seen which way Tom went. She had kept ahead of everyone the whole time; and yet she neither walked nor ran. She went along quite smoothly and grace-fully, while her feet twinkled past each other so fast you could not see which was foremost; till everyone asked the other who the strange woman was; and all agreed, for want of anything better to say, that she must be in league with Tom.

But when she came to the plantation, they lost sight of her; and they could do no less. For she went quietly over the wall after Tom, and followed him wherever he went. Sir John and the rest saw no more of her; and out of sight was out of mind.

And now Tom was right away into the heather, over just such a moor as those in which you have been bred, except that there were rocks and stones lying about everywhere, and that, instead of the moor growing flat as he went upwards, it grew more and more broken and hilly, but not so rough but that little Tom could jog along well enough, and find time, too, to stare about at the strange place, which was like a new world to him.

He saw great spiders there, with crowns and crosses marked on their backs, who sat in the middle of their webs, and when they saw Tom coming, shook them so fast that they became invisible. Then he saw lizards, brown and gray and green, and thought they were snakes, and would sting him; but they were as much frightened as he, and shot away into the heath. And then, under a rock, he saw a pretty sight—a great brown, sharp-nosed creature, with a white tag to her brush and round her four or five smutty little cubs, the funniest fellows Tom ever saw. She lay on her back, rolling about, and stretching out her legs and head and tail in the bright sunshine; and the cubs jumped over her, and run round her, and nibbled her paws, and lugged her about by the tail; and she seemed to enjoy it mightily. But one selfish little fellow stole away from the rest to a dead crow close by, and dragged it off to hide it, though it was nearly as big as he was. Whereat all his little brothers set off after him in full cry, and saw Tom; and then all ran back, and up jumped Mrs Vixen, and caught one up in her mouth, and the rest toddled after her, and into a dark crack in the rocks; and there was an end of the show.

And next he had a fright; for, as he scrambled up a sandy brow—whirr-poof-poof-cock-cock-kick—something went off in his face, with a most horrid noise. He thought the ground had blown up, and the end of the world come.

And when he opened his eyes (for he shut them very tight) it was only an old-cock-grouse, who had been washing himself in sand, like an Arab, for want of water; and who, when Tom had all but trodden on him, jumped up with a noise like the express train, leaving his wife and children to shift for themselves, like an old coward, and went off screaming 'Cur-ru-u-uck, cur-ru-u-uck—murder, thieves, fire—cur-u-uck-cock-kick—the end of the world is come—kick-kick-cock-kick.' He was always fancying that the end of the world was come, when anything happened which was farther off than the end of his own nose. But the end of the world was not come, any more than the twelfth of August was; though the old grouse-cock was quite certain of it.

So the old grouse came back to his wife and family an hour after-wards, and said solemnly, 'Cock-cock-kick; my dears, the end of the world is not quite come; but I assure you it is coming the day after tomorrow—cock.' But his wife had heard so often that she knew all about it, and a little more. And, besides, she was the mother of a family, and had seven little poults to wash and feed every day; and that made her very practical, and a little sharp-tempered; so all she answered was: 'Kick-kick-kick—go and catch spiders, go and catch spiders—kick.'

So Tom went on and on, he hardly knew why; but he liked the great wide strange place, and the cool fresh bracing air. But he went more and more slowly as he got higher up the hill; for now the ground grew very bad indeed. Instead of soft turf and springy heather, he met great patches of flat limestone rock, just like ill-made pavements, with deep cracks between the stones and ledges, filled with ferns; so he had to hop from stone to stone, and now and then he slipped in between and hurt his little bare toes, though they were tolerably tough ones; but still he would go on and up, he could not tell why.

What would Tom have said if he had seen, walking over the moor behind him, the very same Irishwoman who had taken his part upon the road? But whether it was that he looked too little behind him, or whether it was that she kept out of sight behind the rocks and knolls, he never saw her, though she saw him.

And now he began to get a little hungry, and very thirsty; for he had run a long way, and the sun had risen high in the heaven, and the rock was as hot as an oven, and the air danced reels over it, as it does over a limekiln, till everything round seemed quivering and melting in the glare.

But he could see nothing to eat anywhere, and still less to drink.

The heath was full of bilberries and whimberries; but they were only in flower yet, for it was June. And as for water, who can find water, who can find that at the top of a limestone rock? Now and then he passed by a deep dark swallow-hole, going down into the earth, as if it was the chimney of some dwarf's house underground; and more than once, as he passed, he could hear water falling, trickling, tinkling, many many feet below. How he longed to get down to it, and cool his poor baked lips! But, brave little chimney-sweep as he was, he dared not climb down such chimneys as those.

So he went on and on, till his head spun round with the heat, and he thought he heard church-bells ringing, a long way off.

'Ah!' he thought, 'where there is a church there will be houses and people; and, perhaps, someone will give me a bite and a sup.' So he set off again, to look for the church; for he was sure that he heard the bells quite plain.

And in a minute or two, when he looked round, he stopped again, and said, 'Why, what a big place the world is!'

And so it was; for, from the top of the mountain he could see— what could he not see?

Behind him, far below, was Harthover, and the dark woods, and the shining salmon river; and on his left, far below, was the town, and the smoking chimneys of the collieries; and far, far away, the river widened to the shining sea; and little white specks, which were ships, lay on its bosom. Behind him lay, spread out like a map, great plains, and farms, and villages, amid dark knots of trees. They all seemed at his very feet; but he had sense to see that they were long miles away.

And to his right rose moor after moor, hill after hill, till they faded away, blue into the sky. But between him and those moors, and really at his very feet, lay something to which, as soon as Tom saw it, he determined to go, for that was the place for him.

A deep, deep green and rocky valley, very narrow, and filled with wood; but through the wood, hundreds of feet below him, he could see a clear stream glance. Oh, if he could but get down to that stream! Then, by the stream, he saw the roof of a little cottage, and a little garden set out in squares and beds. And there was a tiny little red thing moving about in the garden, no bigger than a fly. As Tom looked down, he saw that it was a woman in a red petticoat. Ah! perhaps she would give him something to eat. And there were the church-bells ringing again. Surely there must be a village down there. Well, nobody would know him, or what had happened at the Place. The news could not have got down there yet, even if Sir John had set all the policemen in the county after him; and he could get down there in five minutes.

Tom was quite right about the hue-and-cry not having got thither; for he had come, without knowing it, the best part of ten miles from Harthover; but he was wrong about getting down in five minutes, for the cottage was more than a mile off, and a good thousand feet below.

However, down he went, like a brave little man as he was, though he was very footsore, and tired, and hungry, and thirsty; while the church-bells rang so loud, he began to think that they must be inside his own head, and the river chimed and twinkled far below; and this was the song which it sang:

Clear and cool, clear and cool,
By laughing shallow, and dreaming pool;
Cool and clear, cool and clear,
By shining shingle, and foaming wear;

Under the crag where the ouzel sings,
And the ivied wall where the church-bell rings,
　Undefiled, for the undefiled;
　Play by me, bathe in me, mother and child.

Dank and foul, dank and foul,
By the smoky town in its murky cowl;
　Foul and dank, foul and dank,
By wharf and sewer and slimy bank;
　Darker and darker the farther I go,
　Baser and baser the river I grow;
　Who dare sport with the sin-defiled?
　Shrink from me, turn from me, mother and child.

Strong and free, strong and free,
The flood-gates are open, away to the sea,
　Free and strong, free and strong,
Cleansing my streams as I hurry along,
To the golden sands, and the leaping bar,
And the taintless tide that awaits me afar.
As I lose myself in the infinite main,
Like a soul that has sinned and is pardoned again.
　Undefiled, for the undefiled,
　Play by me, bathe in me, mother and child.

So Tom went down; and all the while he never saw the Irish-woman going down behind him.

From Chapter 2

When all the world is young, lad,
　And all the trees are green,
And every goose a swan, lad,
　And every lass a queen;
Then hey for boat and horse, lad,
　And round the world away;
Young blood must have its course, lad,
　And every dog his day.

THE KINGSLEYS

When all the world is old, lad,
    And all the trees are brown,
And all the sport is stale, lad,
    And all the wheels run down;
Creep home, and take your place there,
    The spent and maimed among;
God grant you find one face there
    You loved when all was young.

XVI

What, then, does Dr Newman mean?
1864

Writing in the Spectator *its editor, R. H. Hutton, observed: 'Mr Kingsley, in the ordinary steeplechase fashion in which he chooses not so much to think as to* splash up *thoughts, dregs and all—often very healthy and sometimes very noble, but always very loose thought—in one's face, has made a random charge against Father Newman in* Macmillan's Magazine.' *In a review of Froude's* History of England, *Charles had splashed up the remark that 'Truth, for its own sake, has never been a virtue with the Roman clergy. Father Newman informs use that it need not, and on the whole ought not to be; that cunning is the weapon which Heaven has given to saints wherewith to withstand the brute male force of the wicked world which marries and is given in marriage.'*

Father Newman lodged a pained objection, and challenged the writer to give chapter and verse. Charles Kingsley, responding as always to the scent of battle, leapt into the arena, referring to Sermon No. XX in Subjects of the Day *published twenty years earlier. The battle was joined: the clerics went at it hammer and tongs. Kingsley published a retraction which concluded: 'It only remains, therefore, for me to express my hearty regret at having so seriously mistaken him.' Newman was by no means satisfied and published a heavily sarcastic response. 'My object had been throughout to avoid war, because I thought Dr Newman wished for peace,' Kingsley wrote; but this was too much. He replied with a pamphlet, published by Macmillan, from which comes the extract below.*

This somewhat pedantic exchange would have faded, like so many other doctrinal disputes, into undisturbed obscurity had it not been for Newman's response, the lengthy (400 pages) justification for his beliefs and 'History of my religious opinions' which, published under the title Apologia Pro Vita Sua, *became perhaps Newman's best-known and most characteristic work. Beside this large fat mackerel, the sprat that caught it seemed a poor fish indeed. In the intellectual circles of the day it was generally agreed that the Anglican parson had made a great mistake in challenging the formidable Roman priest.*

Kingsley accuses Newman of extreme credulity in elevating medieval superstitions concerning various British saints into divine miracles; and of extreme casuistry in his religious teaching.

A Reply to a Pamphlet Lately Published by Dr Newman

The whole teaching of this lecture and the one following it concerning such matters is, I confess, so utterly beyond my comprehension, that I must ask, in blank astonishment, What does Dr Newman mean? He assures us so earnestly and indignantly that he is an honest man, believing what he says, that we in return are bound, in honour and humanity, to believe him; but still—What does he mean?

He says: 'Take a mere beggar woman, lazy, ragged, and filthy, and not over-scrupulous of truth—(I do not say she has arrived at perfection)—but if she is chaste, sober, and cheerful, and goes to her religious duties (and I am not supposing at all an impossible case)', she will, in the eyes of the Church, have a prospect of heaven, quite closed and refused to the State's pattern-man, the just, the upright, the generous, the honourable, the conscientious, if he be all this, not from a supernatural power (I do not determine whether this is likely to be the fact, but I am contrasting views and principles)—not from a supernatural power, but from mere natural virtue.' (Lecture viii. p. 207).

I must ask again, What does Dr Newman mean by this astounding passage? What I thought that he meant, when I first read it, some twelve years ago, may be guessed easily enough. I said, This man has no real care for truth. Truth for its own sake is no virtue in his eyes, and he teaches that it need not be. I do not say that now: but this I say, that Dr Newman, for the sake of exalting the magical powers of his Church, has committed himself unconsciously to a statement which strikes at the root of all morality. If he answer, that such is the doctrine of his Church concerning 'natural virtues,' as distinguished from 'good works performed by God's grace,' I can only answer, So much the worse for his Church. The sooner it is civilized off the face of the earth, if this be its teaching, the better for mankind. For as for his theory that it may be a 'natural virtue,' I value it as little as I trust every honest Englishman will do. I hold it to be utterly antiscriptual; to border very closely (in theological language) on the Pelagian heresy. Every good gift and every perfect gift comes down from God above. Without Him no man does a right deed, or thinks a right thought; and when Dr Newman says otherwise, he is doing his best (as in this passage) to make the 'State's pattern-man' an atheist, as well as to keep the beggar-woman a lying barbarian. What Dr Newman may have meant to teach by these words, I cannot say; but what he has taught practically is patent. He has the whole Celtic Irish population, that as long as they are chaste (which they cannot well help being, being married almost before they are men and women) and sober (which they cannot well help being, being too poor to get enough whisky to make them drunk), and 'go to their religious duties'—an expression on which I make no comment—they may look down upon the Protestant gentry who send over millions to feed them in famine; who found hospitals and charities to which they are admitted freely; who try to introduce among them capital, industry, civilization, and, above all, that habit of speaking the truth, for which they are what they are, and are likely to remain such, as long as they have Dr Newman for their teacher—that they may look down, I say, on the Protestant gentry as cut off from God, and without hope of heaven, because they do their duty by mere 'natural virtue.'

And Dr Newman has taught them, too, in the very same page, that they confess to the priest thefts which 'would sentence the penitent to transportation if brought into a court of justice; but which the priest knows too' (and it is to be remembered that the priest is bound to conceal his knowledge of the crime), 'in the judgement of the Church, might be pardoned on the man's private contrition, without any confession at all.'

If I said that Dr Newman has, in this page, justified, formally and deliberately, some of the strongest accusations brought by the Exeter Hall party against the Irish priests, I should be answered (and possibly with temporary success) by some of those ingenious special pleadings with which, in spite of plain fact and universal public opinion, black is made to appear, if not white, yet still grey enough to do instead. But this I will say, that if the Roman Catholic hierarchy in these realms had had any sense of their own interests (as far as standing well with the British nation is concerned), they would, instead of sending the man who wrote those words to teach in an Irish Catholic university, have sent him to their furthest mission among the savages of the South Seas.

XVII

Hereward the Wake
1865

When Charles was five years old his father had taken the living of Barnack, near Stamford in Lincolnshire, and installed his family in a rambling fourteenth century rectory haunted by a ghost called Button-Cap. Here they remained for six years. The impression made at an impressionable age upon a boy always sensitive to nature by this quiet bird-haunted, wide-horizoned stretch of England with its Viking traditions emerged nearly forty years later to form the background of Charles' third and last historical novel.

Like Robin Hood and King Arthur, Hereward is a semi-legendary folk hero—in modern terms, the first English nationalist, who headed a rebellion of the native English, descendants of Danes and Saxons, against William the Conqueror. Charles makes him a son of Leofric, ruler of Mercia, and of Lady Godiva. As leader of a band of freedom-fighters he stormed and took Peterborough in 1070, but in the following year was beseiged on the Isle of Ely and, after desperate resistance, driven from it by William's forces. He fled into the Fens, accompanied by his faithful wife Torfrida and his mare Swallow, reputed to be the ugliest and swiftest mount in Christendom. After an interlude as an outlaw in the Lincolnshire maquis *he basely deserted Torfrida for the wily Alftruda—whom he once rescued from a bear—and made his peace with William; but met with his just deserts when, 'fat with the wages of sin', he was murdered at his manor of Bourne by jealous Norman knights.*

Hereward the Wake *is neither so well constructed as* Hypatia *nor does it flow so smoothly as* Westward Ho!, *getting at times somewhat bogged down in Danish and Anglo-Saxon genealogies and dynastic struggles, but it has some spirited pieces of dramatic writing; and, in Hereward, Charles created a character more complex and credible than the simple monk Philammon or the lusty Amyas. The rupugnance Charles felt towards monastic practices finds plenty of expression in this novel of the Fens, although in providing sactuary for Torfrida to end her days in prolonged and, one would think, quite uncalled for penances, he acknowledged one of the functions of the cloister.*

The novel appeared serially in Good Words *in 1865, and was published in book form by Macmillan the following year.*

From Chapter 33

The sun was setting long before they reached Ely: but just as he sank into the western fens, Winter stopped, pointing.—Was that the flash of arms? There, far away, just below Willingham town. Or was it the setting sun upon the ripple of some long water?

'There is not wind enough for such a ripple,' said one. But ere they could satisfy themselves, the sun was down, and all the fen was gray.

Hereward was still more uneasy. If that had been the flash of arms, it must have come off a very large body of men, moving in column, on the road between Cambridge and Ely. He hastened on his men. But ere they were within sight of the minster-tower, they were aware of a horse galloping violently towards them through the dusk. Hereward called a halt. He heard his own heart beat as he stopped. The horse was pulled up short among them. On its back was a lad, with a smaller boy behind him, clasping his waist.

'Hereward? Thank God, I am in time! And the child is safe too. Thanks, thanks, dear saints!' a voice sobbed out.

It was the voice of Torfrida.

'Treason!' she gasped. 'I knew it. The French are in the island. They have got Aldreth. The whole army is marching from Cambridge. The whole fleet is coming up from Southrey. And you have time. . . .'

'To burn Ely over monks' heads. Men! Get bogwood out of yon cottage, make yourselves torches, and onward!' Then rose a babel of questions, which Torfrida answered as she could. But she had nothing to tell. 'Clerks' cunning' she said bitterly, 'was an over-match for woman's wit.' She had sent out a spy: but he had not returned till an hour since. Then he came back breathless, with the news that the French army was on the march from Cambridge, and

that, as he came over the water at Aldreth, he found a party of
French knights in the fort on the Ely side, talking peaceably with
the monks on guard.

She had run up the borough hill—which men call Cherry Hill at
this day—and one look to the north-east had shown her the river
swarming with ships. She had rushed home, put boys' clothes on
herself and her child, hid a few jewels in her bosom, saddled
Swallow, and ridden for her life thither.

'And King Sigtryg?'

He and his men had gone desperately out towards Haddenham,
with what English they could muster: but all were in confusion.
Some were getting the women and children into boats, to hide
them in the reeds; other battering the minster gates, vowing
vengeance on the monks.

'Then Sigtryg will be cut off! Alas for the day that ever brought
his brave heart hither!'

And when the men heard that, a yell of fury and despair burst
from all throats.

Should they go back to their boats?

'No! onward,' cried Hereward. 'Revenge first, and safety after.
Let us leave nothing for the accursed Frenchmen but smoking
ruins, and then gather our comrades, and cut our way back to the
North.'

'Good counsel,' cried Winter. 'We know the roads, and they do
not; and in such a dark night as is coming, we can march out of the
island without their being able to follow us a mile.'

They hurried on: but stopped once more, at the galloping of
another horse.

'Who comes, friend of foe?'

'Alwyn, son of Orgar!' cried a voice under breath. 'Don't make
such a noise, men! The French are within half a mile of you.'

'Then one traitor monk shall die ere I retreat,' cried Hereward,
seizing him by the throat.

'For heaven's sake, hold!' cried Torfrida, seizing his arm. 'You
know not what he may have to say.'

'I am no traitor, Hereward; I have fought by your side as well as
the best; and if any but you had called Alwyn—'

'A curse on your boasting. Tell us the truth.'

'The Abbot has made peace with the King. He would give up the

island, and St Ethelreda should keep all her lands and honours. I
said what I could; but who was I to resist the whole chapter?
Could I alone brave St Ethelreda's wrath?'

Alwyn, the valiant, afraid of a dead girl!'

'Blaspheme not, Hereward! She may hear your at this moment!
Look there!' and pointing up, the monk cowered in terror, as a
meteor flashed through the sky.

'That is St Ethelreda shooting at us, eh? Then all I can say is,
she is a very bad marksman. And the French are in the island?'

'They are.'

'Then forward, men, for one half-hour's pleasure; and then to
die like Englishmen.'

'On?' cried Alwyn. 'You cannot go on. The King is at Whichford
at this moment with all his army, half a mile off! Right across the
road to Ely!'

Hereward grew berserk. 'On! men!' shouted he, 'we shall kill a
few Frenchmen apiece before we die!'

'Hereward,' cried Torfrida, 'you shall not go on! If you go, I
shall be taken. And if I am taken, I shall be burned. And I cannot
burn—I cannot! I shall go mad with terror before I come to the
stake. I cannot go stript my smock before those Frenchmen. I cannot be roasted piecemeal! Hereward, take me away! Take me away!
or kill me, now and here!'

He paused. He had never seen Torfrida thus overcome.

'Let us flee! The stars are against us. God is against us! Let us
hide—escape abroad: beg our bread, go on pilgrimage to Jerusalem
together—for together it must be always: but take me away!'

'We will go back to the boats, men,' said Hereward.

But they did not go. They stood there, irresolute, looking towards
Ely.

The sky was pitchy dark. The minster-roofs, lying north-east,
were utterly invisible against the blackness.

'We may at least save some who escape out,' said Hereward.
'March on quickly to the left, under the hill to the plough-field.'

They did so.

'Lie down, men. There are the French, close on our right. Down
among the bushes.'

And they heard the heavy tramp of men within a quarter of a
mile.

HEREWARD THE WAKE

'Cover the mare's eyes, and hold her mouth, lest she neigh,' said Winter.

Hereward and Torfrida lay side by side upon the heath. She was shivering with cold and horror. He laid his cloak over her; put his arm round her.

'Your stars did not foretell you this, Torfrida,' He spoke not bitterly, but in utter sadness.

She burst into an agony of weeping.

'My stars at least foretold me nothing but woe, since first I saw your face.'

'Why did you marry me then?' asked he half angrily.

'Because I loved you. Because I love you still.'

'Then you do not regret?'

'Never, never, never! I am quite happy—quite happy. Why not?'

A low murmur from the men made them look up. They were near enough to the town to hear—only too much. They heard the tramp of men, shouts and yells. Then the shrill cries of women. All dull and muffled the sounds came to them through the still night; and they lay there spell-bound, as in a nightmare, as men assisting at some horrible tragedy, which they had no power to prevent. Then there was a glare, and a wisp of smoke against the black sky, and then a house began burning brightly, and then another.

'This is the Frenchman's faith!'

And all the while, as the sack raged in the town below, the minster stood above, glaring in the firelight, silent and safe. The church had provided for herself, by sacrificing the children beneath her fostering shadow.

They waited nearly an hour, but no fugitives came out.

'Come, men,' said Hereward, wearily, 'we may as well to the boats.'

And so they went, walking on like men in a dream, as yet too stunned to realize to themselves the hopeless horror of their situation. Only Hereward and Torfrida saw it all, looking back on the splendid past—the splendid hopes for the future: glory, honour, an earldom, a free Danish England—and this was all that was left!

'No it is not!' cried Torfrida suddenly, as if answering her own unspoken thoughts, and his. 'Love is still left. The gallows and the stake cannot take that away.' And she clung closer to her husband's side, and he again to hers.

They reached the shore, and told their tale to their comrades. Whither now?

'To Well. To the wide mere,'* said Hereward.

'But their ships will hunt us out there.'

'We shall need no hunting. We must pick up the men at Cissham. You would not leave them to be murdered, too, as we have left the Ely men?'

No. They would go to Well. And then?

'The Bruneswald, and the merry greenwood,' said Hereward.

'Hey for the merry greenwood!' shouted Leofric the Deacon. And the men, in the sudden delight of finding any place, any purpose, answered with a lusty cheer.

'Brave hearts!' said Hereward. 'We will live and die together like Englishmen.'

'We will, we will, Viking.'

'Where shall we stow the mare?' asked Geri, 'the boats are full already'.

'Leave her to me. On board, Torfrida.'

He got on board last, leading the mare by the bridle.

'Swim, good lass!' said he, as they pushed off; and the good lass, who had done it many a time before, waded in, and was soon swimming behind. Hereward turned, and bent over the side in the darkness. There was a strange gurgle, a splash, and a swirl. He turned round, and sat upright again. They rowed on.

'That mare will never swim all the way to Well,' said one.

'She will not need it,' said Hereward.

'Why?' said Torfrida, feeling in the darkness, 'she is loose. What is this in your hand? Your dagger? and wet?'

'Mare Swallow is at the bottom of the reach. We could never have got her to Well.'

'And you have—' cried a dozen voices.

'Do you think that I would let a cursed Frenchman—ay, even William's self—say that he had bestridden Hereward's mare?'

* Probably near Upwell and Outwell, in the direction of Wisbech. There the old Nene and the old Welney rivers joining, formed vast morasses, now laid dry by the Middle Level and Marshland Drains. The bursting of the Middle Level Sluice in the year 1821, restored for awhile a vast tract in these fens to its primaeval state of 'The Wide Mere'. From this point Hereward could escape north into Lincolnshire, either by Wisbech and the Wash, or by Crowland and Bourne.

None answered: but Torfrida, as she laid her head upon her husband's bosom, felt the great tears running down from his cheek on to her own.

None spoke a word. The men were awe-stricken.

There was something despairing and ill-omened in the deed. And yet there was a savage grandeur in it, which bound their savage hearts still closer to their chief.

And so mare Swallow's bones lie somewhere in the peat unto this day.

They got to Well; they sent out spies to find the men who had been 'wasting Cissham with fire and sword:' and at last brought them in. Ill news, as usual, had travelled fast. They had heard of the fall of Ely, and hidden themselves 'in a certain very small island which is called Stimtench', where, thinking that the friends in search of them were Frenchmen in pursuit, they hid themselves amongst the high reeds. There two of them—one Starkwulf by name, the other Broher—hiding near each other, 'thought that, as they were monks, it might conduce to their safety if they had shaven crowns; and set to work with their swords to shave each other's heads as well as they could. But at last, by their war-cries and their speech, recognizing each other, they left off fighting,' and went after Hereward.

So jokes, grimly enough, the old Chronicler, who may have seen them come in the next morning, with bleeding coxcombs, and could laugh over the thing in after years. But he was in no humour for jesting in the days which they lay at Well. Nor was he in jesting humour when, a week afterwards, hunted by the French from Well, and forced to take to meres and waterways known only to them, and too shallow and narrow for the French ships, they found their way across into the old Nen, and so on toward Crowland, leaving Peterborough far on the left. For as they neared Crowland, they saw before them, rowing slowly, a barge full of men. And as they neared that barge, behold, all they who rowed were blind of both their eyes; and they who sat and guided them, were maimed of both their hands. And as they came alongside, there was not a man in all that ghastly crew but was an ancient friend, by whose side they had fought full many a day, and with whom they had drunk deep full many a night. They were the first fruits of William's vengeance; thrust into that boat, to tell the rest of the fen-men what those had to expect who dared oppose the Norman. And they were going to Crowland, to the sanctuary of the Danish fen-men, that they might cast themselves down before St Guthlac, and ask of him that mercy for their souls which the Conqueror had denied their bodies. Alas for them! They were but a handful among hundreds, perhaps thousands, of mutilated cripples, who swarmed all over England, and especially in the north and east, throughout the reign of the Norman conquerors. They told their comrades' fate, slaughtered in the first attack, or hanged afterwards as rebels and traitors to a foreigner whom they had never seen, and to whom they owned no fealty by law of God or man.

'And Sigtryg Ranaldsson?'

None knew aught of him. He never got home again to his Irish princess.

'And the poor women?' asked Torfrida.

But she received no answer.

And the men swore a great oath, and kept it; never to give quarter to a Frenchman, as long as there was one left on English ground.

XVIII

At Last: A Christmas in the West Indies

1871

In 1869 Charles resigned from his Professorship at Cambridge, remarking that 'the malaria of the river acts as poison on my inside'. Gladstone offered him the Canonry of Chester, a somewhat minor one, and he was glad to accept it and its stipend of £500 a year. To a friend, Raikes Currie, he wrote: 'You were never more right than when you said that I should not like to be a Bishop. I have been too much behind the scenes in Bishops' palaces, their intrigue, vulgarity, toadyism and pretension.'

Tales heard from his mother, Mary Lucas, of her own childhood in Barbados, where her father had served as a judge, had inspired in Charles a longing to see the West Indies. At the end of 1869 he embarked with his daughter Rose for Trinidad, to spend seven delightful weeks as the guest of the Governor, Mr (later Sir Arthur) Gordon. Here he could indulge his passion for natural history amid totally new surroundings and he found the glorious flowering trees and shrubs, the marvellous sea-shells, jewelled butterflies, sinister vipers, raucous birds, all equally enthralling. The hospitality proffered by everyone from nabob to peasant touched his heart. The Governor, their host, even slept on the floor of a cabin in the forest in order that the Canon—'the oldest, least acclimatised and, alas! weakliest of the party'—might occupy the only bed.

He and Rose returned early in 1870 with his health considerably restored, bringing a kinkajou and a vulturine parrot—the ships' doctor brought an alligator, the mate an ant-eater and the chief engineer a tarantula spider—to face the rigours of an English winter but the welcome of a happy home. His impressions were published as a series of letters in Good Words *during 1870, and as a book the following year.*

The Northern Mountains

When we turned out before sunrise next morning, I found myself in perhaps the most charming of all the charming 'camps' of these forests. Its owner, the warden, fearing the unhealthy air of the sea-coast, had bought some hundreds of acres up here in the hills, cleared them, and built, or rather was building, in the midst. As yet the house was rudimentary. A cottage of precious woods cut off the clearing, standing, of course, on stilts, contained two rooms, an inner and an outer. There was no glass in the windows, which occupied half the walls. Doors or shutters, to be closed if the wind and rain were too violent, are all that is needed in a climate where the temperature changes but little, day or night, throughout the year. A table, unpolished, like the wooden walls but, like them, of some precious wood; a few chairs or benches, not forgetting, of course, an American rocking-chair; a shelf or two, with books of law and medicine, and beside them a few books of devotion; a press; a 'perch' for hanging clothes—for they mildew when kept in drawers—just such as would have been seen in a medieval house in England; a covered four-post bed, with gauze curtains, indispens-able for fear of vampires, mosquitoes, and other forest plagues; these make up the furniture of such a bachelor's camp as, to the man who lives doing good work all day out of doors, leaves nothing to be desired. Where is the kitchen? It consists of half a dozen great stones under yonder shed, where as good meals are cooked as in any London kitchen. Other sheds hold the servants and hangers-on, the horses and mules; and as the establishment grows, more will be added, and the house itself will probably expand laterally, like a peripheral Greek temple, by row of posts, probably of palm-stems thatched over with wooden shingle or with the leaves of the Timit[1] palm. If ladies come to inhabit the camp, fresh rooms will be partitioned off by boardings as high as the eaves, leaving the roof within open and common, for the sake of air. Soon, no regular garden, but beautiful flowering shrubs—Crotons, Dracaenas, and Cereuses, will be planted; great bushes of Bauhinia and blue Petraea will roll their long curved shoots over and over each other; Gardenias fill the air with fragrance; and the Bougainvillia or the

[1] Manicaria.

Clerodendron cover some arbour with lilac or white racemes.

But this camp had not yet arrived at so high a state of civilization. All round it, almost up to the very doors, a tangle of logs, stumps, branches, dead ropes and nets or liane lay still in the process of clearing; and the ground was seemingly as waste, as it was difficult —often impossible—to cross. A second glance, however, showed that, amongst the stumps and logs, Indian corn was planted every-where; and that a few months would give a crop which would richly repay the clearing, over and above the fact that the whole materials of the house had been cut on the spot and cost nothing.

As for the situation of the little oasis in the wilderness, it bespoke good sense and good taste. The owner had stumbled, in his forest wanderings, on a spot where two mountain streams, after nearly meeting, parted again, and enclosed in a ring a hill some hundred feet high, before they finally joined each other below. That ring was his estate; which was formally christened on the occasion of our visit, Avoca—the meeting of the waters; a name, as all agreed, full of remembrances of the Old World and the land of his remote ancestors; and yet like enough to one of the graceful and sonorous Indian names of the island not to seem barbarous and out of place. Round the clearing the mountain woods surged up a thousand feet aloft; but so gradually, and so far off, as to allow free circulation of air and a broad sheet of sky overhead; and as the camp stood on the highest point of the rise, it did not give that choking and crushing sensation of being in a ditch, which makes houses in most mountain valleys—to me at least—intolerable. Up one glen, toward the south we had a full view of the green Cerro of Arima, three thousand feet in height; and down another, to the north-east, was a great gate in the mountains, through which we could hear—though not see—the surf rolling upon the rocks three miles away.

I was woke that morning, as often before and afterwards, by a clacking of stones; and, looking out, saw in the dusk a Negro squatting, and hammering, with a round stone on a flat one, the coffee which we were to drink in a quarter of an hour. It was turned into a tin saucepan; put to boil over a firestick between two more great stones; clarified, by some cunning island trick, with a few drops of cold water; and then served up, bearing, in fragrance and taste, the same relation to average English coffee as fresh things usually do to stale ones, or live to dead. After which 'mañana,' and a little quinine for fear of fever, we lounged about waiting for breakfast, and for the arrival of the horses from the village.

Then we inspected a Coolie's great toe, which had been severely bitten by a vampire in the night. And here let me say that the popular disbelief of vampire stories is only owing to English ignorance and disinclination to believe any of the many quaint things which John Bull has not seen, because he does not care to see them. If he comes to these parts, he must be careful not to leave his feet or hands out of bed without mosquito curtains; if he has good horses, he ought not to leave them exposed at night without wire-gauze round the stable-shed—a plan which, to my surprise, I never saw used in the West Indies. Otherwise, he will be but too likely to find in the morning a triangular bit cut out of his own flesh, or even worse, out of his horse's withers or throat, where twisting and lashing cannot shake the tormentor off; and must be content to have himself lamed, or his horses weakened to staggering and thrown out of collar-work for a week, as I have seen happen more than once or twice. The only method of keeping off the vampire yet employed in stables is light; and a lamp is usually kept burning there. But the Negro—not the most careful of men—is apt to fill and trim it; and if it goes out in the small hours, the horses are pretty sure to be sucked, if there is a forest near. So numerous and troublesome, indeed, are the vampires, that there are pastures in Trinidad in which, at least till the adjoining woods were cleared, the cattle would not fatten, or even thrive; being found, morning after morning, weak and sick from the bleedings which they had endured at night.

XIX

Town Geology
1872

*The Canonry of Chester required three months residence a year.
Charles took up the post in May 1870—his first preferment, at the age
of fifty. He did not have to resign his living. 'It enables us to remain at
Eversley and to have a nice change once a year for three months . . . it
will be a rest from the heavy work of the Professorship,' Fanny wrote.
She should have known her husband better. He was never one to rest.
With undiminished vigour he threw himself into his duties, attending
matins and evensong daily, delivering evening lectures twice a week,
preaching sermons to full and enthusiastic congregations, conducting
nature rambles, and finding time into the bargain to found and conduct
the Chester Natural Science Society, which enrolled as founder
members such eminent scientists as Hooker, Tyndall, Huxley and Lyell.*

*In 1872 some of his lectures delivered to the young men of Chester
were published under the title* Town Geology—*'the poor man's science'
as he described it—and in them his ability, when disciplined by science,
to think clearly, expound simply and share his enthusiasm for the
subject are well displayed.*

*The extracts which follow are from the preface in which he urges on
his readers the importance of studying the natural sciences, and gives
his reasons for a devotion to their truths as wholehearted as his devotion
to the truths of God.*

But more: let me urge you to study Natural Science, on grounds
which may be to you new and unexpected—on social, I had almost
said on political grounds.

We all know, and I trust we all love, the names of Liberty,
Equality, and Brotherhood. We feel, I trust, that these words are
too beautiful not to represent true and just ideas; and that therefore
they will come true, and be fulfilled, somewhen, somewhere, somehow.

It may be in a shape very different from that which you, or I, or any man expects; but still they will be fulfilled.

But if they are to come true, it is we, the individual men, who must help them to come true for the whole world, by practising them ourselves, when and where we can. And I tell you—that in becoming scientific men, in studying science and acquiring the scientific habit of mind, you will find yourselves enjoying a freedom, an equality, a brotherhood, such as you will not find elsewhere just now.

Freedom: what do we want freedom for? For this, at least; that we may be each and all able to think what we choose; and to say what we choose also, provided we do not say it rudely, so as to provoke a breach of the peace. That last was my poor friend Mr Buckle's definition of freedom of speech. That was the only limit to it which he would allow; and I think that that is Mr John Stuart Mill's limit also. At all events, it is mine. And I think we have that kind of freedom in these islands, as perfectly as any men are likely to have it on this earth.

But what I complain of is, that when men have got the freedom, three out of four of them will not use it. What?—some one will answer—Do you suppose that I will not say what I choose, and that I dare not speak my own mind to any man? Doubtless. But are you sure first, that you think what you choose, or only what some one else chooses for you? Are you sure that you make up your own mind before you speak, or let some one else make it up for you? Your speech may be free enough, my good friend; and Heaven forbid that it should be anything else; but are your thoughts free likewise? Are you sure that, though you may hate bigotry in others, you are not somewhat of a bigot yourself? That you do not look at only one side of a question, and that the one which pleases you? That you do not take up your opinions at second hand, from some book or some newspaper, which after all only reflects your own feelings, your own opinions? You should ask yourselves that question, seriously and often: 'Are my thoughts really free?'

And I tell you that if you, or I, or any man, want to let our thoughts play freely round questions, and so escape from the tendency to become bigoted and narrow-minded which there is in every human being, then we must acquire something of that inductive habit of mind which the study of Natural Science gives. It is, after all, as Professor Huxley says, only common sense well regulated. But then it is well regulated; and how precious it is, if you can but get it. The art of seeing, the art of knowing what you see; the art of comparing, of perceiving true likenesses and true differences, and so of classifying and arranging what you see; the art of connecting facts together in you own mind in chains of cause and effect, and that accurately, patiently, calmly, without prejudice, vanity, or temper—this is what is wanted for true freedom of mind. But accuracy, patience, freedom from prejudice, carelessness for all except the truth, whatever the truth may be—are not these the virtues of a truly free spirit? Then, as I said just now, I know no study so able to give that free habit of mind as the study of Natural Science.

Equality, too: whatever equality may or may not be just, or possible: this, at least, is just, and I hope possible; that every man, every child, or every rank, should have an equal chance of education; an equal chance of developing all that is in him by nature; an equal chance of acquiring a fair knowledge of those facts of the universe which specially concern him; and of having his reason trained to judge of them. I say, whatever equal rights men may or may not have, they have this right. Let every boy, every girl, have an equal and sound education. If I had my way, I would give the same education to the child of the collier and to the child of the peer. I would see that they were taught the same things, and by the same method. Let them all begin alike, say I. They will be handicapped heavily enough as they go on in life, without our handicapping them in their first race. Whatever stable they come out of, whatever promise they show, let them all train alike, and start fair, and let the best colt win.

Well: but there is a branch of education in which, even now, the poor man can compete fairly against the rich; and that is, Natural Science. In the first place, the rich, blind to their own interest, have neglected it hitherto in their schools; so that they have not the start of the poor man on that subject which they have on many. In the next place, Natural Science is a subject which a man cannot learn by paying for teachers. He must teach it himself, by patient observation, by patient common sense. And if the poor man is not the rich man's equal in those qualities, it must be his own fault, not his purse's. Many shops have I seen about the world, in which fools could buy articles more or less helpful to them: but never saw I yet an observation-shop, nor a common-sense shop either.

Do you wish to be great? Then be great with true greatness; which is,—knowing the facts of nature, and being able to use them. Do you wish to be strong? Then be strong with true strength; which is—knowing the facts of nature, and being able to use them. Do you wish to be wise? Then be wise with true wisdom; which is, —knowing the facts of nature, and being able to use them. Do you wish to be free? Then be free with true freedom; which is again, —knowing the facts of nature, and being able to use them.

When I was young I used to think one could get perfect freedom, and social reforms, and all that I wanted, by altering the arrangements of society and legislation; by constitutions, and Acts of Parliament; by putting society into some sort of freedom-mill, and grinding it all down, and regenerating it so. And that something can be done by Acts of Parliament, I hold still, as every rational man most hold.

But as I grew older, I began to see that if things were to be got right, the freedom-mill would do very little towards grinding them right, however well and amazingly it was made. I began to see what sort of flour came out at one end of the mill, depended mainly on what sort of grain you had put in at the other; and I began to see that the problem was, to get good grain; and then good flour would be turned out, even by a very clumsy old fashioned sort of mill. And what do I mean by good grain? Good men, honest men, accurate men, patient men, self-restraining men, fair men, modest men. Men who are aware of their own vast ignorance compared with the vast amount that there is to be learned in such a universe as this. Men who are accustomed to look at both sides of a question; who, instead of making up their minds in haste like bigots and fanatics, wait like wise men, for more facts, and more thought about the facts. In one word, men who had acquired just the habit of mind which the study of Natural Science can give, and must give; for without it there is no use studying Natural Science; and the man who has not got that habit of mind, if he meddles with science, will merely become a quack and a charlatan, only fit to get his bread as a spirit-rapper, or an inventor of infallible pills.

And when I saw that, I said to myself—I will train myself, by Natural Science, to the truly rational, and therefore truly able and useful, habit of mind; and more, I will, for it is my duty as an Englishman, train every Englishman over whom I can get influence in the same scientific habit of mind; that I may, if possible, make him, too, a rational and an able man.

But now: why should I, as a clergyman, interest myself specially in the spread of Natural Science? Am I not going out of my proper sphere to meddle with secular matters? Am I not, indeed, going into a sphere out of which I had better keep myself, and all over whom I may have influence? For is not science antagonistic to religion? and, if so, what has a clergyman to do, save to warn the young against it, instead of attracting them towards it?

First, as to meddling with secular matters. I grudge that epithet of secular to any matter whatsoever. But I do more; I deny it to anything which God has made, even to the tiniest of insects, the most insignificant atom of dust. To those who believe in God, and try to see all things in God, the most minute natural phenomenon cannot be secular. It must be divine; I say, deliberately, divine; and I can use no less lofty word. The grain of dust is a thought of God; God's power made it; God's wisdom gave it whatsoever properties or qualities it may possess. God's providence has put it in the place where it is now, and has ordained that it should be in that place at that moment, by a train of causes and effects which reaches back to the very creation of the universe. The grain of dust can no more go from God's presence or flee from God's Spirit, than you or I can. If it goes up to the physical heaven, and float (as it actually often does) far above the clouds, in those higher strata of the atmosphere which the aeronaut has never visited, whither the alpine snow-peaks do not rise, even there it will be obeying physical laws, which we term hastily laws of Nature, but which are really the laws of God: and if it go down into the physical abyss; if it be buried fathoms, miles, below the surface, and become an atom of some rock still in the process of consolidation, has it escaped from God, even in the bowels of the earth? Is it not there still obeying physical laws, of pressure, heat, crystallization, and so forth, which are laws of God—the will and mind of God concerning particles of matter? Only look at all created things in this light—look at them as what they are, the expressions of God's mind and will concerning this universe in which we live—'the Word of God,' as Bacon says, 'revealed in facts,'—and then you will not fear physical science; for you will be sure that, the more you know of physical science, the more you will know of the works and of the will of God. At least, you will be in harmony with the teaching of the Psalmist: 'The heavens,' says he, 'declare the glory of God; and the firmament showeth his handiwork. There is neither speech nor language where their voices are not heard among them.' So held the Psalmist concerning astronomy, the knowledge of the heavenly bodies; and what he says of sun and stars is true likewise of the flowers around our feet, of which the greatest Christian poet of modern times has said—

> 'To me the meanest flower that grows may give
> Thoughts that do lie too deep for tears.'

So again, you will be in harmony with the teaching of St Paul, who told the Romans 'that the invisible things of God are clearly seen from the creation of the world, being understood by the things that are made, even his eternal power and Godhead;' and who told the savages of Lycaonia that 'God had not left himself without witness, in that He did good and sent men rain from heaven, and fruitful seasons, filling men's hearts with food and gladness.' Rain and fruitful seasons witnessed to all men of a Father in heaven. And he who wishes to know how truly St Paul spoke, let him study the laws which produce and regulate rain and fruitful seasons, what we now call climatology, meteorology, geography of land and water. Let him read that truly noble Christian work, Maury's 'Physical Geography of the Sea;' and see, if he be a truly rational man, how advanced science, instead of disproving, has only corroborated St Paul's assertion, and how the ocean and the rain-cloud, like the sun and the stars, declare the glory of God. And if any one undervalues the sciences which teach us concerning stones and plants and animals, or thinks that nothing can be learnt from them concerning God—allow one who has been from childhood only a humble, though he trusts a diligent student of these sciences—allow him, I say, to ask in all reverence, but in all frankness, who it was who said, 'Consider the lilies of the field, how they grow.' 'Consider the birds of the air—and how your Heavenly Father feedeth them.'

Consider them. If He has bid you do so, can you do so too much?

XX

Prose Idylls
1873

Recognition came at last, or partial recognition; never a Bishop's mitre, but at least a better Canon's stall than that of Chester: Westminster, in the eye of the world, and with £1000 a year which removed the need to go on grinding out essays and books for money. In the autumn of 1873 Charles entered on his first spell of duty and drew, as at Chester, large and appreciative congregations. But he was ageing, and the sermons tired him; despite 'delicious gleamy weather which quite lifts my poor heart up for a while', he wrote that 'I do not think I could have stood the intense excitement of the Sundays much longer.'

The same year saw the publication of his last book, a collection of Prose Idylls *that had first appeared in* Fraser's Magazine. *In these Charles was at his best, writing with freedom and affection of the sights and scenes he loved: birds, chalk streams, the Fens, French rural life, the moors and shores of his beloved Devon. The extract that follow comes from his essay on The Fens.*

The Fens

But grand enough it was, that black ugly place, when backed by Caistor Hanglands and Holme Wood, and the patches of the primaeval forest; while dark-green alders, and pale-green reeds, stretched for miles round the broad lagoon, where the coot clanked, and the bittern boomed, and the sedge-bird, not content with its own sweet song, mocked the notes of all the birds around; while high overhead hung, motionless, hawk beyond hawk, buzzard beyond buzzard, kite beyond kite, as far as eye could see. Far off, upon the silver mere, would rise a puff of smoke from a punt, invisible from its flatness and its white paint. Then down the wind came the boom of the great stanchion-gun; and after that sound another sound, louder as it neared; a cry as of all the bells of Cambridge, and all the hounds of Cottesmore; and overhead rushed and whirled the skein of terrified wild-fowl, screaming, piping, clacking, filling the air with the hoarse rattle of their wings, while clear above all sounded the wild whistle of the curlew, and the trumpet note of the great wild swan.

They are all gone now. No longer do the ruffs trample the sedge into a hard floor in their fighting-rings, while the sober reeves stand round, admiring the tournament of their lovers, gay with ears and tippets, no two of them alike. Gone are ruffs and reeves, spoonbills, bitterns, avosets; the very snipe, one hears, disdains to breed. Gone too, not only from Whittlesea but from the whole world, is that most exquisite of English butterflies, Lyncoena dispar—the great copper; and many a curious insect more. Ah, well, at least we have wheat and mutton instead, and no more typhus and ague; and, it is hoped, no more brandy-drinking and opium-eating; and children will live and not die. For it was a hard place to live in the old Fen; a place wherein one heard of 'un-exampled instances of longevity,' for the same reason that one hears of them in savage tribes—that few lived to old age at all, save those iron constitutions which nothing could break down.

No one has ever seen a fen-bank break, without honouring the stern quiet temper which there is in these men, when the north-easter is howling above, the spring-tide roaring outside, the brim-ming tide-way lapping up to the dyke-top, or flying over in sheets of spray; when round the one fatal thread is trickling over the dyke —or worse, through some forgotten rat's hole in its side—hundreds of men are clustered, without tumult, without complaint, mar-shalled under their employers, fighting the brute powers of nature, not for their employer's sake alone, but for the sake of their own year's labour and their own year's bread. The sheep have been driven off the land below; the cattle ranged shivering on high dykes inland; they will be saved in punts, if the worst befall. But a hundred spades, wielded by practised hands, cannot stop that tiny rat-hole. The trickle becomes a rush—the rush a roaring water-fall. The dyke-top trembles—gives. The men make efforts, desperate, dangerous, as of sailors in a wreck, with faggots, hurdles, sedge, turf: but the bank will break; and slowly they draw off;

sullen, but uncomplaining; beaten, but not conquered. A new cry rises among them. Up, to save yonder sluice; that will save yonder lode; that again yonder farm; that again some other lode, some other farm, far back inland, but guessed at instantly by men who have studied from their youth, as the necessity of their existence, the labyrinthine drainage of lands which are all below the water level, and where the inner lands, in many cases, are lower still than those outside.

So they hurry away to the nearest farms; the teams are harnessed; the waggons filled, and drawn down and emptied; the beer-cans go round cheerily, and the men work with a sort of savage joy at being able to do something, if not all, and stop the sluice on which so much depends. As for the outer land, it is gone past hope; through the breach pours a roaring salt cataract, digging out a hole on the inside of the bank, which remains as a deep sullen pond for years to come. Hundreds, thousands of pounds are lost already, past all hope. Be it so, then. At the next neap, perhaps, they will be able to mend the dyke, and pump the water out; and begin again, beaten but not conquered, the same everlasting fight with wind and wave which their forefathers have waged for now 800 years.

XXI

Sermons and Essays

Charles Kingsley's Collected Works, published by Macmillan from 1880–5, consist of twenty-eight volumes. Extracts from his novels, verses and natural history essays have been given, but these put together make up only a small part of his published work. The greater part consists of sermons, criticism, topical articles reprinted from magazines, and reprints of lectures, with themes as diverse as 'The Application of Associative Principle and Methods to Agriculture', 'Thoughts on Shelley and Byron', 'The Ancien Regime before the French Revolution', 'The Life of the Rev. Dr John Tauler of Strasbourg', and 'The Birds of Norfolk.' Nothing was either too big or too small to attract his attention and inspire his pen, whether it was sanitation—the theme of an enormous number of articles—or madrepores, history or mythology, education or the paintings in the National Gallery.

Sermons naturally predominate in the collection. He was, according to contemporary accounts, a compelling preacher, so patently sincere, given to homely images and down-to-earth advice, with occasional digressions as when, in the midst of a sermon, he observed an interesting beetle, paused to capture and examine it, released it and then proceeded with his address. In the pulpit his stutter, often so pronounced and embarrassing to others in his social intercourse, disappeared.

Sermons of a past age can be of interest only to theologians and social historians, and it is not for these that Charles Kingsley has been remembered or is still read. A short extract from one of the many, however, is appended, to illustrate his innocence—some would say naivity— and celebration of the natural world he loved, and his capacity to see the hand of God in all His works without too much questioning by His children.

From God's Beautiful World: A Spring Sermon

At this delicious season of the year, when spring time is fast ripening into summer, and every hedge, and field, and garden is full of life and growth, full of beauty and fruitfulness; and we look back on the long winter, and the boughs which stood bare so drearily for six months, as if in a dream; and the blessed spring with its green leaves, and gay flowers, and bright suns has put the winter's frosts out of our thoughts, and we seem to take instinctively to the warmth, as if it were our natural element—as if we were intended, like the bees and butterflies, to live and work only in the summer days, and not to pass, as we do in this climate, one-third of the year, one-third of our whole lives, in mist, cold and gloom. Now, there is a meaning in all this—in our love of bright, warm weather, a very deep and blessed meaning in it. It is a sign to us where we come from—where God would have us go. A sign that we came from God's heaven of light and beauty, that God's heaven of light and beauty is meant for us hereafter. That love which we have for spring, is a sign, that we are the children of the everlasting Spring, children of the light and of the day, in body and in soul; if we would but claim our birthright!

For you must remember that mankind came from a warm country—a country of sunshine and joy. Adam in the Garden of Eden was in no cold or severe climate, he had no need of clothes, not even of the trouble of tilling the ground. The bountiful earth gave him all he wanted. The trees over his head stretched out the luscious fruits to him—the shady glades were his only house, the mossy banks his only bed. He was bred up the child of sunshine and joy. But he was not meant to stay there. God who brings good out of evil, gave man a real blessing when He drove him out of the Garden of Eden. Men were meant to fill the earth and to conquer it, as they are doing at this day. They were meant to become hardy and industrious—to be forced to use their hands and their heads to the utmost stretch, to call into practice all the powers which lay ready to them. They were meant, in short, according to the great law of God's world, to be made perfect through sufferings, and therefore it was God's kindness, and not cruelty, to our forefathers, when He sent them forth into the world; and that He did not send them into any exceedingly hot country, where they would have become utterly lazy and profligate, like the negroes and the South Sea islanders, who have no need to work, because the perpetual summer gives them their bread ready-made to their hands. And it was a kindness, too, that God did not send our forefathers out into any exceedingly cold country, like the Greenlanders and the Esquimaux, where the perpetual winter would have made them greedy, and stunted, and stupid; but that He sent us into this temperate climate, where there is a continual change and variety of seasons.

Here, first, stern and wholesome winter, then bright, cheerful summer, each bringing a message and a lesson from our loving Father in heaven. First comes winter, to make us hardy and daring, and industrious, and strips the trees, and bares the fields, and takes away all food from the earth, and cries to us with the voice of its storms, 'He that will *not work*, neither shall he eat.' 'Go to the ant, thou sluggard; consider her ways, and be wise: who layeth up her meat in the summer, and provideth her food against the time of frosts.' And then comes summer, with her flowers and her fruits, and brings us her message from God, and says to us poor, slaving, hard-worn children of men: 'You are not meant to freeze, and toil, and ache for ever. God loves to see you happy; God is willing to feed your eyes with fair sights, your bodies with pleasant food, to cheer your hearts with warmth and sunshine as much as is good for you. He does not grieve willingly, nor afflict the children of men. See the very bees and gnats, how they dance and bask in the sunbeams! See the very sparrows, how they choose their mates and build their nests, and enjoy themselves as if they were children of the spring! And are ye not of more value than many sparrows? you can understand and enjoy the spring, you men and women who can understand and enjoy God's fair earth ten thousand times more than those dumb creatures can. It is for *you* God has made the Spring. It is for *your* sakes that Christ, the ruler of the earth, sends light and fruitfulness, and beauty over the world year by year. And why? Not merely to warm and feed your bodies, but to stir up your hearts with grateful love for Him, the Blessed One, and to teach you what you are to expect from Him hereafter.

XXII

Finis

Early in 1874, Charles embarked for a tour of North America, again with Rose for a companion. He lectured in the Philadelphia Opera House to 4000 people, met Mark Twain, Longfellow gave a dinner for him, in Washington President Grant invited him to open a session of the House of Representatives with prayer. 'With all his faults,' Charles wrote of the President, 'he was a magnificent *man.' In Ottawa he stayed with the Governor-General and in Quebec received the homage of the French. But in San Francisco he caught a chill which turned to pleurisy and although, after convalescence in Colorado Springs, he resumed his lecturing, he was a sick man when he returned to Eversley in August 1874. Worse still, Fanny's health had broken down and he was told she had angina pectoris. Despite this he preached at West-minster in November, but on the night of their return to Eversley Fanny had a heart attack from which the doctors said that she could not recover.*

A macabre three weeks followed, with both Kingsleys apparently dying in adjoining rooms in the damp and horrid rectory. At first, Charles read aloud their favourite poems, but he developed pneumonia and was kept under drugs. One day he dragged himself out of bed to kneel beside his wife and hold her hand. He died on 23 January, 1875. Dean Stanley telegraphed to offer burial in Westminter Abbey, but Fanny refused. He was buried at Eversley, with a spray of passion flowers engraved on his tombstone and the words with which Charles had summed up their marriage: Amavimus, Amamus, Amababimus. *Fanny recovered, and survived for many years.*

Max Muller, Professor of Modern Languages at Oxford and one of Charles' greatest admirers, summed up his friend's virtues and failings as a writer in words which, by and large, hold good a century later.

THE KINGSLEYS

From the preface to the Roman and the Teuton

'When an author or a poet dies, the better part of him, it is often said, is left in his works. So it is in many cases. But with Kingsley his life and works were one. All he wrote he meant for the day when he wrote it. That was enough for him. Compared with a good work done, a good word spoken, with a silent grasp of the hand from a young man he had saved from mischief, or with a "Thank you, sir," from a poor woman to whom he had been a comfort, he would have despised what people call glory, like incense curling away in smoke. He did his best at the time and for the time. He did it with a concentrated energy of will which broke through all difficulties. In his flights of imagination, in the light and fire of his language he had few equals, if any: but the perfection and classical finish which can be obtained by a sustained effort only, and by a patience which shrinks from no drudgery, these are wanting in most of his works.'

PART TWO

HENRY KINGSLEY
1830–76

XXIII

Henry Kingsley

The Rev. Charles Kingsley's son Henry, youngest of five boys and one girl, was born on 2 January, 1830, at Barnack in Lincolnshire, and brought up at Clovelly and then at Chelsea, where his father became rector of St Luke's in Sydney Street. Like his famous elder brother he gave his heart to Devon and in many of his novels the scenery and natives of the West Country are lovingly described. He followed his elder brother to Kings College, and then matriculated at Worcester College, Oxford, in 1850. Here he spent three gay, extravagant and athletic years, and left without sitting for a degree. As an oarsman he excelled, winning the Diamond Sculls at Henley. He also won a bet that he could not row a mile, run a mile and trot a mile in fifteen minutes.

With his contemporary Edwin Arnold, poet and orientalist, he founded the Fez club, composed of fifty members pledged to celibacy and misogyny. Lavish club breakfasts were held at Dickenson's Coffee House in the Turl when members wore, in addition to their fezes, secret insignia, and smoked ornate oriental pipes. Arnold described him at this period as 'always generous, manly, and of an inner temper nobler than his external manners', adding that 'beneath his levity there lay that love of nature and that passion for honourable development which made him an Australian colonist and gave the world his novels'.

The youngest Kingsley was poor and his tastes expensive; he got into debt, but a timely legacy of £300 enabled him to clear the debts and buy a ticket to Australia. No one in England heard of him for five years. Then, in 1858, a shabby, stocky, weather-beaten man (he was a foot shorter than his clerical brother) with threadbare clothes and a fringe of beard rang the doorbell of St Luke's rectory, to be told that the Kingsley parents had retired to Eversley. There they were re-united with a son who brought no fortune, but the unfinished manuscript of a novel, probably started at a station called Langa-willi near Ballarat,

171

where the owner had befriended the down-and-out young Englishman who had failed at the diggings.

Affection, encouragement and practical help awaited the prodigal. Charles' enthusiasm was immediately kindled by the novel, which he pronounced to be much better than any of his own, and which he re-read frequently. He sent the manuscript to Alexander Macmillan who accepted it without hesitation, and published it in 1859.

XXIV

Geoffrey Hamlyn
1859

Geoffrey Hamlyn was the first and, for a time, the only Australian novel. Its freshness and spontaneity owed everything to personal experience and nothing to reconstruction, and were seldom matched in Henry's later writing. A combination of an unfamiliar, exciting colonial setting, plenty of action, characters credible to British readers because they were transplanted Britons, vivid scenic descriptions, touches of humour, and a fine narrative sweep, proved the recipe for a best-seller and won the younger Kingsley instant renown. Mudies' ordered 500 copies and Henry's native land seemed ready to offer him the fortune he had failed to win at Ballarat.

Two extracts follow. One presents Australian society, or one segment of it, in a new and gentle light, far removed from convict brutalities and gold-digging squalor. The other deals with a more conventional aspect of Australian life—the bushrangers of whom Henry probably had personal experience when a trooper in the Sydney Mounted Police.

The Golden Vineyard

Garoopna is an exceedingly pretty station; in fact, one of the most beautiful I have ever seen. It stands at a point where the vast forests, which surround the mountains in a belt from ten to twenty miles broad, run down into the plains and touch the river. As at Baroona, the stream runs in through a deep cleft in the table-land, which here, though precipitous on the eastern bank, on the western breaks away into a small natural amphitheatre bordered by a fine hanging wood, just in advance of which, about two hundred yards from the river, stands the house, a long, low building densely covered with creepers of all sorts, and fronted by a beautiful garden. Right and left of it are the woolsheds, sheepyards, stockyards, men's huts, etc. giving it almost the appearance of a little village; and behind the wooded ranges begin to rise, in some places broken beautifully by sheer scarps of grey rock. The forest crosses the river a little way; so that Sam, gradually descending from the plains to cross, went the last quarter of a mile through a shady sandy forest tract, fringed with bracken, which led down to a broad crossing place, where the river sparkled under tall over-arching red gums and box-trees; and then following the garden fence, found himself before a deep cool-looking porch, in a broad neatly-kept court-yard behind the house.

A groom came out and took his horse. Rover has enough to do; for there are three or four sheep dogs in the yard, who walk round him on tiptoe, slowly, with their frills out and their tails arched, growling. Rover, also, walks about on tiptoe, arches his tail, and growls with the best of them. He knows that the slightest mistake would be disastrous, and so manoeuvres till he gets to the porch, where, a deal of gravel having been kicked backwards, in the same way as the ancients poured out their wine when they drank a toast, or else (as I think more probable) as a symbol that animosities were to be buried, Rover is admitted as a guest, and Sam feels it safer to enter the house.

A cool, shady hall, hung around with coats, hats, stockwhips; a gun in the corner, and on a slab, the most beautiful nosegay you can imagine. Remarkable, that, for a bachelor's establishment;—but there is not time to think about it, for a tall, comfortable-looking housekeeper, whom Sam has never seen before, comes in from the kitchen and curtseys.

'Captain Brentwood not at home, is he?' said Sam.

'No, sir! Away on the run with Mr James.'

'Oh! very well,' says Sam; 'I am going to stay a few days.'

'Very well, sir; will you take anything before lunch?'

'Nothing, thank you.'

'Miss Alice is somewhere about, sir. I expect her in every minute.'

'Miss Alice!' says Sam, astonished. 'Is she come home?'

'Came home last week, sir. Will you walk in and sit down?'

Sam got his coat out of his valise, and went in. He wished that he had put on his plain blue necktie instead of the blue one with white spots. He would have liked to have worn his new yellow riding-trousers, instead of breeches and boots. He hoped his hair was in order, and tried to arrange his handsome brown curls without a glass, but, in the end, concluded that things could not be mended now, so he looked round the room.

What a charming room it was! A couple of good pictures, and several fine prints on the walls. Over the chimneypiece, a sword, and an old gold-laced cap, on which Sam looked with reverence. Three French windows opened on to a dark cool verandah, beyond which was a beautiful flower-garden. The floor of the room, un-carpeted, shone dark and smooth, and the air was perfumed by vases of magnificent flowers, a hundred pounds worth of them, I should say, if you could have taken them to Covent-garden that December morning. But what took Sam's attention more than any-thing was an open piano, in a shady recess, and on the keys a little fairy white glove.

'White kid gloves, eh, my lady?' says Sam; 'that don't look well.' So he looked through the book-shelves, and, having lighted on Boswell's *Johnson*, proceeded into the verandah. A colley she-dog was lying at one end who banged her tail against the floor in welcome, but was too utterly prostrated by the heat and by the persecution of her puppy to get up and make friends. The pup, however, a ball of curly black wool, with a brown-striped face, who was sitting on the top of her with his head on one side, seemed to conclude that a game of play was to be got out of Sam, and came blundering towards him; but Sam was, by this time, deep in a luxurious rocking-chair, so the puppy stopped halfway, and did battle with a great black tarantula spider who happened to be abroad on business.

Sam went to the club with his immortal namesake, bullied Bennet Langton, argued with Beauclerk, put down Goldsmith, and extinguished Boswell. But it was too hot to read; so he let the book fall on his lap, and lay a dreaming.

What a delicious verandah is this to dream in! Through the tangled passion-flowers, jessamines and magnolias, what a soft gleam of bright hazy distance, over the plains and far away! The deep river-glen cleaves the table-land, which, here and there, swells into breezy downs. Beyond, miles away to the North, is a great forest-barrier, above which there is a blaze of late snow, send-ing strange light aloft into the burning haze. All this is seen through an arch in the dark mass of verdure which clothes the trellis-work, only broken through in this one place, as though to make a frame for the picture. He leans back, and gives himself up to watching trifles.

See here. A magpie comes furtively out of the house with a key in his mouth, and seeing Sam, stops to consider if he is likely to betray him. On the whole, he thinks not; so he hides the key in a crevice, and whistles a tune.

Now enters a cockatoo, waddling along comfortably and talking to himself. He tries to enter into coversation with the magpie, who, however, cuts him dead, and walks off to look at the prospect.

Flop! flop! A great foolish-looking kangaroo comes through the house and peers round him. The cockatoo addresses a few remarks to him which he takes no notice of, but goes blundering out into the garden, right over the contemplative magpie, who gives him two or three indignant pecks on his clumsy feet, and sends him flying down the gravel walk.

Two bright-eyed little kangaroo rats come out of their box peering and blinking. The cockatoo finds an audience in them, for they sit listening to him, now and then catching a flea, or rubbing the backs of their heads with their fore-paws. But a buck 'possum, who stealthily descends by a pillar from unknown realms of mischief on the top of the house, evidently discredits cockey's stories, and departs down the garden to see if he can find something to eat.

An old cat comes up the garden walk, accompanied by a wicked kitten, who ambushes round the corner of the flowerbed, and pounces out on her mother, knocking her down and severely maltreating her. But the old lady picks herself up without a murmur, and comes into the verandah followed by her unnatural offspring, ready for any mischief. The kangaroo rats retire into their box, and the cockatoo, rather nervous, lays himself out to be agreeable.

But the puppy, born under an unlucky star, who has been watching all these things from behind his mother, thinks at last, 'Here is some one to play with,' so he comes staggering forth and challenges the kitten to a lark.

She receives him with every symptom of disgust and abhorrence; but he, regardless of all spitting, and tail swelling, rolls her over, spurring and swearing, and makes believe he will worry her to death. Her scratching and biting tell but little on his woolly hide, and he seems to have the best of it out and out, till a new ally appears unexpectedly, and quite turns the tables. The magpie hops up, ranges alongside of the combatants, and catches the puppy such a dig over the tail as sends him howling to his mother with a flea in his ear.

Sam lay sleepily amused by this little drama; then he looked at the bright green arch which separated the dark verandah from the bright hot garden. The arch was darkened, and looking he saw something which made his heart move strangely, something that he has not forgotten yet, and never will.

Under the arch between the sunlight and the shade, bareheaded, dressed in white, stood a girl, so amazingly beautiful, that Sam wondered for a few minutes whether he was asleep or awake. Her hat, which she had just taken off, hung on her left arm, and with her delicate right hand she arranged a vagrant tendril of the passion-flower, which in its luxuriant growth had broken bounds and fallen from its place above.—A girl so beautiful that I in all my life never saw her superior. They showed me the other day, in a carriage in the park, one they said was the most beautiful girl in England, a descendant of I know not how many noblemen. But, looking back to the times I am speaking of now, I said at once and decidedly, 'Alice Brentwood twenty years ago was more beautiful than she.'

A Norman style of beauty, I believe you would call it. Light hair, deep brilliant blue eyes, and a very fair complexion. Beauty and high-bred grace in every limb and every motion. She stood there an instant on tip-toe, with the sunlight full upon her, while Sam, buried in gloom, had time for a delighted look, before she stepped into the verandah and saw him.

She floated towards him through the deep shadow. 'I think,' she said in the sweetest, most musical little voice, 'that you are Mr Buckley. If so, you are a very old friend of mine by report.' So she held out her little hand, and with one bold kind look from the happy eyes, finished Sam for life.

Father and mother, retire into the chimney corner and watch. Your day is done. Doctor Mulhaus, put your good advice into your pocket and smoke your pipe. Here is one who can exert a greater power for good and evil than all of you put together. It was written of old,—'A man shall leave his father and mother and cleave unto his—' Hallo! I am getting on rather fast, I am afraid.

He had risen to meet her. 'And you, Miss Brentwood,' he said, 'are tolerably well known to me. Do you know that I believe by an exertion of memory I could tell you the year and the month when you began to learn the harp? My dear old friend Jim has kept me quite *au fait* with all your accomplishments.'

'I hope you are not disappointed in me,' said Alice, laughing.

'No,' said Sam. 'I think rather the contrary. Are you?'

'I have not had time to tell yet,' she said. 'I will see how you behave at lunch, which we shall have in half an hour *tête-à-tête*. You have been often here before, I believe? Do you see much change?'

'Not much. I noticed a new piano, and a little glove that I had never seen before. Jim's menagerie of wild beasts is as numerous as ever, I see. He would have liked to be in Noah's Ark.'

'And so would you and I, Mr Buckley,' she answered, laughing, 'if we had been caught in the flood.'

Good Gracious! Think of being in Noah's Ark with her!

'You find them a little troublesome, don't you, Miss Brentwood?'

'Well, it requires a good deal of administrative faculty to keep the kitten and the puppy from open collision, and to prevent the magpie from pecking out the cockatoo's eye and hiding it in the flower bed. Last Sunday morning he (the magpie) got into my father's room, and stole thirty-one shillings and sixpence. We got it all back but half a sovereign, and that we shall never see.'

The bird thus alluded to broke into a gush of melody, so rich, full, and metallic, that they both turned to look at him. Having attracted attention, he began dancing, crooning a little song to himself, as though he would say, 'I know where it is.' And lastly he puffed out his breast, put back his bill, and swore two or three oaths that would have disgraced a London scavenger, with such remarkable distinctness too, that there was no misunderstanding him; so Sam's affectation of not having caught what the bird said, was a dead failure.

'Mr Buckley,' said she, 'if you will excuse me I will go and see about lunch. Can you amuse yourself here for half an hour?' Well, he would try. So he retired again to the rocking-chair, about ten years older than when he rose from it. For he had grown from a boy into a man.

He had fallen over head and ears in love, and all in five minutes.

*　　*　　*

But lunch! Don't let us starve our new pair of turtle-doves, in the outset. Sam is but a growing lad, and needs carbon for his muscles, lime for his bones, and all that sort of thing; a glass of wine won't do him any harm either, and let us hope that his new passion is not of such a lamentable sort as to prevent him using a knife and fork with credit and satisfaction to himself.

Here, in the dark, cool parlour, stands a banquet for the gods, white damask, pretty bright china, and clean silver. In the corner of the table is a frosted claret-jug, standing, with freezing polite-ness, upright, his hand on his hip, waiting to be poured out. In the centre, the grandfather of watermelons, half-hidden by peaches and pomegranates, the whole heaped over by a confusion of ruby cherries (oh! for Lance to paint it!). Are you hungry, though? If so, here is a mould of potted-head and a cold wild duck, while, on the side-board, I see a bottle of pale ale. My brother let us breakfast in Scotland, lunch in Australia, and dine in France, till our lives' end.

And the banquet being over, she said, as pleasantly as possible, 'Now, I know you want to smoke in the verandah. For my part, I should like to bring my work there, and sit with you, but, if you had rather not have me, you have only to say that "you could not think," etc., etc., and I will obediently take myself off.'

But Sam didn't say that. He said that he couldn't conceive any-thing more delightful, if she was quite sure she did not mind.

Not she, indeed! So she brought her work out, and they sat to-gether. A cool wind came up, bending the flowers, swinging the creepers to and fro, and raising a rushing sound, like the sea, from the distant forest. The magpie having been down the garden when the wind came on, and having been blown over, soon joined them in a very captious frame of mind; and, when Alice dropped a ball of red worsted, he seized it as lawful prize, and away in the house with a hop and a flutter. So both Sam and Alice had to go after him, and hunt under the sofa, and the bird, finding that he must yield, dropped the ball suddenly, and gave Sam two vicious digs on the fingers to remember him by. But when Alice just touched his hand in taking it from him, he wished it had been a whipsnake instead of a magpie.

So the ball or worsted was recovered, and they sat down again. He watched her nimble fingers on the delicate embroidery; he glanced at her quiet face and down-turned eyelids, wondering who she was thinking of. Suddenly she raised her eyes and caught him in the fact. You would not swear she blushed; it might only be a trifling reflection from one of the red China roses that hung between her and the sun; yet, when she spoke, it was not quite with her usual self-possession; a little hurriedly perhaps.

'Are you going to be a soldier, as your father was ?'

San had thought for an instant of saying 'yes,' and then to prove his words true of going to Sydney, and enlisting in the 'Half Hundred'.[1] Truth, however, prompting him to say 'no', he compromised the matter by saying he had not thought of it.

'I am rather glad of that, do you know,' she said. 'Unless in India, now, a man had better be anything than a soldier. I am afraid my brother Jim will be begging for a commission some day. I wish he would stay quietly at home.'

That was comforting. He gave up all thoughts of enlisting at once. But now the afternoon shadows were beginning to slant longer and longer, and it was nearly time that the Captain and Jim should make their appearance. So Alice proposed to walk out to meet them, and as Sam did not say no, they went forth together.

Down the garden, faint with the afternoon scents of the flowers before the western sun, among petunias and roses, oleander and magnolia; here a towering Indian lily, there a thicket of scarlet geranium and fuschia. By shady young orange trees, covered with fruit and blossom, between rows of trellised vines, bearing rich promise of a purple vintage. Among fig trees and pomegranates, and so leaving the garden, along the dry slippery grass, towards the hoarse rushing river, both silent till they reached it. There is a silence that is golden.

They stood gazing on the foaming tide an instant, and then Alice said,—

'My father and Jim will come home by the track across there. Shall we cross and meet them ? We can get over just below.'

A little lower down, all the river was collected into one headlong race; and a giant tree, undermined by winter floods, had fallen from one bank to the other, offering a giddy footway across the foaming water.

'Now,' said Alice, 'if you will go over, I will follow you.'

So he ran across, and then looked back to see the beautiful figure

[1] The fiftieth, buffs.

tripping fearlessly over, with outstretched arms, and held out his great brown hand to take her tiny fingers as she steeped down from the upturned roots, on to the soft white sand. He would like to have taken them again, to help her up the bank, but she sprang up like a deer, and would not give him the opportunity. Then they had a merry laugh at the magpie, who had fluttered down all this way before them, to see if they were on a foraging expedition, and if there were any plunder going, and now could not summon courage to cross the river, but stood crooning and cursing by the brink. Then they sauntered away through the forest, side by side, along the sandy track, among the knolls of bracken, with the sunlit boughs overhead whispering knowingly to one another in the evening breeze, as they passed beneath.—An evening walk long remembered by both of them.

> 'Oh see ye not that pleasant road,
>   That winds along the ferny brae?
> Oh that's the road to fairy land,
>   Where thou and I e'en must gae.'

'And so you cannot remember England, Mr Buckley?' says Alice.

'Oh dear, no. Stay though, I am speaking too fast. I can remember some few place. I remember a steep, red road, that led up to the church, and have some dim recollection of a vast grey building, with a dark porch, which must have been the church itself. I can see too, at this moment, a broad green flat, beside a creek, which was covered with yellow and purple flowers, which mother and I made into nosegays. That must be the place my father speaks of as the Hatherleigh Meadows, where he used to go fishing, and, although I must have been there often, yet I can only remember it on one occasion, when he emptied out a basket of fish on the grass for me to look at. My impression of England is, that everything was of a brighter colour than here; and they tell me I am right.'

'A glorious country,' said Alice; 'what would I give to see it?—so ancient and venerable, and yet so amazingly young and vigorous. It seemed like a waste of existence for a man to stay here tending sheep, when his birthright is that of an Englishman; the right to move among his peers, and find his fit place in the greatest empire in the world. Never had any woman such as noble destiny before her as this young lady who has just ascended the throne.'

But the conversation changed here, and her Majesty escaped criticism for the time. They came to an open space in the forest, thickly grown with thickets of bracken fern, prickly acacia, and here and there a solitary dark-foliaged lightwood. In the centre rose a few blackened posts, the supports of what had once been a hut, and as you looked, you were surprised to see an English rose or two, flowering among the dull-coloured prickly shrubs, which were growing around. A place, as any casual traveller would have guessed, which had a history, and Sam, seeing Alice pause, asked her, 'what old hut was this?'

'This,' she said, 'is the Donovans' old station, where they were burnt out by the blacks.'

Sam knew the story well enough, but he would like to hear her tell it; so he made believe to have heard some faint reports of the occurrence, and what could she do, but give him the particulars?

'They had not been here a year,' she said; 'and Mrs Donovan had been confined only three days; there was not a soul on the station but herself, her son Murtagh, and Miss Burke. All day the blackfellows were prowling about, and getting more and more insolent, and at night, just as Murtagh shut the door, they raised their yell, and rushed against it. Murtagh Donovan and Miss Burke had guessed what was coming all day, but had kept it from the sick woman, and now, when the time came, they were cool and prepared. They had two double-barrelled guns loaded with slugs, and with these they did such fearful execution from two loop-holes they had made in the slabs, that the savages quickly retired; but poor Miss Burke, incautiously looking out to get a shot, received a spear-wound in her shoulder, which she bears the mark of to this day. But the worst was to come. The blackfellows mounted on the roof, tried to take off the bark and throw their spears into the hut, but they were foiled again. Wherever a sheet of bark was seen to move they watched, and on the first appearance of an enemy, a charge of shot at a few yards' distance told with deadly effect. Mrs Donovan, who lay in bed and saw the whole, told my father that Lesbia Burke loaded and fired with greater rapidity and precision than did her cousin. A noble woman, I say.'

'Good old Lesbia!' said Sam; 'and how did it end?'

'Why, the foolish blacks fired the woolshed, and brought the Delisles upon them; they tried to fire the roof of the hut, but it was raining too hard: otherwise it would have gone hard with poor Miss Burke. See, here is a peach-tree they planted, covered with fruit; let us gather some; it is pretty good, for the Donovans have kept it pruned in memory of their escape.'

'But the hut was not burnt,' said Sam, 'where did it stand?'

'That pile of earth there, is the remains of the old turf chimney. They moved across the river after it happened.'

But peaches, when they grow on a high tree, must be climbed for, particularly if a young and pretty girl expresses a wish for them. And so it fell out, that Sam was soon astride of one of the lower boughs, throwing the fruit down to Alice, who put them one by one into the neatest conceivable little basket that hung on her arm.

And so they were employed, busy and merry, when they heard a loud cheery voice, which made both of them start.

'Quite a scene from *Paradise Lost*, I declare; only Eve ought to be up the tree handing down the apples to Adam, and not *vice versa*. I miss a carpet snake, too, who would represent the Deuce, and make the thing complete.—Sam Buckley, how are you?'

It was Captain Brentwood who had come on them so inaudibly along the sandy track, on horseback, and beside him was son Jim, looking rather mischievously at Sam, who did not show to the best of advantage up in the peach-tree; but, having descended, and greetings being exchanged, father and son rode on to dress for dinner, the hour for which was now approaching, leaving Sam and Alice to follow at leisure, which they did; for Captain Brentwood and Jim had time to dress and meet in the verandah, before they saw the pair come sauntering up the garden.

'Father,' said Jim, taking the Captain's hand, 'how would that do?'

'Marvellous well, I should say;' replied the Captain.

'And so I think, too,' said Jim. 'Hallo! you two; dinner is ready, so look sharp.'

Widderin shows clearly that he is worth all the money Sam gave for him

The Sergeant, as I said, broke in upon us with the fearful news as we sat at wine. For a minute no man spoke, but all sat silent and horror-struck. Only the Doctor rose quietly, and slipped out of the room unnoticed.

Desborough spoke first. He rose up with deadly wrath in his face, and swore a fearful oath, an oath so fearful, that he who endorsed every word of it then, will not write it down now. To the effect, 'That he would take neither meat, nor drink, nor pleasure, nor rest, beyond what was necessary to keep body and soul together, before he had purged the land of these treacherous villains!'

Charles Hawker went up to the Sergeant, with a livid face and shaking hands. 'Will you tell me again, Robinson, *are they all dead* ?'

The Sergeant looked at him compassionately. 'Well, sir', he said; 'the boy seemed to think Mrs and Miss Mayford had escaped. But you mustn't trust what he says, sir.'

'You are deceiving me,' said Charles. 'There is something you are hiding from me. I shall go down there this minute, and see.'

'You will do nothing of the kind, sir,' said Mrs Buckley, coming into the doorway and confronting him; 'your place is with Captain Desborough. I am going down to look after Ellen.'

During these few moments, Sam had stood stupefied. He stepped up to the Sergeant, and said,—

'Would you tell me which way they went from the Mayfords' ?'

'Down the river, sir.'

'Ah!' said Sam; 'towards Captain Brentwood's, and Alice at home, and alone!—There may be time yet.'

He ran out of the room and I after him. 'His first trouble,' I thought—'his first trial. How will our boy behave now ?'

Let me mention again that the distance from the Mayfords' to Captain Brentwood's following the windings of the river on its right bank, was nearly twenty miles. From Major Buckley's to the same point, across the plains, was barely ten; so that there was still a chance that a brave man on a good horse, might reach Captain Brentwood's before the bushrangers, in spite of the start they had got.

Sam's noble horse, Widderin, a horse with a pedigree a hundred years old, stood in the stable. The buying of that horse had been Sam's only extravagance, for which he had often reproached himself, and now this day, he would see whether he would get his money's worth out of that horse, or no.

I followed him up to the stable, and found him putting the bridle on Widderin's beautiful little head. Neither of us spoke, only when I handed him the saddle, and helped him with the girths, he said, 'God bless you.'

I ran out and got down the slip-rails for him. As he rode by he said, 'Good-bye, Uncle Jeff, perhaps you won't see me again;' and I cried out, 'Remember your God and your mother, Sam, and don't do anything foolish.'

The he was gone; and looking across the plains the way he should go, I saw another horseman toiling far away, and recognized Doctor Mulhaus. Good Doctor! he had seen the danger in a moment, and by his ready wit had got a start of every one else by ten minutes.

The Doctor, on his handsome long-bodied Arabian mare, was making good work of it across the plains, when he heard the rush of horses feet behind him, and turning, he saw tall Widderin bestridden by Sam, springing over the turf, gaining on him stride after stride. In a few minutes they were along side one another.

'Good lad!' cried the Doctor; 'On, forwards; catch her, and away to the woods with her. Bloodhound Desborough will be on their trail in half-an-hour. Save her, and we will have noble vengeance.'

Sam only waved his hand in good-bye, and sped on across the plain like a solitary ship at sea. He steered for a single tree, now becoming dimly visible, at the foot of the Organ Hill.

The good horse, with elastic and easy motion, fled on his course like a bird; lifting his feet clearly and rapidly through the grass. The brisk south wind filled his wide nostrils as he turned his graceful neck from side to side, till, finding that work was meant, and not play, he began to hold his head straight before him, and rush steadily forward.

And Sam, poor Sam! all his hopes for life are now brought down to this: to depend on the wind and pluck of an unconscious horse. One stumble now, and it were better to lie down on the plain and die. He was in the hands of God and he felt it. He said one short prayer, but that towards the end was interrupted by the wild current of thoughts.

Was there any hope? They, the devils, would have been drinking at the Mayfords', and perhaps would go slow; or would they ride fast and wild? After thinking a short time, he feared the latter.

They had tasted blood, and knew that the country would be roused on them shortly. On, on, good horse!

The lonely shepherd on the plains, sleepily watching his feeding sheep, looked up as Sam went speeding by, and thought how fine a thing it would be dressed like that, and have nothing to do but to ride blood-horses to death. Mind your sheep, good shepherd; perhaps it were better for you to do that and nothing more all your life, than to carry in your breast for one short hour such a volcano of rage, indignation, and terror, as he does who hurries unheeding through your scattered flock.

Here are a brace of good pistols, and they, with care, shall give account, if need be, of two men. After that, nothing. It were better, so much better, not to live if one were only ten minutes too late. The Doctor would be up soon; not much matter if he were, though, only another life gone.

The Organ Hill, a cloud of misty blue when he started, now hung in aerial fluted cliffs above his head. As he raced across the long glacis which lay below the hill, he could see a solitary eagle wheeling round the topmost pinnacles, against the clear blue sky; then the hill was behind him, and before him another stretch of plain, bounded by timber, which marked the course of the river.

Brave Widderin had his ears back now, and was throwing his breath regularly through his nostrils in deep sighs. Good horse, only a little longer; bear thyself bravely this day, and then pleasant pastures for thee till thou shalt go the way of all horses. Many a time has she patted, with kind words, thy rainbow neck, my horse; help us to save her now.

Alas! good willing brute, he cannot understand; only he knows that his kind master is on his back, and so he will run till he drop. Good Widderin! think of the time when thy sire rushed triumphant through the shouting thousands at Epsom, and all England heard that Arcturus had won the Derby. Think of the time when thy grandam, carrying Sheik Abdullah, bore down in a whirlwind of sand on the toiling affrighted caravan. Ah! thou knowest not of these things, but yet thy speed flags not. We are not far off now, good horse, we shall know all soon.

Now he was in the forest again, and now, as he rode quickly down the steep sandy road among the bracken, he heard the hoarse rush of the river in his ears, and knew the end was well-nigh come.

No drink now, good Widderin! a bucket of champagne in an hour's time, if thou wilt only stay now to bend thy neck down to the clear gleaming water; flounder through the ford, and just twenty yards up the bank by the cherry-tree, we shall catch sight of the house, and know our fate.

Now the house was in sight, and now he cried aloud some wild inarticulate sound of thankfulness and joy. All was as peaceful as ever, and Alice, unconscious, stood white-robed in the verandah, feeding her birds.

As he rode up he shouted out to her and beckoned. She came running through the house, and met him breathless at the doorway.

'The bushrangers! Alice, my love,' he said. 'We must fly this instant, they are close to us now.'

She had been prepared for this. She knew her duty well, for her father had often told her what to do. No tears! no hysterics! She took Sam's hand without a word, and placing her fairy foot upon his boot, vaulted up into the saddle before him, crying,—'Eleanor, Eleanor!'

Eleanor, the cook, came running out. 'Fly!' said Alice.

'Get away into the bush. The gang are coming; close by.' She, and old Vandemonian, needed no second warning, and as the two young people rode away, they saw her clearing the paddock rapidly, and making for a dense clump of wattles, which grew beyond the fence.

'Whither now, Sam?' said Alice, the moment they were started.

'I should feel safer across the river,' he replied; 'that little wooded knoll would be a fine hiding-place, and they will come down this side of the river from Mayford's.'

'From Mayford's! why, have they been there?'

'They have, indeed. Alas! poor Cecil.'

'What has happened to him? nothing serious?'

'Dead! my love, dead.'

'Oh! poor little Cecil,' she cried, 'that we were all so fond of. And Mrs Mayford and Ellen?'

'They have escaped!—they are not to be found—they have hidden away somewhere.'

They crossed the river, and dismounting, they led the tired horse up the steep slope of turf that surrounded a little castellated tor of bluestone. Here they would hide till the storm was gone by, for from here they could see the windings of the river, and all the broad plain stretched out beneath their feet.

'I do not see them anywhere, Alice,' said Sam presently. 'I see no one coming across the plains. They must be either very near us in the hollow of the river-valley, or else a long way off. I have very little doubt they will come here, though, sooner or later.'

'There they are!' said Alice. 'Surely there are a large party of horsemen on the plain, but they are seven or eight miles off.'

'Ay, ten,' said Sam. 'I am not sure they are horsemen.' Then he said suddenly in a whisper, 'Lie down, my love, in God's name! Here they are, close to us!'

There burst on his ear a confused sound of talking and laughing, and out of one of the rocky gullies leading towards the river, came the men they had been flying from, in number about fourteen. They had crossed the river, for some unknown reason, and to the fear-struck hiders it seemed as though they were making straight towards their lair.

He had got Widderin's head in his breast, blindfolding him with his coat, for should he neigh now, they were undone, indeed! As the bushrangers approached, the horse began to get uneasy, and paw the ground, putting Sam in such an agony of terror that the sweat rolled down his face. In the midst of this he felt a hand on his arm, and Alice's voice, which he scarcely recognized, said, in a fierce whisper,—

'Give me one of your pistols, sir!'

'Leave that to me!' he replied in the same tone.

'As you please,' she said; 'but I must not fall alive into their hands. Never look your mother in the face again if I do.'

He gave one more glance round, and saw that the enemy would come within a hundred yards of their hiding-place. Then he held the horse faster than ever, and shut his eyes.

The Fight among the Fern-Trees

Then Captain Desborough cried aloud to ride at them, and spare no man. And, as he spoke, every golden fern-bough, and every coign of vantage among the rocks, began to blaze and cackle with gun and pistol shot. Jim's horse sprung aloft and fell, hurling him forcibly to the ground, and a tall young trooper, dropping his carbine, rolled heavily of his saddle, and lay on the grass face downward, quite still, as if asleep.

'That's the first man killed,' said the Major, very quietly. 'Sam, my boy, don't get excited, but close on the first fellow you see a chance at.' And Sam, looking in his father's face as he spoke, saw a light in his eyes, that he had never seen there before—the light of battle. The Major caught a carbine from the hands of a trooper who rode beside him, and took a snap-shot, quick as lightning, at a man whom they saw running from one cover to another. The poor wretch staggered and put his hands to his head, then stumbled and fell heavily down.

Now the fight became general and confused. All about among the fern and the flowers, among the lemon-shrubs, and the tangled vines, men fought, and fired, and struck, and cursed; while the little brown bandicoots scuddled swiftly away, and the deadly snake hid himself in his darkest lair, affrighted. Shots were cracking on all sides, two riderless horses, confused in the *mêlée*, were galloping about neighing, and a third lay squealing on the ground in the agonies of death.

Sam saw a man fire at his father, whose horse went down, while the Major arose unhurt. He rode at the ruffian, who was dismounted, and cut him so deep between the shoulder and neck, that he fell and never spoke again. Then seeing Halbert and the Doctor on the right, fiercely engaged with four men who were fighting with clubbed muskets and knives, he turned to help them, but ere he reached them, a tall, handsome young fellow dashed out of the shrub, and pulling his horse short up, took deliberate aim at him, and fired.

Sam heard the bullet go hissing past his ear, and got mad. 'That young dog shall go down,' said he. 'I know him. He is one of the two who rode first yesterday.' And as this passed through his mind, he rode straight at him, with his sword upon his left shoulder. He came full against him in a moment, and as the men held up his gun to guard himself, his cut descended, so full and hard, that it shore through the gunbarrel as through a stick,[1] and ere he could

---

[1] Lieutenant Anderson, unless I am mistaken, performed the same feat at the capture of a bushranger in '52.

bring his hand to his cheek, his opponent had grappled him, and the two rolled off their horses together, locked in a deadly embrace.

Then began an awful and deadly fight between these two young fellows. Sam's sword had gone from his hand in the fall, and he was defenceless, save by such splendid physical powers as he had by nature. But his adversary, though perhaps a little lighter, was a terrible enemy, and fought with the strength and litheness of a leopard. He had his hand at Sam's throat, and was trying to choke him. Sam saw that one great effort was necessary, and with a heave of his whole body, threw the other beneath him, and struck downwards, three quick blows, with the whole strength of his ponderous fist, on the face of the man, as he lay beneath him. The hold on his throat loosened, and seeing that they had rolled within reach of his sword, in a moment he had clutched it, and drawing back his elbow, prepared to plunge it into his adversary's chest.

But he hesitated. He could not do it. Maddened as he was with fighting, the sight of that bloody face, bruised beyond recognition by his terrible blows, and the wild fierce eyes, full of rage and terror, looking into his own, stayed his hand, and while he paused the man spoke, thick and indistinctly, for his jaw was broken.

'If you will spare me,' he said, 'I will be king's evidence.'

'Then turn on your face', said Sam; 'and I will tie you up.'

And, as he spoke a trooper ran up, and secured the prisoner, who appealed to Sam for his handkerchief. 'I fought you fair', he said; 'and you're a man worth fighting. But you have broken something in my face with your fist. Give me something to tie it up with.'

'God save us all!' said Sam, giving him his handkerchief. 'This is miserable work! I hope it is all over.'

It seemed so. All he heard were the fearful screams of a wounded man lying somewhere among the fern.

'Where are they all, Jackson?' said he.

'All away to the right sir,' said the trooper. 'One of my comrades is killed, your father has had his horse shot, the Doctor is hit in the arm, and Mr James Brentwood has got his leg broken with the fall of his horse. They are minding him now. We've got all the gang, alive or dead, except two. Captain Desborough is up the valley now after the head man, and young Mr Hawker is with him. D . . . n it all, hark at that.'

Two shots were fired in quick succession in the direction indicated; and Sam, having caught his horse, galloped off to see what was going on.

Desborough fought neither against small nor great, but only against one man, and he was George Hawker. Him he had sworn he would bring home, dead or alive. When he and his party had first broken through the fern, he had caught sight of his quarry, and had instantly made towards him, as quick as the broken scrub-tangled ground would allow.

They knew one another; and, as soon as Hawker saw that he was recognized, he made to the left, away from the rest of his gang, trying to reach, as Desborough could plainly see, the only practicable way that led from the amphitheatre in which they were back into mountains.

They fired at one another without effect at the first. Hawker was now pushing in full flight, though the scrub was so dense that neither made much way. Now the ground got more open and easier travelled, when Desborough was aware of one who came charging recklessly up along side of him, and, looking around, he recognized Charles Hawker.

'Good lad,' he said; 'come on. I must have that fellow before us there. He is the arch-devil of the lot. If we follow him to h-ll, we must have him!'

'We'll have him safe enough!' said Charles. 'Push to the left, Captain, and we shall get him against those fallen rocks.'

Desborough saw the excellence of this advice. This was the last piece of broken ground there was. On the right the cliff rose precipitous, and from its side had tumbled a confused heap of broken rock, running out into the glen. Once past this, the man they were pursuing would have the advantage, for he was splendidly mounted, and beyond was clear galloping ground. As it was, he was in a recess, and Desborough and Charles pushing forward, succeeded in bringing him to bay. Alas, too well!

George Hawker reined up his horse when he saw escape was impossible, and waited their coming with a double-barrelled pistol in his hand. As the other two came on, calling on him to surrender, Desborough's horse received a bullet in his chest, and down went horse and man together. But Charles pushed on till he was within ten yards of the bushranger, and levelled his pistol to fire.

So met father and son, the second time in their lives, all

unconsciously. For an instant they glared at one another with wild threatening eyes, as the father made his aim more certain and deadly. Was there no lightning in heaven to strike him dead, and save him from this last horrid crime? Was there no warning voice to tell him that this was his son?

None. The bullet sped, and the poor boy tumbled from his saddle, clutching wildly, with crooked, convulsive fingers, at the grass and flowers—shot through the chest!

Then, ere Desborough had disentangled himself from his fallen horse, George Hawker rode off laughing—out through the upper rock walls into the presence of the broad bald snowline that rolled above his head in endless lofty tiers towards the sky.

XXV

Ravenshoe
1862

Settled in a cottage next to brother Charles at Eversley, Henry went to work immediately on a more ambitious novel, set mainly in England and especially in the Devon he remembered from his early boyhood. Ravenshoe is the seat of an ancient Roman Catholic family of the same name, on the edge of Dartmoor close to the sea. A complicated plot hinges on such topics, dear to the Victorians, as the heir's legitimacy, secret marriages, changelings, and the schemings of a Jesuit priest to keep the name and property in Catholic hands. (Henry took a less jaundiced view of Roman priests than did his brother, but was nevertheless firmly in the Protestant camp.) 'The plot is very intricate and so overborne by incident,' its contriver rightly remarked, 'that it would be difficult to give a précis of it.'

Henry was a great admirer of Thackeray, whom he once met at dinner when a schoolboy, and evidently borrowed from the master an indulgence in discursiveness, and a habit of keeping up a running commentary on the behaviour of his characters, which often hold up the action of Ravenshoe. *But there is a rich inventiveness, both in episodes which follow each other as closely as raindrops, and in the characters who crowd the scene: mostly rich upper-class characters, leavened by respectful peasantry and grooms, of whom Henry can have had little first-hand experience since Oxford days, but whom he depicted with considerable fluency and skill. In particular Charles Ravenshoe, the hero, is brought to life by the affection borne him by his creator; he remained the author's favourite character, no doubt an idealized version of himself: generous, open-hearted, loyal and brave, but quixotically foolish and possessed of a stubborn pride that hurts others more than it hurts him.*

Not everyone would endorse the judgement of one of Henry's biographers, S. M. Ellis, that this is 'one of the great stories of the world', still less that of Joseph Pulitzer who called it the best novel in

193

the English language; but it is probably Henry's main achievement, and was widely praised in its day. It was serialized in Macmillan's Magazine *in 1861–2.*

About a third of the way through the novel Charles, brought up as the heir of Ravenshoe, learns that he is not the heir after all, but the son of a keeper. Cutting himself off from his friends and relatives he takes service as a groom with a Lieutenant Hornby, and eventually enlists as a trooper in the 140th Hussars. The first extract describes his departure with his regiment for the Crimea, and his first taste of action. In the second extract the scene reverts to Ravenshoe where the rich and highborn Lord Saltire, concealing beneath his polished cynicism a heart of gold, converses with Mary, apart from the vessel's captain the sole survivor of a shipwreck off the Devon coast, who was brought up in the Ravenshoe household to become a governess, and is in love with Charles. The action of the book at this stage alternates between the Crimea and the purlieus of Ravenshoe. The third extract describes how Charles takes part in the charge of the Light Brigade; this led his biographer Sir Michael Sadleir to suggest that Henry might have seen the Crimean war at first-hand, perhaps as a newspaper correspondent, during his Australian sojourn. There is, however, no evidence of this.

In which Charles comes to life again

Ha! This was a life again. Better this than dawdling about at the heels of a dandy, or sitting on a wheelbarrow in a mews! There is a scent here sweeter than that of the dung-hill, or the dandy's essences—what is it? The smell of tar, and bilge water, and red herrings. There is a fresh whiff of air up this narrow street, which moves your hair, and makes your pulse quicken. It is the free wind of the sea. At the end of the street are ships, from which comes the clinking of cranes; pleasanter music sometimes than the song of nightingales.

Down the narrow street towards the wharf come the hussars. Charles is among them. On the wharf, in the confusion, foremost, as far as he dare, to assist. He was known as the best horseman in the troop, and, as such, was put into dangerous places. He had attracted great attention among the officers by his fearlessness and dexterity. The captain had openly praised him; and, when the last horse had been slung in, and last cheer given, and the great ship was away down the river, on her message of wrath, and woe, and glory, Charles was looking back at Southampton spires, a new man with a new career before him.

The few months of degradation, of brooding misery, of listlessness and helplessness he had gone through, made this short episode in his life appear the most happy and most beautiful of all. The merest clod of a recruit in the regiment felt in some way ennobled and exalted; but as for Charles, with his intensely, sensitive, romantic nature, he was quite, as the French say, *tête montée*. The lowest menial drudgery was exalted and glorified. Groom his horse and help clean the deck? Why not? That horse must carry him in the day of the merry meeting of heroes. Hard living, hard work, bad weather, disease, death: what were they, with his youth, health, strength, and nerve? Not to be thought of save with a smile. Yes! this expedition of his to the Crimea was the noblest, and possibly the happiest in his life. To use a borrowed simile, it was like the mournful, beautiful autumn sunset, before the dark night closes in. He felt like a boy at midsummer, exploring some wood, or distant valley, watched from a distance long, and at last attained; or as one feels when, a stranger in a new land, one first rides forth alone into the forest on some distant expedition, and sees the new world, dreamt of and longed for all one's life, realized in all its beauty and wonder at last; and expanding leaf by leaf before one. In a romantic state of mind. I can express it no better.

And really it is no wonder that a man, not sea-sick, should have been in a state of wonder, eager curiosity, kindliness, and, above all, high excitement—which four states of mind, I take it, make up together the state of mind called romantic, quixotic, or chivalrous; which is a very pleasant state of mind indeed. For curiosity, there was enough to make the dullest man curious. Where were they going? Where would the blow be struck? Where would the dogs of war first fix their teeth? Would it be a campaign in the field, or a siege, or what? For kindliness: were not his comrades a good set of brave, free-hearted lads, and was not he the favourite among them? As for wonder and excitement, there was plenty of that, and it promised to last. Why, the ship herself was a wonder. The biggest in the world, carrying 500 men and horses; and every man in the ship knew, before she had been five hours at sea, that that quiet-looking commander of hers was going to race her out under steam the whole way. Who could tire of wondering at the glimpse one got down the ironrailed well into the machinery, at the busy cranks and leaping pistons, or, when tired of that, at the strange dim vista of swinging horses between decks? Wonder and excitement enough here to keep twenty Don Quixotes going! Her very name too was romantic—HIMALAYA.

A north-east wind and a mountain of rustling white canvas over head. Blue water that seethed and creamed, and roared past to leeward. A calm, and the Lizard to the north, a dim grey cape. A south-west wind, and above a mighty cobweb of sailless rigging. Top-gallant masts sent down and yards close hauled. Still, through it all, the busy clack and rattle of the untiring engine.

A dim wild sunset, and scudding prophet clouds that hurried from the west across the crimson zenith, like witches towards a sabbath. A wind that rose and grew as the sun went down, and hummed loud in the rigging as the bows of the ship dipped into the trough of the waves, and failed almost into silence as she raised them. A night of storm and terror: in the morning, the tumbling broken seas of Biscay. A few fruit brigs scudding wildly here and there; and a cape on a new land. A high round down, showing a gleam of green among the flying mists.

Sail set again before a northerly wind, and the ship rolling before it like a jolly drunkard. Then a dim cloud of smoke before them. Then the great steamer *Bussorah*, thundering forward against the wind, tearing furiously at the leaping seas with her iron teeth. A hurried glimpse of fluttering signals, and bare wet empty decks; and, before you had time to say what a noble ship she was, and what good weather she was making of it, only a cloud of smoke miles astern.

Now, a dark line, too faint for landsmen's eyes, far ahead, which changed into a loom of land, which changed into a cloud, which changed into a dim peak towering above the sea mists, which changed into a tall crag, with a town, and endless tiers of white fortification—Gibraltar.

Then a strong west wind for three days, carrying the ship flying before it with all plain sail set. And each day, at noon, a great

excitement on the quarter-deck, among the officers. On the third
day much cheering and laughter, and shaking of hands with the
commander. Charles, catching an opportunity, took leave to ask
his little friend the cornet, what it meant. The *Himalaya* had run a
thousand miles in sixty-three hours.[1]

★   ★   ★

I suppose that, if I knew my business properly, I should at this
point represent Charles as falling down the companion ladder and
spraining his ankle, or as having over-eaten himself, or something
of that sort, and so pass over the rest of the voyage by saying that he
was confined to his bunk, and saw no more of it. But I am going to
do nothing of the sort, for two reasons. In the first place, because
he did not do anything of the kind; and in the next, because he
saw somebody at Constantinople, of whom I am sure you will be
glad to hear again.

Charles had seen Tenedos golden in the east, and Lemnos purple
in the west, as the sun went down; then, after having steamed at
half-speed through the Dardanelles, was looking the next evening
at Constantinople, and at the sun going down behind the minarets,
and all that sort of thing, which is no doubt very beautiful, but of
which one seems to have heard once or twice before. The ship was
laying at anchor, with fires banked, and it was understood that they
were waiting for a Queen's messenger.

They could see their own boat, which they had sent to wait for
him at Seraglio Point. One of the sailors had lent Charles a telescope—a regular old brute of a telescope, with a crack across the
object-glass. Charles was looking at the boat with it, and suddenly
said, 'There he is.'

He saw a small grey-headed man, with moustaches, come quickly
down and get into the boat, followed by some Turks with his
luggage. This was Colonel Oldhoss, the Queen's messenger; but
there was another man with him, whom Charles recognized at once.
He handed the telescope to the man next him, and walked up and
down the deck rapidly.

[1] The most famous voyage of the *Himalaya*, from Cork to Varna in twelve
days with the Fifth Dragoon Guards, took place in June. The voyage
here described, is, as will be perceived a subsequent one, but equally
successful, apparently.

'I *should* like to speak to him,' he thought, 'if it were only one word. Dear old fellow. But then he will betray me, and they will begin persecuting me at home, dear souls. I suppose I had better not. No. If I am wounded and dying I will send for him. I will not speak to him now.'

The Queen's messenger and his companion came on board, and the ship got under way and steamed through the Bosphorus out into the wild seething waves of the 'Fena Kara degniz', and Charles turned in without having come near either of them. But in the chill morning, when the ship's head was north-west, and the dawn was flushing up on the distant Thracian sierra, Charles was on deck, and, while pausing for an instant in his duties, to look westward, and try to remember what country and what mountains lay to the north-west of Constantinople, a voice behind him said quietly, 'Go find me Captain Crocker, my man.' He turned, and was face to face with General Mainwaring.

It was only for an instant, but their eyes met; the general started, but he did not recognize him. Charles's moustache had altered him so much that it was no great wonder. He was afraid that the general would seek him out again, but he did not. These were busy times. They were at Varna that night.

Men were looking sourly at one another. The French expedition had just come in from Kustendji in a lamentable state, and the army was rotting in its inactivity. You know all about that as well as I can tell you; what is of more importance to us is, that Lieutenant Hornby had been down with typhus, and was recovering very slowly, so that Charles's chances of meeting him were very small.

What am I to do with this three weeks or more at Varna to which I have reduced Charles, you, and myself? Say as little about it as need be, I should say. Charles and his company were, of course, moved up at once to the cavalry camp at Devna, eighteen miles off, among the pleasant hills and woodlands. Once, his little friend, the young cornet, who had taken a fancy for him, made him come out shooting with him to carry his bag. And they scrambled and clambered, and they tore themselves with thorns, and they fell down steep places, and utterly forgot their social positions towards one another. And they tried to carry home every object which was new to them, including a live turtle and a basaltic column. And they saw a green lizard, who arched his tail and galloped away like a racehorse, and a grey lizard, who let down a bag under his chin and barked at them like a dog. And the cornet shot a quail, and a hare, and a longtailed francolin, like a pheasant, and a wood-pigeon. And, lastly, they found out that, if you turned over the stones, there were scorpions under them, who tucked their claws under their armpits, as a man folds his arms, and sparred at them with their tails, drawing their sting in and out, as an experienced boxer moves his left hand when waiting for an attack. Altogether, they had a glorious day in a new country, and did not remember in what relation they were to one another till they topped the hill above Devna by moonlight, and saw the two long lakes, stretching towards the sea, broken here and there into silver ripples by the oars of the commissariat boats. A happy innocent schoolboy day— the sort of day which never comes if we prepare for it and anticipate it, but which comes without warning, and is never forgotten.

★   ★   ★

In the evening of the nineteenth there was a rumble of artillery over the hill in front of them, which died away in half an hour. Most of the rest of the cavalry were further to the front of the extreme left, and were 'at it,' so it was understood, with the Cossacks. But the 140th were still idle.

On the morning of the twentieth, Charles and the rest of them, sitting in their saddles, heard the guns booming in front and on the right. It became understood among the men that the fleet were attacking some batteries. Also, it was whispered that the Russians were going to stand and fight. Charles was sixth man from the right of the rear rank of the third troop. He could see the tails of the horses immediately before him, and could remark that his front-rank man had a great patch of oil on the right shoulder of his uniform. He could also see Hornby in the troop before him.

These guns went moaning on in the distance till half-past one; but still they sat there idle. About that time there was a new sound in the air, close on their right, which made them prick up their ears and look at one another. Even the head of the column could have seen nothing, for they were behind the hill. But all could hear, and guess. We all know that sound well enough now. You hear it now, thank God, on every village green in England when the cricket is

over. Crack, crack! Crack, crack! The noise of advancing skirmishers.

And so it grew from the right towards the front, towards the left,
till the air was filled with the shrill treble of musketry. Then, as the
French skirmished within reach of the artillery, the deep bass
roared up, and the men, who dared not whisper before, could
shout at one another without rebuke.

Louder again, as our artillery came into range. All the air was
tortured with concussion. Charles would have given ten years of
his life to know what was going on on the other side of the hill. But
no. There they stay, and he had to look at the back of the man
before him; and at this time he came to the conclusion that the
patch of grease on his right shoulder was of the same shape as the
map of Sweden.

A long weary two hours or more was spent like this. Charles, by
looking forward and to the right, between the two right-hand men
of the troop before him, could see the ridge of the hill, and see the
smoke rising from beyond it, and drifting away to the left before
the sea-breeze. He saw an aid-de-camp come over that ridge and
dismount beside the captain of Hornby's troop, loosening his girths.
They laughed together; then the captain shouted to Hornby, and
he laughed and waved his sword over his head. After this, he was
reduced to watching the back of the man before him, and studying
the map of Sweden. It was becoming evident that the map of
North America, if it existed, must be on his left shoulder, under
his hussar jacket, and that the Pacific Islands must be round in
front, about his left breast, when the word was given to go forward.

They advanced to the top of the hill, and wheeled. Charles, for
one instant, had a glimpse of the valley below, seething and roaring
like a volcano. Everywhere bright flashes of flame, single, or running along in lines, or blazing out in volleys. The smoke, driven to
the left by the wind, hung across the valley like a curtain. On the
opposite hill a ring of smoke and fire, and in front of it a thin
scarlet line disappearing. That was all. The next moment they
wheeled to the right, and Charles saw only the back of the man
before him, and the patch of grease on his shoulder.

But that night was a night of spurs for them. Hard riding for them
far into the night. The field of the Alma had been won, and they

were ordered forward to harass the Cossacks, who were covering the rear of the Russian army. They never got near them. But ever after, when the battle of the Alma was mentioned before him, Charles at once used to begin thinking of the map of Sweden.

Captain Archer turns up

'Do not betray me, my lord,' said Mary, from out of the gloom.

'I will declare your malpractices to the four winds of heaven, Miss Corby, as soon as I know what they are. Why? why do you come rustling into the room, like a mouse in the dark? Tell me at once what this hole-and-corner work means.'

'I will not, unless you promise not to betray me, Lord Saltire.'

'Now just think how foolish you are. How can I possibly make myself *particeps*, of what is evidently a most dark and nefarious business, without knowing beforehand what benefit I am to receive. You offer me no share of booty; you offer me no advantage, direct or indirect, in exchange for my silence, except that of being put into possession of facts which it is probably dangerous to know anything about. How can you expect to buy me on such terms as these?'

'Well, then, I will throw myself on your generosity. I want *Blackwood*. If I can find *Blackwood* now, I shall get a full hour at it to myself while you are all at dinner. Do you know where it is?'

'Yes,' said Lord Saltire.

'Do tell me, please. I do so want to finish a story in it. Please to tell me where it is.'

'I won't.'

'Why not? How very unkind. We have been friends eight months now, and you are just beginning to be cross to me. You see how familiarity breeds contempt; you used to be so polite.'

'I shan't tell you where *Blackwood* is,' said Lord Saltire, 'because I don't choose. I don't want you to have it. I want you to sit here in the dark and talk to me, instead of reading it.'

'I will sit and talk to you in the dark; only you must not tell ghost stories.'

'I want you to sit in the dark,' said Lord Saltire, 'because I want to be *'vox et praeterea nihil.'* You will see why, directly. My dear

Mary Corby, I want to have some very serious talk with you. Let us joke no more.'

Mary settled herself at once into the arm-chair opposite Lord Saltire, and, resting her cheek on her hand, turned her face towards the empty fire-place. 'Now, my dear Lord Saltire,' she said, 'go on. I think I can anticipate what you are going to say.'

'You mean about Charles.'

'Yes.'

'Ah, that is only a part of what I have to say. I want to consult you there, certainly; but that is but a small part of the business.'

'Then I am curious.'

'Do you know, then, I am between eighty and ninety years old?'

'I have heard so, my lord.'

'Well then, I think that the voice to which you are now listening will soon be silent for ever; and do not take offence; consider it as a dead man's voice, if you will.'

'I will listen to it as the voice of a kind living friend,' said Mary. 'A friend who has always treated me as a reasonable being and an equal.'

'That is true, Mary; you are so gentle and so clever, that is no wonder. See here, you have no private fortune.'

'I have my profession,' said Mary, laughing.

'Yes, but your profession is one in which it is difficult to rise,' said Lord Saltire, 'and so I have thought it necessary to provide for you in my will. For I must make a new one.'

Poor Mary gave a start. The announcement was so utterly unexpected. She did not know what to say or what to think. She had had long night thoughts about poverty, old age, a life in a garret as a needlewoman, and so on; and had many a good cry over them, and had never found any remedy for them except saying her prayers, which she always found a perfect specific. And here, all of a sudden, was the question solved! She would have like to thank Lord Saltire. She would have liked to kiss his hand; but words were rather deficient. She tried to keep her tears back, and she in a way succeeded; then in the honesty of her soul she spoke.

'I will thank you more heartily, my lord, than if I went down on my knees and kissed your feet. All my present has been darkened by a great cloud of old age and poverty in the distance. You have swept that cloud away. Can I say more?'

'On your life, not another word. I could have over-burdened you with wealth, but I have chosen not to do so. Twenty thousand pounds will enable you to live as you have been brought up. Believe an old man when he says that more would be a plague to you.'

'Twenty thousand pounds!'

'Yes. That will bring you in, you will find, about six hundred a year. Take my word for it, it is quite enough. You will be able to keep your broughham, and all that sort of thing. Believe me, you would not be happy with more.'

'More!' said Mary, quietly. 'My lord, look here, and see what you have done. When the children are going to sleep, I sit, and sew, and sing, and, when they are gone to sleep, I still sit, and sew, and think. Then I build my Spanish castles; but the highest tower of my castle has risen to this—that in my old age I should have ten shillings a week left me by some one, and be able to keep a canary bird, and have some old woman as pensioner. And now—now—now. Oh! I'll be quiet in a moment. Don't speak to me for a moment. God is very good.'

I hope Lord Saltire enjoyed his snuff. I think that, if he did not, he deserved to. After a pause Mary began again.

'Have I left on you the impression that I am selfish? I am almost afraid I have. Is it not so? I have one favour to ask of you. Will you grant it?'

'Certainly I will.'

'On your honour, my lord.'

'On my honour.'

'Reduce the sum you have mentioned to one-fourth. I have bound you by your honour. Oh, don't make me a great heiress; I am not fit for it.'

Lord Saltire said, 'Pish! If you say another word I will leave you ten thousand more. To the deuce with my honour; don't talk nonsense.'

'You said you were going to be quiet in a moment,' he resumed presently. 'Are you quiet now?'

'Yes, my lord, quiet and happy.'

'Are you glad I spoke to you in the dark?'

'Yes.'

'You will be more glad that it was in the dark directly. Is Charles Ravenshoe quite the same to you as other men?'

'No,' said Mary; 'that he most certainly is not. I could have answered that question *to you* in the brightest daylight.'

'Humph!' said Lord Saltire. 'I wish I could see him and you comfortably married, do you know? I hope I speak plain enough. If I don't, perhaps you will be so good as to mention it, and I'll try to speak a little plainer.'

'Nay; I quite understand you. I wonder if you will understand me, when I say that such a thing is utterly and totally out of the question.'

'I was afraid so. You are a pair of simpletons. My dear daughter (you must let me call you so), you must contemplate the contingency I have hinted at in the dark. I know that the best way to get a man rejected, is to recommend him; I therefore, only say, that John Marston loves you with his whole heart and soul, and that he is a *protégé* of mine.'

'I am speaking to you as I would to my own father. John Marston asked me to be his wife last Christmas, and I refused him.'

'Oh, yes. I knew all about that the same evening. It was the evening after they were nearly drowned out fishing. Then there is no hope for a reconsideration there?'

'Not the least,' said Mary. 'My lord, I will never marry.'

'I have not distressed you?'

'Certainly not. You have a right to speak as you have. I am not a silly hysterical girl either, that I cannot talk on such subjects without affection. But I will never marry; I will be an old maid. I will write novels, or something of that sort. I will not even marry Captain Archer, charm he never so wisely.'

'Captain Archer! Who on earth is Captain Archer?'

'Don't you know Captain Archer, my lord?' replied Mary, laughing heartily but ending her laugh with a short sob. 'Avast heaving! Bear a hand, my hearties, and let us light this taper. I think you ought to read his letter. He is the man who swam with me out of the cruel sea, when the *Warren Hastings* went down. That is who he is, Lord Saltire.' At this point, little Mary, thoroughly unhinged by this strange conversation, broke down, and began crying her eyes out, and putting a letter into his hand, rose to leave the room.

He held the door open for her. 'My dear Mary,' he said, 'if I have been coarse or rude, you must try to forgive me.'

'Your straightforward kindness,' she said, 'is less confusing than the most delicate finesse.' And so she went.

Chapter 54

Balaclava was not such a pleasant place as Devna. It was bare and rocky, and everything was in confusion, and the men were dying in heaps of cholera. The nights were beginning to grow chill, too, and Charles began to dream regularly that he was sleeping on the bare hill-side, in a sharp frost, and that he was agonisingly cold about the small of his back. And the most singular thing was, that he always woke and found his dream come true. At first he only used to dream this dream towards morning; but, as October began to creep on, he used to wake with it several times in the night, and at last hardly used to go to sleep at all for fear of dreaming it.

Were there no other dreams? No. No dreams, but one ever-present reality. A dull aching regret for a past for ever gone. A heavy deadly grief, lost for a time among the woods of Devna, but come back to him now amidst the cold, and the squalor, and the sickness of Balaclava. A brooding over missed opportunities, and the things that might have been. Sometimes a tangled puzzled train of thought, as to how much of this ghastly misery was his own fault, and how much accident. And above all, a growing desire for death, unknown before.

And all this time, behind the hill, the great guns—which had begun a fitful muttering when they first came there, often dying off into silence—now day by day, as trench after trench was opened, grew louder and more continuous, till hearing and thought were deadened, and the soul was sick of their never-ceasing melancholy thunder.

And at six o'clock on the morning of the seventeenth, such an infernal din began as no man there had ever heard before, which grew louder and louder till nine, when it seemed impossible that the ear could bear the accumulation of sound; and then suddenly doubled, as the *Agamemnon* and the *Montebello*, followed by the fleets, steamed in, and laid broadside-to under the forts. Four thousand pieces of the heaviest ordnance in the world were doing their work over that hill, and the 140th stood dismounted and listened.

At ten o'clock the earth shook, and a column of smoke towered up in the air above the hill, and as it began to hang motionless, the sound of it reached them. It was different from the noise of guns. It was something new and terrible. An angry hissing roar. An hour after they heard that twenty tons of powder were blown up in the French lines.

Soon after this, though, there was work to be done, and plenty of it. The wounded were being carried to the rear. Some cavalry were dismounted, and told off for the work. Charles was one of them.

The wind had not yet sprung up, and all that Charles saw for the moment was a valley full of smoke, and fire, and sound. He caught a glimpse of the spars and funnel of a great liner above the smoke to the left; but directly after they were under fire, and the sickening day's work began.

Death and horror in every form, of course. The wounded lying about in heaps. Officers trying to compose their faces, and die like gentlemen. Old Indian soldiers dying grimly as they had lived; and lads, fresh from the plough last year, listed at the market-cross some unlucky Saturday, sitting up staring before them with a look of terror and wonder: sadder sight than either. But everywhere all the day, where the shot screamed loudest, where the shell fell thickest, with his shako gone, with his ambrosial curls tangled with blood, with his splendid gaudy fripperies soiled with dust and sweat, was Hornby, the dandy, the fop, the dicer; doing the work of ten, carrying out the wounded in his arms, encouraging the dying, cheering on the living.

'I knew there was some stuff in him,' said Charles, as he followed him into the Crown battery; just at that time the worse place of all, for the *The Twelve Apostles* had begun dropping red-hot shot into it, and exploded some ammunition, and killed some men. And they had met a naval officer, known to Hornby, wounded, staggering to the rear, who said, 'that his brother was knocked over, and that they wanted to make out he was dead, but he had only fainted.' So they went back with him. The officer's brother was dead enough, poor fellow; but as Charles and Hornby bent suddenly over to look at him, their faces actually touched.

Hornby did not recognize him. He was in a state of excitement, and was thinking of no one less than Charles, and Charles's

206

moustaches had altered him, as I said before. If their eyes had met,
I believe Hornby would have known him; but it was not to be till
the 25th, and this was only the 17th. If Hornby could have only
known him, if they could have had ten minutes' talk together,
Charles would have known all that we know about the previous
marriage of his grandfather; and, if that conversation had taken
place, he would have known more than any of them, for Hornby
knew something which he thought of no importance, which was
very important indeed. He knew where Ellen was.

But Charles turned his face away, and the recognition did not
take place. Poor Charles said afterwards that it was all a piece of
luck—that 'the stars in their courses fought against Sisera.' It is not
the case. He turned away his eyes, and avoided the recognition.
What he meant is this—

As Hornby's face was touching his, and they were both bending
over the dead man, whom they could hardly believe to be dead, the
men behind them fired off the great Lancaster in the next one-gun
battery. 'Crack!' and they heard the shell go piff, piff, piff, and
strike something. And then one man close to them cried, 'God
Almighty!' and another cried, 'Christ!' as sailors will at such awful
times; and they both leapt to their feet. Above the smoke there
hung, a hundred feet in the air, a something like a vast black pine-
tree; and before they had time to realize what had happened, there
was a horrible roar, and a concussion which made them stagger on
their legs. A shell from the Lancaster had blown up the great re-
doubt in front of the Redan wall, and every Russian gun ceased
firing. And above the sound of the Allied guns rose the cheering
of our own men, sounding, amidst the awful bass, like the shrill
treble of school-children at play.

Charles said afterwards that this glorious accident prevented
their recognition. It is not true. He prevented it himself, and took
the consequences. But Hornby recognized him on the twenty-fifth
in this wise—

The first thing in the morning, they saw, on the hills to the right,
Russian skirmishers creeping about towards them, apparently
without an object. They had breakfast, and took no notice of them
till about eight o'clock, when a great body of cavalry came slowly,
regiment by regiment, from behind a hill near the Turks. Then
gleaming batteries of artillery; and lastly, an endless column of grey

infantry, which began to wheel into line. And when Charles had seen some five or six grey battalions come swinging out, the word was given to mount, and he saw no more, but contemplated the tails of horses. And at the same moment the guns began an irregular fire on their right.

Almost immediately the word was given to advance, which they did slowly. Charles could see Hornby just before him, in his old place, for they were in column. They crossed the plain, and went up the crest of the hill, halting on the high road. Here they sat for some time, and the more fortunate could see the battle raging below to the right. The English seemed getting rather the worst of it.

They sat there about an hour and a half; and all in a moment, before anyone seemed to expect it, some guns opened on them from the right; so close that it made their right ears tingle. A horse from the squadron in front of Charles bolted from the ranks, and nearly knocked down Hornby. The horse had need to bolt, for he carried a dead man, who in the last spasm had pulled him on his haunches, and struck his spurs deep into his sides.

Charles began to guess that they were 'in for it' at last. He had no idea, of course, whether it was a great battle or a little one; but he saw that the 140th had work before them. I, of course, have only to speak of what Charles saw with his own eyes, and what therefore bears upon the story I am telling you. That was the only man he saw killed at that time, though the whole brigade suffered rather heavily by the Russian cannonade at that spot.

Very shortly after this they were told to form line. Of course, when this manoeuvre was accomplished, Charles had lost sight of Hornby. He was sorry for this. He would have liked to know where he was; to help him if possible, should anything happen to him; but there was not much time to think of it, for directly after they moved forward at a canter. In the front line were the 11th Hussars and the 13th Light Dragoons, and in the second were the 140th Hussars, the 8th Hussars, and the 4th Dragoons. Charles could see thus much, now they were in line.

They went down hill, straight towards the guns, and almost at once the shot from them began to tell. The men of the 11th and 13th began to fall terribly fast. The men in the second line, in which Charles was, were falling nearly as fast, but this he could not remark. He missed the man next to him on the right, one of his favourite comrades, but it did not strike him that the poor fellow was cut in two by a shot. He kept on wishing that he could see Hornby. He judged that the affair was getting serious. He little knew what was to come.

He had his wish of seeing Hornby, for they were riding up hill into a narrowing valley, and it was impossible to keep line. They formed into column again, though men and horses were rolling over and over at every stride, and there was Hornby before him, sailing along as gallant and gay as ever. A fine beacon to lead a man to a glorious death.

And, almost the next moment, the batteries right and left opened on them. Those who were there engaged can give us very little idea of what followed in the next quarter of an hour. They were soon among guns—the very guns that had annoyed them from the first; and infantry beyond opened fire on them. There seems to have been a degree of confusion at this point. Charles, and two or three others known to him, were hunting some Russian artillery-men round their guns, for a minute or so. Hornby was among them. He saw also at this time his little friend cornet, on foot, and rode to his assistance. He caught a riderless horse, and the cornet mounted. Then the word was given to get back again; I know not how; I have nothing to do with it. But, as they turned their faces to get out of this horrible hell, poor Charles gave a short, sharp scream, and bent down in his saddle over his horse's neck.

It was nothing. It was only as if one were to have twenty teeth pulled out at once. The pain was over in an instant. What a fool he was to cry out. The pain was gone again, and they were still under fire, and Hornby was before him.

How long? How many minutes, how many hours? His left arm was nearly dead, but he could hold his reins in a way, and rode hard after Hornby, from some wild instinct. The pain had stopped, but was coming on again as if ten thousand red-hot devils were pulling at his flesh, and twenty thousand were arriving each moment to help them.

His own friends were beside him again, and there was a rally and a charge. At what? he thought for an instant. At guns? No. At men this time, Russian hussars—right valiant fellows, too. He saw Hornby in the thick of the *mêlée*, with his sword flickering about his head like lightning. He could do but little himself; he rode at a Russian and unhorsed him; he remembers seeing the man go down, though whether he struck at him, or whether he went down by the mere superior weight of his horse, he cannot say. This I can say, though, that, whatever he did, he did his duty as a valiant gentleman; I will go bail for that much.

They beat them back, and then turned. Then they turned again and beat them back once more. And then they turned and rode. For it was time. Charles lost sight of Hornby till the last, when some one caught his rein and turned his horse, and then he saw they were getting into order again, and that Hornby was before him, reeling in his saddle.

As the noise of the battle grew fainter behind them, he looked round to see who was riding beside him, and holding him by the right arm. It was the little cornet. Charles wonder why he did so. 'You're hard hit, Simpson,' said the cornet. 'Never mind. Keep your saddle a little longer. We shall be all right directly.'

His faculties were perfectly acute, and, having thanked the cornet he looked down and noticed that he was riding between him and a trooper, that his left arm was hanging numbed by his side, and that the trooper was guiding his horse. He saw that they had saved him, and even in his deadly agony he was so far his own old courteous self, that he turned right and left to them, and thanked them for what they had done for him.

But he had kept his eyes fixed on Hornby, for he saw that he was desperately hit, and he wanted to say one or two words to him before either of them died. Soon they were among English faces, and English cheers rang out in welcome to their return, but it was nothing to him; he kept his eye, which was growing dim, on Hornby, and, when he saw him fall off his saddle into the arms of a trooper, he dismounted too and staggered towards him.

The world seemed to go round and round, and he felt about him like a blind man. But he found Hornby somehow. A doctor, all scarlet and gold, was bending over him, and Charles knelt down on the other side, and looked into the dying man's face.

'Do you know me, lieutenant?' he said, speaking thick like a drunken man but determined to hold out. 'You know your old servant, don't you?'

Hornby smiled as he recognized him, and said, 'Ravenshoe.' But then his face grew anxious, and he said, 'Why did you hide your-self from me? You have ruined everything.'

He could get no further for a minute, and then he said—

'Take this from round my neck and carry it to her. Tell her that you saw me die, and that I was true to our compact. Tell her that my share of our purification was complete, for I followed duty to death, as I promised her. She has a long life of weary penance before her to fulfil our bargain. Say I should wish her to be happy, only that I know she cannot be. And also say that I see now, that there is something better and more desirable than what we call hap-piness. I don't know what it is, but I suspect it is what we call duty.'

Here the doctor said, 'They are at it again, and I must go with them. I can do no good here for the poor dear fellow. Take what he tells you off his neck, in my presence, and let me go.'

The doctor did it himself. When the great heavy gold stock was unbuttoned, Hornby seemed to breathe more freely. The doctor found round his neck a gold chain, from which hung a photograph of Ellen, and a black cross. He gave them to Charles, and departed.

Once more Charles spoke to Hornby. He said, 'Where shall I find her?'

Hornby said, 'Why, at Hackney, to be sure; did you not know she was there?' And afterwards, at the very last, 'Ravenshoe, I should have loved you; you are like her, my boy. Don't forget.'

But Charles never heard that. They found Hornby dead and cold, with his head on Charles's lap, and Charles looked so like him that they said, 'This man is dead too; let us bury him.' But a skilful doctor there present said, 'This man is not dead, and will not die;' and he was right.

Oh, but the sabres bit deep that autumn afternoon! There were women in Minsk, in Moglef, in Tehernigof, in Jitemir, in Polimva, whose husbands were Hussars—and women in Taganrog, in Tcherkask, in Sanepta, which lies under the pleasant slate moun-tains, whose husbands and sons were Cossacks—who were made widows that day. For that day's work there was weeping in the reed-thatched hovels of the Don, and in the mud-built shanties of the Dnieper. For the 17th Lancers, the Scots Greys, the 1st Royals, and the 6th Enniskillens—'these terrible beef-fed islanders' (to use the words of the *Northern Bee*)—were upon them; and Volhynia and Hampshire, Renfrewshire and Grodno, Podolia and Fermanagh, were mixed together in one common ruin.

Still, they say, the Princess Petrovich, on certain days, leaves her carriage, and walks a mile through the snow barefoot, into Alexandroski, in memory of her light-haired handsome young son, whom Hornby slew at Balaclava. And I myself know the place where Lady Allerton makes her pilgrimage for those two merry boys of hers who lie out on the Crimean hill. Alas! not side by side. Up and down, in all weathers, along a certain gravel walk, where the chalk brook, having flooded the park with its dammed-up waters, comes foaming and spouting over a cascade, and hurries past between the smooth-mown lawns of the pleasance. In the very place where she stood when the second letter came. And there, they say, she will walk at times, until her beauty and her strength are gone, and her limbs refuse to carry her.

Karlin Karlinoff was herding strange-looking goats on the Suratow hill-side, which looks towards the melancholy Volga on one side, and the reedy Ural on the other, when the Pulk came back, and her son was not with them. Eliza Jones had got on her husband's smock-frock, and was a-setting of beans, when the rector's wife came struggling over the heavy lands and water-furrows, and broke the news gently, and with many tears. Karlin Karlinoff drove her goats into the mud-walled yard that night, though the bittern in the melancholy fen may have been startled from his reeds by a cry more wild and doleful than his own; and Eliza Jones went on setting her beans, though they were watered with her tears.

What a strange, wild business it was! The extreme east of Europe against the extreme west. Men without a word, an idea, a habit, or a hope in common, thrown suddenly together to fight and slay; and then to part, having learned to respect one another better, in one year of war, then ever they had in a hundred years of peace. Since that year we have understood Eylau and Borodino, which battles were a puzzle to some of us before that time. The French did better than we, which was provoking, because the curs began to bark—Spanish curs, for instance; American curs; the lower sort of French cur; and the Irish curs, who have the strange habit of barking the louder the more they are laughed at, and who now, being represented by about two hundred men among six million, have rather a hard time of it. They barked louder of course, at the Indian mutiny. But they have all got their tails between their legs now, and are likely to keep them there. We have had our lesson. We have learnt that what our fathers told us was true—that we are the most powerful nation on the face of the earth.

This, you will see, bears all upon the story I am telling you. Well, in a sort of way. Though I do not exactly see how. I could find a reason, if you gave me time. If you gave me time, I could find a reason for anything. However, the result is this, that our poor Charles had been struck by a ball in the bone of his arm, and that the splinters were driven into the flesh, though the arm was not broken. It was a nasty business, said the doctors. All sorts of things might happen to him. Only one thing was certain, and that was that Charles Ravenshoe's career in the army was over for ever.

XXVI

Austin Elliot
1863

The years from 1860 until 1864 were probably the happiest of Henry's life. For the first and last time he was free of financial worries, and apparently on the road to fame and fortune. He lived agreeably in his Eversley cottage cultivating roses, and working to a routine which would seem eccentric to many but proved congenial to him. After dinner he repaired to his study with a jug of rum and water and wrote steadily until 6 a.m., when he went to bed until lunch time. Then he walked, worked in the garden or fished until dinner came round again. Scenes, characters, episodes, dialogue flowed easily over the pages; young men were handsome, young women were fair and both were rich, if not to start with then generally by some fortunate legacy or marriage. The novels of this period were creations of a good-humoured man in love with life and content to mirror the surface of a high society he can scarcely have known, rather than to probe the depths of a reality which he knew at first-hand.

Suspense in Austin Elliot *is again contrived by means of a family secret withheld from the headstrong young hero by his beloved, for the noblest of motives but with disastrous results. The scene is laid in 1844–6, possibly to enable Henry to work in a duel before the practice was finally quashed. Politics, the* Corn Law *debates, London life, and scenes in Wales and in the Hebrides form a background for the author's amiable or villainous puppets.*

Love of animals was a Kingsley trait, and Henry wrote of dogs, especially, with humour and affection. The noblest character in Austin Elliot *is the sheepdog Robin, round whose adventures the following extracts from this slight, light-hearted novel revolve. Robin is chosen; is lost (to be found again); and awaits his master outside the gaol in which that unlucky young gentleman must serve a sentence for having, as a matter of honour, taken part in a duel.*

I

There was, in and about the kennel, almost every variety of dog conceivable. There were deep-jowled dogs, with sunken eyes and wrinkled foreheads, at the first distant note of whose bell-like voice the hunted slave in the Cuban jungle lies down and prays for death; yet who here is a stupid, blundering, affectionate brute, who will let you do as you like with him, and casts himself on his back at Miss Cecil's feet. English bloodhounds, too—stupid, sleepy, goodnatured, slobbering. St Bernard's, too—dogs of the snow-storm and the avalanche, wise-looking dogs, self-contained, appearing to know more than they choose to say, but idiots withal notwithstanding, and very great idiots, as are many self-contained and wise-looking animals beside they. A great rough Newfoundland dog, chained up. Marry, why? Because he had been the pet of the house, until one day he had become *Must, Berserk*, or what you choose to call it, until the devil, or the seven devils, which lurk in *all* Newfoundland dogs, gentle and docile as they are, had broken loose, and Mr Cecil had had to fight with him for his life in his own dressing-room. There were two French poodles, which, as Mr Sala says somewhere, so truly, 'you can teach to do everything but love you.' There was a British bulldog, white, with small eyes, so short-sighted as to be obliged to examine everything with his nose (which gave Austin a creeping up his back), and with a wicked, lowering, face; yet which bull-dog turned out, like most other British bull-dogs, to be a good-natured, kind-hearted fellow, and a firm friend, as soon as he had (by smelling the calves of their legs, a nervous proceeding) found out his friends from his enemies.

And Austin, finding that the bull-dog, instead of biting his legs, wagged his tail at him, and proposed to accompany him further, broke out into raptures.

'Miss Cecil, I have never seen such a collection of dogs as this! And I am a great fancier of dogs.'

'You have not seen them nearly all yet,' she said. 'This, is, I believe, the best collection of dogs in England; or rather, I should say, better than any in England, for we are in Wales. You know how they came here?'

'No.'

'My poor brother chose to have the best dogs in England; it was a passion with him; and since his death, my father has chosen to pursue his hobby. You know about my brother's death?'

'Oh, yes', said Austin, who knew nothing at all about it, but who did what was possibly the best thing he could do, utter a *façon de parler* (for it was nothing more), and try to turn the subject. At the same time he reflected, that it would be well for young men like himself, not in society, before they went into a house, to inform themselves somewhat about the history of that house, to prevent mistakes.

'Do you really know about my brother, Mr Elliot?' said Miss Cecil.

'Well, no,' said Austin, 'I do not, since you ask me twice. Remember, I am only an undergraduate at Oxford, and that I knew nothing even of Mr Cecil, except that he was one of the first men in England, and had given such and such votes, until he asked me here.'

'I like you very much,' said she; 'you are so well-bred, and have so little pretension. I only wanted to mention my poor brother, whom I hardly remember, to warn you what not to talk about with my father. He was drowned boating at Eton. And you will find that it is as well to know all this sort of thing in the world.'

Miss Cecil, the oracle, was much younger than Austin; but she had been out two seasons, and knew a great deal of the world; and he was at the University and knew absolutely and entirely nothing. If he had, he would have known what a consummate fool he was to fall in love with her, recklessly to go on feeding his passion; and above all, what an utter fool he was to hope that it would have any other than one conclusion.

'I know nothing of the world, or about people, yet,' he said; 'I suppose the knowledge of people and their belongings will come to one in time. It seems tiresome to get it up. Do you know that none of the best fellows who I know are up in that sort of thing? Now, there is Lord Charles Barty, he is coming on very well indeed; but, mind you, I believe if you were to put him into a corner he would not be able to tell you who his grandmother's father was.'

Miss Cecil laughed. 'I daresay not' said she. '*I* know. His grandmother was a Leyton, daughter of Sir Robert Leyton, of Broadash. Leave the pedigrees to the women. One of the great uses of a woman in society is, I take it, to tell her husband who people are.'

So she talked to him, as one would talk to an intelligent boy sent to one for a holiday; and yet the fool loved on more madly than ever.

'Come on', she said, 'and let us see the rest of the dogs;' for this conversation took place at the fountain in the centre of the kennels, and they had only come up one avenue, and only seen one fourth of the dogs as yet.

And as they turned to go she said:

'I like you very much, as I told you before. And to prove to you how much I like you, I will give you, out of these hundreds of beautiful dogs, the dog you choose—the dog you think that you will love best; and I only annex one condition—that whenever your heart warms towards that dog, you will think of me, and think how much I like you. I have heard a great deal of you. I rather believe that you did not know of my existence before you came here. But I have been in love with you for a long time.'

Miss Cecil and Eleanor had been friends and correspondents; Austin did not know this. He was not coxcomb enough to take her cool free-and-easy expressions as advances to himself, and yet he was foolish enough to think that they formed a basis of operations. He had hopes.

*   *   *

Now they began looking at the terriers. There was one snow-white English terrier of such amazing beauty, that Austin very nearly chose it, but fortunately did not. Then there were some black and tans, equal in beauty to the white; Dandy Dinmont terriers, as long and as lithe as otters; and pert, merry, sharp little Sykes; rough, long-legged English fox terriers which ran on three legs, like Scotch terriers, and held their heads on one side knowingly. Austin was more and more delighted every step. He knew all about every dog; but at the last he was stopped. He came across four little dogs, the like of which he had never seen before.

Little long-bodied, short-legged dogs, a dull blue-grey colour, with clouded black spots; sharp, merry little fellows.

'What dogs can these be, Miss Cecil?' he said. 'I am quite at fault.'

'Cannot you guess? Why, they are turnspits, and all with the turnspit peculiarity. The right eye is not the same colour as the left. I suppose you will hardly see such dogs as these in England. Will you choose one?'

Although one of the queer merry little rogues begged at him, he said No. 'They are a sight,' he said, 'a sight worth seeing, but I will not choose one. In an artistic point of view, they are ugly, and they suggest to one the blue dogs which the Chinese fatten for table. No. I hardly dare to say so, but of all the dogs here I would soonest have that incomparable white terrier. I have dreamed of such a dog as that, but I never saw such a one.'

'It is hardly possible that you can have. He is yours, with a thousand welcomes. I hope he may live long to remind you of me.'

'I need no dog to do that,' said Austin; 'but I cannot take such a princely present.'

She laughed. 'It is done,' she said; 'the election is made for good or evil. Come and take possession.'

*　　*　　*

The white terrier was so nearly chosen, in spite of Austin's strong repugnance to accept such a valuable present, that they had turned, and Austin's hands were eager to seize the beautiful little animal, and call him his own, when, in the wood behind them, there was a wild jubilant bark; in another instant there was a rush past them, as of an eagle coming through a forest; in the next, a dog, different to any they had seen before, was madly, joyously careering round and round them in ever-narrowing circles; and in another he was leaping on both of them, and covering them with caresses.

But he saw that Austin was a stranger, and paused to look at him, and after a moment he reared up against him, and said with his beautiful soft hazel eyes, as Austin thought, 'Choose me, choose me, and I will follow you through it all, even to the very end.'

It was a most beautiful Scotch sheep dog, black and tan and white, with a delicate smooth head, the hair of which began to wave about the ears, until it developed into a deep mane upon the shoulders. The author has described such a dog before. The Scotch sheep dog is the highest development of the brute creation, in beauty, in sagacity, and in other qualities, which one dares, by leave of Messieurs of the Holy Office, to call moral. This was the most beautiful dog of that variety ever seen. If the reader wishes to realize the dog to himself he can do so thus. In Landseer's picture of 'The Shepherd's Bible,' the dog which is standing up is very like him; though the dog I am describing is drawn from the life, and from a handsomer dog than he.

'This is the dog for me,' cried Austin. 'Why, you beauty! Miss Cecil, I would give anything for this dog. Just look at his eyes, will you? Can I have him? Does he belong to any one?'

'Yes,' she said laughing. 'He belongs to you. He is worth all the white terriers that ever were born. I like you the better for your choice of Robin.'

II

Austin had a very good habit of riding out early in the morning before the streets were full, and the smoke had settled down; and on the 15th of April he woke early, and said that he would ride out.

He rang the bell, and when his servant came he ordered his horse to be saddled while he dressed, and called 'Robin.'

The servant called 'Robin', too, but Robin was not in his usual place at the foot of the bed, and on further search it became evident that Robin was not in the house, nor in the street either.

'I brought him in last night,' said Austin. 'Run round to Miss Hilton's, and see if he is there.'

By the time Austin had done dressing, and was standing on the doorstep, in a pair of yellow riding trousers, and a blue neck-cloth, his man came back. The dog was not there. It became evident that the dog was stolen.

Austin was vexed and resolute. At last a foolish scullion-wench, in the lower regions, incautiously volunteered information. Austin's servants immediately claimed that she should be haled before him, and interrogated.

She came upstairs in pattens, with a mop in her hand, and her hair all tumbled and tangled, in a dreadful fright. Austin's valet offered to hold her mop for her: she refused. He tried to take it from her; she fought him and beat him, and was ushered into Austin's presence, red, triumphant, with her mop in her hand.

Her mysterious communication about the dog amounted to very

little indeed. She had found the dog scratching at the door, and had let him out for a run, 'Which the Milk had seen her.'

'Find the policeman, and tell him,' said Austin; 'as I come home I will ride round by James's.'

Riding about the west end of London before nine o'clock on an April morning is a very pleasant pastime. The streets are nearly empty, and you can dawdle as much as you like; while in Piccadilly and such places, the air—should the wind have anything of the west in it—is as fresh as it is in the country. Everybody's horses are out exercising, too: and you can see their legs, eyes, tails, and noses showing out of their clothes, and may, if you like, drive yourself mad, by calculating, on the '*ex pede Herculem*' plan,—by an effort of comparative anatomy far beyond Owen—what sort of horses they are, and how much they are worth apiece. You can also see the British cabman free from the cares of office, and many other strange sights, not to be met with later in the day.

It was a very pleasant ride that Austin had on this spring morning. He rode slowly over the piece of wood pavement between Sackville Street and Bond Street, and then trotted till he came to the small patch opposite Devonshire House (both these are laid down in good granite now), where there was a horse down as usual. Then he walked slowly down the hill, and, turning into the newly-opened park, had a gallop along Rotten Row, and, passing out by Kensington Gate, began to feel his way slowly eastward once more.

Through fresh squares, where the lilac was already budding, through squares and streets which grew grander and grander, till they culminated in Belgrave Square itself, and then into the lower part of the town which lies south-east of it.

It is astonishing how rapidly the town degenerates to the south-east of Belgrave Square towards Vauxhall Bridge; or, to be more correct, did degenerate, in those days. From great mansions you suddenly find yourself among ten-roomed houses. So you rapidly deteriorate to six rooms, to four, to old bankrupt show vans taken off their wheels, and moved on the waste ground, like worn-out hulks; and, after them, dust and ashes, and old paper-hangings, and piles of lath and plaster, and pots and kettles, and swarms of wild children; to whom this waste of ash-heaps are mountains, and the stagnant fever-pools, lakes—who build here for themselves the fairy castles of childhood, with potsherds and oystershells, and who seem to enjoy more shrill wild happiness, than the children of any other class in the community.

Austin paused before he came to this range of dust Alps. At the junction of two low streets, between Vauxhall Bridge and Millbank, there stood a house by itself, with a garden in front, and a leafless arbour. This was James's, and James himself, in his shirt sleeves, was in the front garden, drowning some puppies in a bucket.

As Austin reined up, and paused before this house, the population turned out to see the splendid apparition. Such a handsome young gentleman, so nobly dressed, on such a beautiful horse, before half-past ten, was really something to look at. Was there never a lady of Shalott among those busy worn needlewomen, stitching behind the dirty blinds, who looked out and fell in love with this noble young Camelot? Who knows?

> 'She left the web, she left the loom,
> She made three paces through the room,
> She saw the helmet and the plume,
>   And she looked down to Camelot.'

Poor things! Sitting there feeding on their own fancies, month by month, it is a wonder how respectable, as a class, these poor folks are. If it were not for the cheap novels, what would become of them?

Austin drew up. Mr James was so busy drowning the puppies that he did not hear him. So Austin cried out, 'Hallo!'

Immediately he heard an unknown number (he says nine hundred, but that is an exaggeration) of dogs, dash out of barrels in the back yard, and choke themselves with their collars. Before they had got wind to bark, a sound was heard as of a strong man swearing. At which these dogs (number unknown, Austin saw afterwards thirty-five bull-dogs, and a cloud of black and tan terriers, which, to use his own vigorous expression, darkened the air) all, rattled their chains and went silently back among the straw.

All except an invisible small dog, who, from the volume of his voice seemed to be the very dog in the 'Arabian Nights', which came out of the walnut-shell. He continuing to bark, was audibly kicked by the strong man, and Mr James, having drowned the last puppy, came towards Austin, hat in hand.

Mr James, a great, handsome giant, was, and is, one of the most remarkable men in the country. He was the greatest and most successful cynoclept, or dog-dealer, in England, and consequently in the world. If a Chinese Mandarin had sent an order to Mr James for a dozen fat, blue, hairless dogs, to be cooked for a *fete champêtre* at Pekin, Mr James would have executed the order by the next mail, without winking his eye. Mr James was the greatest dog-fancier in England, and, I am exeedingly sorry to say, that Austin was one of his best customers.

I have hinted at Austin's low taste for dogs before this. With all his high political ambition, this low taste was one black spot in his character. He had an ambition to possess the smallest black-and-tan terrier in England, apparently for the delectation of his groom, for they were always kept at the Mews with his horses. The groom became, to a certain extent, debauched through these dogs. Prize-fighters and far worse, used to make court to that young man, and take him to public-houses, free of expense, for the mere privilege of handling these wonderful dogs, the largest of which did not weigh more than four pounds. Austin had sometimes given at the rate of four guineas a pound for them. Robin had never considered them to be dogs at all, and had treated them accordingly.

The enormous sums paid for these dogs, and the fact of their being regularly stolen once a week, and recovered and sent home by Mr James, had ended in Mr James, great man as he was, being a creature of Austin's. He considered Austin to be a type of real English gentleman, the last hope of a degenerate age. Consequently, when he had done drowning his puppies and saw Austin at his gate, he advanced towards him with a very low bow.

'James,' said Austin, 'I have lost Robin.'

'What o'clock, sir?'

'About seven.'

'Then I can't let you have him before tomorrow morning, sir. My cads were all out before that. Will half-past eight tomorrow morning do, sir?'

'It must, I suppose,' said Austin, 'unless he comes home by himself.'

Mr James was much amused by this supposition. He said Mr Elliot would have his joke; and requested that Austin would dismount.

Austin did so, and Mr James called for Sam. Sam came. The invisible strong man before mentioned—a young man, in his shirt and trousers, who had not washed himself, and who looked like a prize fighter under a cloud—which indeed he was. With him came Mr James's own favourite dog—a white bull-terrier, who smelt Austin's legs and gave him a creeping up his back. After which he went into James's yard and bought the dog which came out of the walnut-shell for seven guineas.

III

'One year's imprisonment.'

The turnkey tapped him on the shoulder, and he followed the turnkey out, and was given over to a policeman. He brushed the shoulder of the next prisoner, a young man, a burglar, who looked at him curiously, and laughed, and said that it was a good thing that the swells got it sometimes, though if he had the giving on it to 'em—. Austin didn't hear any more than that, and did not appreciate or care about what he had heard. He was confused, and felt as if he was going to be ill. He asked for some water, and they gave it to him, and then he sat down and began thinking.

A year. This was 1846. Then it would be 1847. What was the day of the month? He could not remember, and asked the policeman.

The eleventh of June. The policeman repeated it twice, and then Austin thanked him, but his mind was elsewhere. A woman who sat opposite to him, a weary witness, had got on odd boots. They were both black jean boots, and were both for the right foot. One was trodden on one side, and the other was gone at the toes, but Austin was wide awake enough to see that they were both right-foot boots. You couldn't take *him* in. What a fool the woman must be; perhaps she was drunk when she put them on. She looked a drunken sort of drab. But there was something funny in it. Austin, God help him, had a quiet laugh over it; and soon they told him it was time to go.

And so he went, patient and contented enough, for happily he was just now past feeling anything acutely. As he was going down the corridor, something struck him. When he had started from home that morning, his dog Robin had followed him, and would not be driven back He remembered that now. He asked a police-man, who was standing by, to see after the dog for him, and take him to Miss Hilton's, in Wilton Crescent, and said she would give him five shillings. The man said, 'Yes, he would,' and thanked him, and as he stepped through the crowd into the prison van, he looked round for his dog, but could not see him.

Robin had seen him, though, and was quite contented. His master, thought he, was busy to-day, and was now going for a drive. Robin had waited for Austin in all sorts of places, for all sorts of times, and had seen Austin get into all sorts of carriages and drive away without thinking about him. His custom, on these occasions, was to tear along the street, in front of the vehicle into which Austin had got—be it cab, carriage, or omnibus—with joyous bark, ready to take his part in the next pleasant adventure which should befall. So now he dashed through the crowded Old Bailey at the hazard of his life, racing and leaping in front of the prison-van which held his ruined and desperate master, as if this were the best fun of all.

The van took Austin to the great bald prison by the river-side, and he was hurried in. The cruel iron door clanged behind him, and sent its echoes booming through the long dismal white-washed corridors. And the clang of that door fell like a death-knell on his ear. 'I am condemning you,' said the judge, 'to social and political death.' He knew it now. The door jarred, and clanged; and the world knew Austin Elliot no more.

Outside that great prison-door all was glorious June sunshine; the river flashing on, covered with busy craft, towards the tall blue dome which rose into the air above the drifting smoke, far away eastward. The June sun smote fiercely on the long prison-wall, on the quiet road which passed it, on the great iron door which had shut in Austin Elliot and all his high-built hopes and fancies. There is not a duller place in London than that river-terrace beneath the prison-wall. There is never anything to see there. People who have cause to go that way generally hurry past; there is nothing to see there in general.

But for many days after this, people who had passed in a hurry came dawdling back again: for there was something to attract them, though they would have been troubled to tell you what. There sat at this time, a dog against the prison-door, in the burning sunshine—a dog who sat patient and spoke to no other dogs, but who propped himself up against the nails and bars, and panted in the heat, and snapped sometimes at the flies. Those who turned and came back again knew, by their mother wit, that the dog had seen some one go into that prison, and had sat himself to wait till he came out again; and they spoke in low tones the one to the other, and tried to get the dog away, but he would not come. And one slipshod drunken woman, whose husband was also behind that door, urged by some feeling of sickly sentimentality, which we will charitably attribute to gin, if you please, lest we should be accused of sentimentality ourselves; brought the dog what we strongly suspect to have been her own dinner, and stood by while he ate it. Robin, poor dog! made many friends during his solitary watch under the burning prison-wall; for the people who pass by Millbank are mostly of the class whose highest idea of virtue is a certain blind self-sacrificing devotion—(reasons of such devotion, or merit of object, not to be inquired into by respectable folks, if you please.)

So Robin kept watch in the burning sun, and got himself precariously fed by thieves and thieves' wives. Sometimes the great door behind him would be opened, and then he would lope out into the middle of the street, and, with his head on one side, peer eagerly up the dim vista of white-washed passages beyond. The blue-coated warders would whistle to him, and say, 'Here, poor fellow!' but he would only shake his long drooping tail for an instant, almost imperceptibly, and stand where he was. If there was a stranger present, the blue-coated warders would tell him, that that was the dog of a young swell, they had got inside for duelling, and that that dog had been there for above a week. Then the door would be shut again, and Robin would take his old post in the sun, and catch the flies.

For more than ten days he stayed there. At the end of that time he went away. The great door was open one day, and three or four warders were standing about. Robin had gone into the middle of the street, when a very tall handsome young man came walking by with his eyes fixed on the prison.

He nearly stumbled over Robin. When Robin saw him, he leaped upon him, and the young man caught him in his bosom. And the young man was of the Scotch nation, for he said—

'It's his ain dog, if it's no his ain self. What, Robin, boy, do ye mind Gil Macdonald, and the bonny hill-sides of Ronaldsay!'

XXVII

The Hillyars and the Burtons
1865

'*Charles has fallen in love with* The Hillyars and the Burtons,' *Henry wrote to Alexander Macmillan. 'A very bad sign, for he never likes a popular book.' The brothers' approach to novel-writing was remarkably similar. Both flung themselves headlong upon their story much as an impetuous, rollicking, woolly-coated young dog will fall upon an old slipper, tossing bits of plot hither and yon and scattering characters in all directions; to be retrieved on occasion in a perfunctory way: 'All this time there was a Sir George Hillyar somewhere. But where? That is a question which will never be answered with any accuracy, even if it were worth answering.' Both Kingsleys were in love with their story, with the people in it and especially with the scenes in which their people moved. Both looked first for the moral qualities of their characters; there were Good Women and Bad Men, the former beyond reproach but the latter never beyond redemption. Both writers accepted society as it was, believed in a divine order, and liked to nudge their readers into enjoyment of an arch or of a ponderous joke.*

In this, his fourth novel, Henry combined memories of his Chelsea boyhood with those of his Australian adventures into a saga of two families, one poor and humble and the other aristocratic and rich, whose fortunes intertwined. Amid the usual fruitful Kingsley mixture of bastard sons, stolen wills, low life and high life, politics—colonial in this instance—bushrangers, convicts, shipwrecks and typhoons, the story hops about like a busy kangaroo, impeded here and there by the usual running commentary in whose use, however, Henry was growing more restrained. This was the last product of his tranquil Eversley routine, pursued under his brother's sheltering wing and free of major worries. Before it was completed, he had married, moved, and shaped his life to a different and more anxious pattern.

James Burton the elder is an honest, industrious, kind-hearted black-smith who inhabits, with a numerous family which includes a hunch-

226

back Joe, a big semi-derelict house in Church Street, Chelsea, that had once belonged to the Earl of Essex. The tale is told partly by his son James, apprenticed to his father, who makes friends with Sir George Hillyar's sheltered and sweet-tempered younger son Erne (called after the lake in Ireland), who in turn falls in love with Jim's sister Emma. The manner of James' and Erne's meeting at Stanlake is the subject of the first extract; the second tells how the Burton family reached their new home in Australia; and the third of how their fortunes were made.

I
At Stanlake

It was September, but it was summer still. Those who live in the country, they tell me, can see the difference between a summer-day in September and a summer-day in June; but we town-folks cannot. The country-folks have got tired of their flowers, and have begun to think of early fires, and shortening days, and turnips, and deep cover, and hollies standing brave and green under showering oak-leaves, which fall on the swift wings of flitting wood-cocks; but to town-folks September is even as June. The same shadows on the grass, the same tossing plumage on the elms, the same dull silver on the willows. More silence in the brooks perhaps, and more still-ness in the woods; but the town-bred eye does not recognize the happy doze before the winter's sleep. The country is the country to them, and September is as June.

On a bright September day, Joe and I came, well directed, to some park palings, and after a short consultation we—in for a penny in for a pound, demoralized by the domestic differences of Mr and Mrs Bill Avery—climbed over them, and stood, tres-passing flagrantly in the park which they enclosed. We had no business there. We knew we were doing wrong. We knew that we ought to have gone to church that morning. We were guilty beings for, I really think, the first time in our lives. William Avery's having thrown his wife down stairs on to the top of Emma and Fred had been such a wonderful disturbance of old order and law, that we were in a revolutionary frame of mind. We knew that order would be once more restored, some time or another, but, meanwhile, the barricades were up, and the jails were burning; so we were determined to taste the full pleasure derivable from a violent disturbance of the political balance.

First of all we came on a bright broad stream, in which we could see brown spotted fish, scudding about in the shallows, which Joe said must be trout. And, after an unsuccessful attempt to increase the measure of our sins by adding poaching to trespass, we passed on towards a dark wood, from which the stream issued.

It was a deep dark wood of lofty elms, and, as we passed on into it, the gloom grew deeper. Far aloft the sun gleamed on the highest boughs; but, beneath, the stream swept on through the shadows, with scarcely a gleam of light upon the surface. At last we came on a waterfall, and, on our climbing the high bank on one side of it, the lake opened on our view. It was about a quarter of a mile long, hemmed in by a wood on all sides, with a boathouse, built like a Swiss chalet, halfway along it.

The silence and solitude were profound; nothing seemed moving but the great dragon-flies; it was the most beautiful place we had ever seen; nothing would have stopped us now short of a policeman.

We determined to wait, and go further before we gathered the water-lilies; then, suddenly, up rose a great red-and-black butterfly, and Joe cried out to me for heaven's sake to get it for him. Away went the butterfly, and I after it, headlong, not seeing where I went, only intent on the chase. At one time I chambered over a sunk fence, and found myself out of the wood; then I vaulted over an iron hurdle, then barely saved myself from falling into a basin of crystal water, with a fountain in the middle; then I was on a gravel walk, and at last got my prize under my cap, in the middle of a bed of scarlet geraniums and blue lobelia.

'Hang it!' I thought, 'I must be out of this pretty quick. *This* won't do! We shan't get through this Sunday without a blessed row, I *know*.'

A voice behind me said, with every kind of sarcastic emphasis—

'*Upon* my veracity, young gentleman. *Upon* my word and honour! Now do let me beg and pray of you, my dear creature, to make yourself entirely at home. Trample, and crush, and utterly destroy, three or four more of my flower-beds, and then come in and have some lunch. *Upon* my word and honour!'

I turned, and saw behind me a very handsome gentleman, of

about fifty-five or so, in a blue coat, a white waistcoat, and drab trousers, exquisitely neat, who stood and looked at me, with his hands spread abroad interrogatively, and his delicate eyebrows arched into an expression of sarcastic enquiry. 'He won't hit me,' was my first thought; and so I brought my elbows down from behind my ears, rolled up my cap with the butterfly inside it, and began to think about flight.

I couldn't take my eyes off him. He was a strange figure to me. So very much like a perfect piece of waxwork. His coat was so blue, his waistcoat so white, his buttons so golden, his face so smoothly shaven, and his close-cropped grey hair so wonderfully sleek. His hands, too, such a delicate mixture of brown and white, with one blazing diamond on the right one. I saw a grand gentleman for the first time, and this, combined with a slightly guilty conscience, took the edge off my London 'prentice audacity, and made me just the least bit in the world afraid.

I had refinement enough (thanks to my association with Joe, a gentleman born) not to be impudent. I said—'I am very, very, sorry sir. The truth is, sir, I wanted this butterfly, and I followed it into your grounds. I meant no harm, indeed sir. (As I *said* it, in those old times, it ran something like this—'I wanted that ere betterfly, sir, and I follered of it into your little place, which I didn't mean no harm, I do assure you.')

'Well! well! well!' said Sir George Hillyar, 'I don't say you did. When I was at Eton, I have bee-hunted into all sorts of strange places. To the very feet of royalty, on one occasion. Indeed, you are forgiven. See here, Erne: here is a contrast to your lazy style of life; here is a—'

'Blacksmith,' I said.

'Blacksmith,' said Sir George, 'I beg your pardon; who will—will—do *all kinds of things* (he said this with steady severity) in pursuit of a butterfly. An example, my child.'

Taking my eyes from Sir George Hillyar, for the first time I saw that a boy, about my own age apparently (I was nearly seventeen), had come up and was standing beside him, looking at me, with his arm passed through his father's, and his head leaning against his shoulder.

Such a glorious lad. As graceful as a deer. Dark brown hair, that wandered about his forehead like the wild boughs of a neglected vine; features regular and beautiful; a complexion well-toned, but glazed over with rich sun-brown; a most beautiful youth, yet whose beauty was extinguished and lost in the blaze of two great blue-black eyes, which forced you to look at them, and which made you smile as you looked.

So I saw him first. How well I remember his first words, 'Who is this?'

I answered promptly for myself. I wanted Joe to see him, for we had never seen anything like him before, and Joe was now visible in the dim distance, uncertain what to do. I said, 'I hunted this butterfly, sir, from the corner of the lake into this garden; and if you will come to my brother Joe, he will confirm me. May I go sir?'

'You may go, my boy,' said Sir George; 'and, Erne, you may show him off the place, if you please. This seems an honest lad, Erne. You may walk with him, if you will.'

So he turned and went towards the house, which I now had time to look at. A bald, bare, white place, after all; with a great expanse of shadeless flower-garden round it. What you would call a very great place, but a very melancholy one, which looked as though it must be very damp in winter. The lake in the wood was the part of that estate which pleased me best.

Erne and I walked away together, towards the dark inscrutable future, and never said a word till we joined Joe. Then we three walked on through the wood, Joe very much puzzled by what had happened; and at last Erne said to me—

'What is your name?'

'Jim.'

'I say, Jim, what did you come here for, old fellow?'

'We came after the water-lilies,' I said. 'We were told there were yellow ones here.'

'So there were', he said; 'but we have rooted them all up. If you will come here next Sunday, I will get you some.'

'I am afraid we can't sir,' I said. 'If it hadn't been for Bill Avery hitting his missis down stairs, we couldn't have come here today. And we shall catch it now.'

'Do you go to school?' said Erne.

'No, sir; I am apprenticed to father. Joe here does.'

'Do the fellows like you, Joe? Have you got any friends?'

Joe stopped, and looked at him. He said:

'Yes, sir. Many friends, God be praised! though I am only a poor hunchback. Have you many, sir?'

'Not one single one, God help me, Joe. Not one single one.'

It came on to rain, but he would not leave us. We walked to the station together; and, as we walked, Joe, the poet, told us tales, so that the way seemed short. Tales of sudden friendships made in summer gardens, which outlive death. Of long-sought love; of lands far off; lands of peace and wealth, where there was no sorrow, no care; only an eternal, dull, aching regret for home, never satisfied; and of the great heaving ocean, which thundered and burst everlastingly on the pitiless coast, and sent its echoes booming up the long-drawn corridors of the dark storm-shaken forest capes.

Did Joe tell us all these stories, or has my memory become confused? I forget, good reader, I forget; it is so long ago.

2
Trevittick's Latent Madness Begins to Appear

The fierce summer was blazing overhead; the forests were parched and crisp; the plains were yellow and dry; and the rivers at their lowest, some barely whispering, others absolutely silent, as we passed away to the southward, towards our new home, and our strange new fortunes.

To the west and north of the town, the dun-grey grass wolds rolled off in melancholy waves towards the great interior; but to the south, on our track, the vast wood-clad mountains, dimly visible in the south-west, had thrown out a spur, which carried the dark forest with it down to the sea, and ended not ten miles from the town in the two noble promontories, Cape Horner and Cape Huskisson. And so we had barely got clear of the enclosures when we found ourselves out of sight of the melancholy plains, travelling along a dusty winding track, fringed on each side with bracken fern, through a majestic open forest of lofty trees.

'I like this better than the plains,' said Erne to me. 'And yet I believe that I am going to live in the most dreary part of all the plains. The Secretary says that they have to send five miles for firewood.'

'Then you have decided what to do, sir?'

'Yes, I was going to tell you as we started, but your natural anxiety about getting on horseback for the first time rendered you rather a bad listener. How do you feel now?'

'Comfortable enough for you to go on; time is getting short.'

'Well, I am going to one of the stations belonging to Mr Charles Morton for three years, to learn the squatting trade. The Secretary wanted me very much; but I took Morton's offer, because this particular station of his lies more in a particular direction than any one of the brother-in-law's; and the Secretary said one station was as good as another, though he was a little offended.'

'I suppose it is nearer to us.'

'It is *only* sixty miles; but it is nearer than any other.'

'What did *she* say this morning?'

'The old word "*never*", Jim. She used the old argument about Joe's deformity, and the impossibility of his marrying, and the necessity of some one devoting herself to him. And I said, "Suppose that obstacle could be removed," and she said there was a greater one still. She would never consent to drag me down to her level— that I was made for another sphere of life; and, when I impatiently interrupted her, she said, "Mr Hillyar, would Mr Oxton or Mrs Oxton receive me? And don't you know you would be cut off from the best society here by marrying me, and have nothing left but the billiard-rooms?" And I hesitated one instant, and she broke out into a laugh at me. And she let me kiss her hand, and then we separated; and that is the end of all, Jim.'

'Not for ever,' I said. 'If time or chance could remove those two obstacles—'

'I am faithful for ever,' said Erne, in a low voice, 'but I am losing hope. If I did not know she loved me, I could bear it better—'

I knew what was coming, by experience—a furious tirade against ranks and proprieties; but he was interrupted, for a horse came brushing rapidly along through the short fern, and rattling amongst the fallen bark, which lay about like vast sticks of cinnamon, and up came the Hon. Charles Morton at a slinging trot, on a big chestnut, with a blazed face, and four white stockings; a 'Romeo.' His shining butcher's boots fitted him like a glove, or like Custance's; his spurs were fresh from the plate-brush; his fawn-coloured breeches fitted to perfection; his shirt was as white as the

Secretary's, and his light drab riding coat (he wore no waistcoat) was met by a bright blue scarf, with a diamond pin; his Indian pith helmet was wound round with a white veil; his whiskers and moustache were carefully trimmed; and altogether he was one of the most perfect dandies ever seen. This was Charles Morton of the towns; Charles Morton of the bush—the pioneer—was a very different object.

'Hallo, Hillyar, my boy. Well, blacksmith, how are you to-day? Confoundedly hot in these forests, is it not? Hillyar and I shall be out on the breezy plains in an hour; you will have forest for sixty miles or thereabouts.'

I touched my hat for the information.

'You'll soon leave off doing that,' he said, looking at me, laughing. And I though if I never touched my hat to a less gallant-looking gentleman I shouldn't care.

'I am sorry to advise you to come up country so soon,' said Mr Morton to Erne. 'But, as my principal overseer in those parts is going back, it will be a great opportunity for you. He will introduce you to station after station on the road. He is not a gentleman by birth, but he is always received as one. I wish I could introduce you in those parts myself; but, considering your close connection with the Secretary, he will do as well. Clayton will prove your identity.'

When I heard the name 'Clayton' I gave a violent start, and cried out, 'Good gracious!' which made my horse move forward a little faster, and which, consequently, nearly laid me on my back in the road. I lost both my stirrups, and hauled myself upright again by the reins. But my horse didn't care a bit. He only thought I was drunk. He was an aged stockhorse, which I had bought very cheap, as being a secure animal to begin with. He had been many years on the road, and had carried many stock-riders out of Palmerston, but never, hitherto, a sober one. He had been very much surprised at my not setting off full gallop for the first mile or two, yelling like a Bedlamite; and had shown that he expected that to happen on two or three occasions, to my infinite horror. He had long since come to the conclusion that I was too far gone in liquor to gallop; and, after my last reel, he concluded that I should soon fall off, and go to sleep in the road for an hour or two, after the manner of stockmen returning from town; in which case he would have a quiet graze until I got sober. He was so fully persuaded of this, that

I had (with infinite caution, as though I was letting off a large and dangerous firework) to give him, now and then, a gentle reminder with the spur to make him keep up with the others.

'Hallo! blacksmith!' said Mr Morton. 'We must teach you to ride better than that before we have done with you. But, Hillyar, you will find Clayton a very good, honest fellow. His wife is a woman of low origin, but well-behaved, who sings ballads, if you care about that; there are no children, which, perhaps, you will be glad of. You will, however, find some books there. I am sorry to put you in a house where there is no society of your own rank; but it was your choice, remember. As soon as you feel able to undertake the thing, I will put you in charge of one of the other stations thereabout, and then you will have a table and a cellar of your own. It is time to say good-bye to your friend now; here is Wattle Creek, and we take the road to the right; I will ride on; you will soon pick me up. Good-bye, blacksmith. God speed you heartily, my boy.'

So, in his delicacy, he rode on, and left Erne and me alone together. There were many last words; and then the last of all—

'Good-bye.'

'Good-bye, Jim. Keep her in mind of me. Good-bye.'

And he rode slowly away, and I saw him passing on from sunlight to shade, from shade to sunlight again, through an aisle in the dim forest cathedral, whose pillars were trunks of the box-trees, and whose roof was their whispering foliage. Farther and farther yet, until he was lost among the thickening stems and denser boskage of some rising ground beyond. And then I sat upon my grazing horse, alone in this strange forest, foolishly wondering if I should see him, or any one I had ever known, again; for all the past seemed more like reality than the present.

But I have noticed as a curious fact that town-bred blacksmith boys, however affectionate, are not given to sentiment; and, the moment Erne was out of sight, I began to make such a series of remarkable discoveries, that Erne, and the awful fact of his going to live in the house with Mrs Clayton, some time Avery, *née* Martin, went clean out of my mind. I gave myself up to the wild delight of being for the first time in a new and strange land.

Conceive my awe and delight at finding that the whole place was swarming with parrots. Hundreds of little green ones, with short tails, who were amazingly industrious and busy, and who talked cheerily to one another all the time; others still more beautiful, with long tails (shell parrots, we call them, but now so popular in London as Zebra parakeets), who crowded in long rows, kissed one another, and wheetled idiotically; larger and more glorious ones yet—green, orange, scarlet, and blue (mountain blues)—who came driving swiftly through the forest in flocks, whistling and screaming; and, lastly, gentle lories, more beautiful in colour than any, who sat on the Banksias like a crop of crimson and purple flowers.

Then I made another discovery. I crossed the creek, and, blundering up the other bank, struck my spurs deep into the old horse's side, and away he went full gallop, and I did not fall off. As soon as I recovered my presence of mind, by using certain directions given me by Erne and others, I made the wonderful discovery that I could stick on, and that I rather liked it. It was in a colonial-made saddle, with great pads in front of the knee, and I found that by keeping my toes slightly in, and raising my heels, I could sit as easily as in a rocking-chair. I assisted myself with the pom—our space is limited—but I was most perfectly at home after a mile, and found it the most delightful thing I had ever experienced, to go charging on ten miles an hour through a primaeval forest towards unknown surprises and unknown dangers.

Whether the old horse thought my intoxication had, like some recorded cases of hydrophia, broken out after a long period of incubation; or whether he thought I was the victim of an acute attack of skyblues (as he would have called the malady known to the faculty as delirium tremens), I am unable to say; but he went like the wind.

The road turned and wound about very much among the tree stems, but the old horse took care of me. I was prepared for any adventure or surprise, from a lion downwards, when I was startled by the shrill cry of familiar voices, and, pulled up, found myself in the bosom of my family.

There were the dear old Chelsea group, a little older, sitting by themselves in this strange forest, just as they used to sit in old times in the great old room at home—my father and mother on a box side by side, Emma and Martha on the ground, with the children grouped round them, and Joe leaning against a tree, musing, just as he used to lean against the mantelpiece in old times.

'And poor Reuben,' I thought, 'where was he?' But I said

nothing. I asked my father how he found himself, and my father replied, 'Bustin' '; and really the dear old fellow did look most remarkably radiant, as did the others, save Joe and Emma.

'We've been a having such a game a coming along, old man,' said my father. 'We seen a alligator as hooked it up a tree; didn't us, Fred ?'

'And Harry, he's a drawed it in his book beautiful,' said my mother, complacently. 'And now he's a drawing his own Jim a horseback, full gallop, as we see you a coming along just now. And Frank has been talking beautiful, and—'

I had dismounted, and Tom Williams had kindly taken my horse from me, and I was looking over my mother's shoulder at Harry's drawing of the great Monitor lizard and my humble self, rather uncertain, I confess, which was the lizard and which was me; but my mother had succeeded in getting my head against hers, and I asked in a whisper, 'How are they ?'

'Joe's terrible low,' said my mother; 'lower than ever I saw him. But Emma's keeping up noble. Did he send her any message ?'

'No. How could he ? He has got his final answer.'

'I wish he had sent some message or other to her,' said my mother; 'for her heart's a breaking for him, and a few words would have been so precious. Couldn't you, eh, Jim ?—didn't he say anything ?'

I did not wait for my dear mother to propose point blank that we should coin a message together, but I went over and sat beside Emma, and took Fred on my lap.

'He is gone,' I said in a low voice.

There was only a catch in her breath. She made no answer.

'Shall I tell you his last words ?'

The poor girl only nodded her head.

'He said, "Good-bye, Jim. Don't let her forget me." And no more I will.'

There was the slightest possible suspicion of scorn in the look she gave me as she said, 'Is that very likely ?'

Perhaps I was nettled; perhaps it was only owing to my clumsy eagerness about the matter which lay nearest to my heart. I cannot decide which it was; but I said—

'Would you not recall him now if you could ?'

She did not answer in words, but she turned and looked at me;

and, when she had caught my eye, she carried it with hers, until they rested on the figure of poor Joe, who had sat down on a log, with his great head buried in his hands. I understood her, and said no more, but quietly drew her to me and kissed her.

'If those two obstacles could be removed,' I found myself saying a dozen times that day, and for many days.

We were travelling with a caravan of bullock drays, seven in number, each drawn by eight bullocks, all the property of our friend the Hon. Mr Dawson, which were returning empty to one of his many stations, Karra Karra, after taking to Palmerston a trifle of fourteen tons of fine merino wool, to swell his gigantic wealth. It was a very pleasant, lazy way of travelling, and I think that, when the long 270 miles of it came to an end, there was not one of us who did not wish that we could have gone a few miles farther.

If the road was smooth, you could sit on the dray. If it was rough, you could walk, and walk faster than the dray went; so much faster that some of us would walk forward along the track, which still wandered through dense and magnificent forest, as much as a mile or two, into the unknown land before us; and, forewarned of snakes, gather such flowers as we could find, which at this time of year were not many. We had very few adventures. Sometimes we would meet a solitary horseman; sometimes a flock or two of two or three thousand sheep going to market, whose three shepherds rode on horseback, and whose dogs, beautiful Scotch sheep-dogs, alert and watchful, but gasping with thirst, would find a moment to come to Fred or Harry and rub themselves against them complacently, and tell them how hot, hot, hot, it was. Sometimes again would come a great drove of fat cattle, guided by three or four wild-looking stock-men, in breeches and boots, which in this hot weather were the principal part of their clothing, for they had nothing else but shirts without buttons, and hats generally without any ribbons. These men were accompanied by horrid great dogs, who cut Fred and Harry dead; but, in spite of their incivility, their masters were very good-humoured and kind, keeping their cattle away from us with their terrible great stock-whips. The head stockman would always stay behind and talk to us—sometimes for a long while—generally asking us question about England— questions which seemed almost trivial to us. I remember that one wild, handsome fellow, who told Emma in pure chivalrous admiration that looking at her was as good as gathering cowslips, was very anxious, when he heard we were from Chelsea, to find out if we had ever met his mother, whose name was Brown, and who lived at Putney. He was afraid something was wrong with the old lady, he said, for he hadn't heard from her this ten years, and then she was seventy-five. He would go home some of these days, he added, and knock the old girl up.

After a few of these expeditions ahead of the drays, we began to take Trevittick the sulky with us. For Trevittick, thirsting madly after knowledge, in the manner of his fair-haired fellow-Phoenicians, had spent more than he could very well afford in buying a book on the colonial flora. He now began to identify the flowers as fast as we got them; and, as the whole of us went at the novel amusement with a will, and talked immensely about it afterwards, we attracted poor Joe's attention, and, to my great delight, he began to join us, and to enter somewhat into the pleasure with us.

The forest continued nearly level; the only irregularities were the banks of the creeks which we crossed at intervals of about ten miles —chains of still ponds walled by dark shrubs, shut in on all sides by the hot forest, so that no breath of air troubled their gleaming surface. But when a hundred miles were gone, the land began to rise and roll into sharp ascents and descents; and one forenoon we came to a steep and dangerous hill. And, while we were going cautiously down through the thick hanging trees, we heard the voice of a great river rushing through the wood below us. As we struggled through it, with the cattle belly-deep in the turbid green water, we had a glimpse right and left of a glorious glen, high piled with grey rocks, with trees hanging in every cranny and crag, and solemn pines which shot their slender shafts aloft in confused interlacing groups, beautiful beyond expression. Only for a minute did we see this divine glen; instantly after, we were struggling up the opposite cliff, in the darksome forest once more.

'Why,' I asked one of the bullock-drivers, who volunteered that evening to show me a place to bathe, 'why is the water so ghastly cold? I can scarcely swim.'

'Snow, mate, snow. This water was brought down from Mount Hampden by yesterday's sun.'

The next morning the scene changed strangely, and Trevittick walked like one in a dream. As we went up a hill we saw the light between the tree stems at the top, and the wind began to come more freshly to our cheeks. When we reached the summit the forest had come to an end, and we were looking over into Flinder's Land.

A glorious country indeed; sheets of high rolling down, and vast stretches of table-land, bounded by belts of forest, and cut into by deep glens everywhere—channels for the snow-water from the mountains. Two great lakes gleamed among dark woodlands at different elevations, and far to the left was a glimpse of distant sea. A fair, beautiful, smiling land, and yet one of the most awful the eye ever rested on: for there was one feature in it which absorbed all the others, and made waving wood, gleaming lake, and flashing torrent, but secondary objects for the eye to rest on—just as the ribbed cliffs of stone which formed the nave of Winchester make the chantries of Wykeham and Edyngton appear like children's toys.

For to the right, towering horrible and dark, rose, thousands of feet in the air, high above everything, a scarped rampart of dolomite, as level as a wall; of a lurid grey colour with deep brown shadows. It dominated the lower country so entirely that the snow mountains beyond were invisible for it, and nothing gave notice of their presence but a lighter gleam in the air, above the dark wall. It stretched away, this wall, into the farthest distance the eye could penetrate. It had bays in it, and sometimes horrid rents, which seemed to lead up into the heart of the mountains—rents steep and abrupt, ending soon and suddenly—glens bounded with steep lawns of gleaming green. Sometimes it bent its level outline down, and then from the lowest point of the dip streamed eternally a silvery waterfall, which, snow-fed, waxed and waned as the sun rose or fell. But there hung the great rock wall, frowning over the lovely country below; which, like Pitt's face at the last, reflected in some sort of way smiles of sunshine and frowns of cloud, yet bore the ghastly look of Austerlitz through it all.

So for twelve days this dark rampart haunted us, and led our eyes to it at all times, never allowing us to forget its presence. In the still cool night it was black, in the morning it was purple, at noon it was heavy pearly grey, and at sunset gleaming copper-colour. Sometimes, when we were down a deep glen, or crossing some rushing river, we could only catch a glimpse of the level wall cutting the bright blue sky; sometimes, again, when we were aloft on a breezy down, the whole of the great rampart would be in sight at once, stretching north and south as far as the eye could reach; but for twelve days it bent its horrid frown upon us, until we grew tired of it, and wished it would end.

At last it ended. Gradually, for three days, a peaked mountain grew upon our sight, until we reached it, and begun passing over the smooth short turf which formed its glacis; a mountain which rose out of the lower land in advance of, and separate from, the great wall which I have been describing; a mountain which heaved a smooth sharp cone aloft out of the beautiful slate country through which we have been travelling, and whose apex pierced the heavens with one solitary needle-like crag. It was the last remnant of the walls of an old crater; of a volcano which had been in action long after the great cliff, which we had watched so long, had been scorched and ruined into its present form. The men called the peak Nicnicararlah; and, when we had rounded the shoulder of it, we saw that our journey's end was near; for a beautiful fantastic mountain range hurled itself abruptly into the sea across our path, and barred our further progress, and as soon as we sighted it the men called out at once, 'There you are, mates; there is Cape Wilberforce!'

3

Everybody was up early, with a full determination to make holiday of it; for land sales were few and far between in those days; and this one, coming a few days before Christmas, would make a very good starting-point for the Christmas saturnalia. The young men caught their horses, and rode about; or, if they had no horses of their own, borrowed some one else's. At the same time was begun a long, objectless, and incomprehensible game of cricket, in which a man, by dexterous manoeuvring, might have sixteen or seventeen innings; and which lasted from cockcrow to long after curfew. At the same time also everybody began to bathe, and kept on bathing, while they were not riding about or cricketing, all day. Harry confided in me that he had been 'in' eight times. At about nine o'clock the black fellows arrived and the dogs began barking 'as though there were bears in the town', and barked on until the black fellows left late in the afternoon.

At about ten the auctioneer arrived, and with him the Hon. Mr

Dawson. Soon after this all the elders of the township adjourned into the little court-house to look at the plans, and I, having been married a week, felt several degrees more dignified than the Governor, and took my place among the others with becoming gravity. After some time the court was filled, and the business began. Mr Dawson sat next the auctioneer, and just as he began to speak, my cousin Samuel, dressed in black, came up and thrust himself among the foremost.

'Here's the devil come for old Jack Dawson,' said some one who was standing in the crowd, and everybody laughed, for my friend Mr Dawson's popularity was not high in the township. The auctioneer began: 'Silence, gentlemen, pray silence.'

'Silence yourself, you old scrubber,' was the polite rejoinder, the gentleman who spoke being slightly in liquor, 'What's the good of such a farce as this here? Why, there sits old Jack Dawson, the blacksmith, with his pockets full of money, ready to buy up the whole boiling, scot and lot; while a poor man can't get a bit of land to put his foot on. He is going to be king at Port Romilly, mates; and we're to be his humble servants. Blow that, I say!'

There was a murmur of discontent through the hall. I saw Mr Dawson wince; for he could not bear unpopularity. The first lot was put up, a lot of twenty acres, with frontage on the Erskine. After a brisk competition it was knocked down to my cousin Samuel, for the high sum of ten pounds an acre. Mr Dawson did not compete.

Neither did he for the next lot, or the next. It was plain that he had been affected by the sarcasms of the drunken man, and the evident applause with which they were received. All the lots with wharfage along the Erskine went without a sign from him: and next the land further back towards the Cape Wilberforce mountain was put up. 'Your father is mad,' Erne said to me. 'He is letting his fortune slip away under his eyes: why on earth don't he bid? All the best land is going. Do pray him to bid for this she-oak lot; it's only 640. Why, it would grow 40 bushels to the acre; I was over it yesterday.'

My father's folly did seem to me incomprehensible. I pushed through to him, and pointed out what Erne had said. He was very pale and anxious; but all I could get out of him was, 'All right, old man, leave it to me.'

THE KINGSLEYS

As the sale went on there was less and less competition, as the land grew both poorer in quality from being nearer the mountain, and being further removed from the river and the bay. Several lots just under the mountain went for the upset price; and at last the sale was nearly concluded, and the people began to go out. Three lots remained to be sold, and these three comprised a large portion of the mountain itself. As lot 67 was mentioned, I saw my father and Mr Dawson exchange glances, and everybody began to be funny.

'Lot 67, gentlemen,' began the auctioneer, 'a most eligible lot gentlemen. If you were to ask me my opinion, as between man and man, I should say the most eligible lot which I have had the honour of tempting you with to-day. 1,280 acres, or shall we say, two of 640. The soil, though not fertile, is dry, the situation is elevated, the air invigorating and salubrious, and the scenery romantic. On a clear day, as I am informed by our venerable and respected harbour-master, the lighthouse on Cape Pit is distinctly visible to the naked eye.'

Somebody said that with a glass you might see old Jack Dawson sanding the men's sugar at Myrnong, sixty miles off. This un-expected attack on my unoffending friend resulted in a violent and personal fracas between Mr Dawson and the gentleman who had so rudely assailed him, in which several joined; during which the honourable gentleman so far forgot himself in the heat of debate as to say, that 'if he got any more cheek from him, or any other carroty-haired, 'possum-headed, forty-acre, post and rail son of a seacock, he would knock his head into the shape of a slushdump in about two minutes.' Peace being restored in about ten minutes, and the Hon. Mr Dawson being left in a great heat, the auctioneer went on with the description of the lot, only once interrupted by the Hon. Mr Dawson, suddenly, irrelevantly, and gratuitously in-forming the company in a loud and defiant voice, that he would find a young smith, not twenty-one, who should fight the best man in that room for a hundred pounds a side.

Much as I was flattered at this proof of my friend's confidence, I was glad no one came forward. The auctioneer concluded—

'Now whom can I tempt with this lot? Can I tempt you, Mr Dawson?'

'Yes, you can, sir!' retorted the still angry Mr Dawson. 'And

242

I'll have this lot, sir, and my friend Mr Burton shall have the next, sir, if it cost fifty thousand pounds, sir. Now. And, if any individual chooses to run this lot up out of spite, sir, whether that individual has red hair or green hair sir, I will punch that individual's head immediately after the termination of these proceedings, sir, and knock it against the blue stone and mortar which compose the walls of this court house. Now, sir.'

However, nobody, I suppose, caring to get his head punched for a whim, the lot was knocked down to him, and immediately afterwards my father stepped forward looking as white as a sheet.

'Now we come to lot 68, commonly known by your fellow-townsmen as the Burnt Hut lot; exactly similar to lot 67 just knocked down to the Hon. Mr Dawson, as a site for his new country house. Now who would like to have our honoured legislative councillor for a neighbour ? What gentleman of fortune can I tempt with this lot ? The lot is up. At one pound an acre. Will any one bid one pound an acre ?'

'I will,' said my father, in a queer, hoarse voice. I saw that he was moistening his lips with his tongue. I began to grow deeply interested, half frightened.

'Going at a pound. Come, gentlemen, if any one is going to bid, be quick. It is the last lot.'

There were but few left: and no one of them spoke. The hammer came down, and I saw Mr Dawson clutch my father's arm.

'The land is yours, Mr Burton. If you'll be good enough to step up and sign, I'll be able to get on as far as Stawell tonight. There is a good deal of snow-water coming down the Eldon this hot weather, and I don't like that crossing-place after dark.'

Thanks to James Oxton's excellent conveyancing bill, land with a title direct from the Crown were transferred to the purchaser in about ten minutes. In that time my father was standing outside the court-house, with his papers in his hand, with Mr Dawson beside him.

'Where's Trevittick ?' almost whispered Mr Dawson.

'Go seek him at home, Jim, and fetch him here,' said my father in the same tone.

I went quickly home with a growing awe upon me. Every one was behaving so queerly. My awe was not dissipated by my finding Trevittick, with his head buried in the blankets, praying eagerly and rapidly, and Tom Williams standing by as pale as a ghost.

'This is the way he has been carrying on this last hour,' said poor Tom. 'I can't make nothing of him at all.'

I went up to him and roused him. 'Trevittick,' I said, 'father has got the bit of land he wanted.'

He jumped up and clutched me by both arms. 'Jim,' he said, 'if you're lying—. If you're lying—. If you're lying—.'

We went out and joined the two others, and all walked away towards the hill in silence. The boys were bathing, the cricketers were shouting, and the quaint-scattered village bore a holiday look. The neighbours were all sitting out at their doors, and greeted me as we went by: but yet everything seemed changed to me since the morning. I almost dreaded what was to come, and it seems to me now that it all happened instantaneously.

We crossed the low-lying lands which had been sold that day, and came to our own—a desolate, unpromising tract, stretching up the side of the mountain which formed Cape Wilberforce, about three miles from the sea. The land bought by Mr Dawson was similar to our own, separated from it by a rib of trap rock; both lots were just as Erne described them, but ours was rather the rockier of the two.

It was soon over. Trevittick took a hammer and some gads from behind a rock, and going up to a low ledge, set them in, and began working furiously. Once he struck aside and hit the rock and the rock, instead of clinking, gave forth a dull thud. In a few minutes Trevittick had succeeded in detaching a piece about two feet square, the broken side of which shone strangely in the sun. It was a mass of solid, gleaming virgin copper.

The murder was out now. With the exception of one on Lake Superior, and one in South Australia, my father was the proprietor of the richest copper mine in the world.

XXVIII

Silcote of Silcotes
1867

When revisiting his old Chelsea haunts, Henry encountered a lively, intelligent and penniless girl of twenty-two, in fact a distant cousin, employed as governess to the rector's family. On 19 July, 1864, he and Sarah Haselwood were married at the Chelsea church where his father had formerly presided. So far as we know the marriage was a happy one, and yet it proved disastrous to Henry. The couple took a house at Wargrave by the Thames and overspent on moving, furnishing and settling in—a terraced garden, poultry, rabbits, dogs, surrounded them—and on entertaining their friends. Sarah's ill-health, first a persistent cough and then several miscarriages, added to their worries. For the first time the sales of Henry's books became a matter of survival rather than a measure of success.

He completed The Hillyars and the Burtons *at Wargrave and in the following year, 1866, brought out* Leighton Court, *described by the* Spectator *as a 'little comedy of high life in the country' and moderately commended, although it was 'sufficiently slight'. Then came* Silcote of Silcotes *on which Henry lavished great care. 'Every sentence will be polished,' he promised his publisher, 'as it passes out of my hands.' Also he had other aims. 'I want to write a story about good things and good people without being "goody" . . . I want to write a story which shall be interesting and exciting, and to make everyone the better for having read it.'*

This excellent motive does not supply the best recipe for a novel. Henry himself was nagged by doubt. 'Silcotes is all hard-bitten, earnest work,' he wrote, 'but it must be made more lively. There is a dreary purism about the earlier numbers which is, even to myself who understand it, very dull.' In its central character, the 'dark squire' of Silcotes, Henry endeavoured to create a memorable and forceful figure: morose, tyrannical, withdrawn and abrupt, possessed of a biting tongue, but at heart a perfect gentleman: a man in whom the milk of human

THE KINGSLEYS

kindness has been curdled by a secret grief too horrible to be contemplated, let alone revealed. Sisters, sons, nephews, nieces, uncles and aunts and a host of domestics weave around him an incredibly intricate plot, or series of plots, with the inheritance of Silcotes at stake; and they talk and behave in a manner that dimly foreshadows the characters created, in a similar milieu, nearly a century later by Ivy Compton Burnett. Incongruously, the denouement is reached with the battle of Solferino, fought in 1859, when Tom Silcote is killed leaving James as the heir.

Perhaps it was Henry's anxiety to write a 'polished' novel, well constructed and with vigorous dialogue, that led him to over-elaboration, loss of spontaneity and a pasteboard quality that was pounced upon by critics. Silcote of Silcotes was not well received. 'Must the muscular villain inevitably reappear ?' complained the Saturday Review, *referring to the squire's son Tom; adding that the author's 'puppets throughout are active as fleas, but their activity leads to nothing'; this was 'a novel without a purpose'. This harsh judgment ignores Henry's inventiveness, good humour and sheer readability, as well as his hopes of making the good as lively as the wicked, hopes which have been disappointed in many excellent writers both before and since.*

In the following extract the business of unveiling secrets is begun. A Mrs Morgan has taken up her duties as matron of a charity school of which the squire is chairman, one of his sons is headmaster and the sturdy lad James Sugden, supposedly the son of one of Silcote's farm labourers—voted the most popular boy in the academy—is his favourite. The squire calls to make her acquaintance.

Silcote saw before him a grey-headed woman, dressed in grey, with a long grey shawl, with her head turned away from him, bending over baskets of linen which she was sorting. She attracted his attention at once, and he began, 'I beg your pardon, madam,—' when she turned and looked at him.

Silcote was transfixed with unutterable astonishment. He burst out, 'Why, what the . . .!' when she suddenly raised her right hand, and with her left pointed to the boy beside him. Silcote understood in a moment, as he put it to himself mentally, 'The cub has not recognized her then.' He changed his manner at once. 'Madam,' he said, 'I have come, as chairman, to have a talk with you on various matters. Are you at leisure ?'

'I am at leisure, sir; at least, if you will allow me to go on with my work. When the hands are idle the memory gets busy. You have found that yourself, sir, I do not doubt.'

The Squire swung himself round towards James, and, standing squarer and broader than ever before him, pointed his finger at him, and said—

'Go, and shut the door after you.'

Which things James did.

'Now, my dear Mrs Sugden,' said he, pulling up a chair, and sitting down in front of her, 'would you be kind enough to let me know the meaning of this?'

'Certainly. First of all, how did you call me just now?'

'I called you Mrs Sugden.'

'That is not my name. It *was*, and is still, that of my half-brother, who passed for my husband when I lived in your little cottage at Beechwood; but it is not mine.'

'Your half-brother?' said Silcote. 'Was not Sugden your husband, then?'

'No, only half-brother. His mother was not the same as mine. Our common father, a twenty-acre freeholder in Devonshire, married twice. The name of his first wife, of my brother's mother, was Coplestone; the name of his second wife, *my* mother, was Lee.'

'Then how shall I call you? Mrs Morgan?'

'Not at all. A mere *nom de guerre*, which I assumed when they objected to the title I bore at St Peter's, "Sister Mary." Nothing more than that.'

'Then perhaps, madam, to facilitate conversation, you would put me in possession of your style and titles.'

'I am Mrs Thomas Silcote, your unworthy, but dutiful daughter-in-law,' she said very quietly.

The Squire fell back in his chair. 'Don't regard me, my dear madam; I have the constitution of a horse. If I had not, I should have been in Bedlam or the grave, years ago. Let us have it out, madam. I thought there were Silcotes enough encumbering the face of the earth. There don't happen to be any more of you, I suppose?'

'There is James, you know,' said Mrs Thomas Silcote, smiling. 'He makes another. I don't think there are any more.'

'Quite so,' said Silcote. 'James. I begin to collect myself. James, then, is my lawful grandson?'

'Most certainly. Do you desire proofs?'

'Not if you assert it. You yourself are a standing proof of every proposition that comes out of your mouth.'

'I was a labourer's daughter,' said Mrs Thomas. 'A twenty-acre freeholder *is* a labourer, is he not?'

'I don't believe a word of it,' said Silcote.

'I thought you were bound to believe everything I said a minute ago?'

'Don't fence with me. It is not fair. You utterly ruin my nerves, and then begin what these low boys here call "chaffing." Will you explain to me how all this came about?'

'Not tonight.'

'You really must in part. How on earth did you come here?'

'Merely by answering an advertisement.'

'Does Betts know nothing?'

'Not a word. It is all between you and me. And it must remain there.'

'How was it that the boy did not recognize you?'

'Time, time, time!'

Silcote sat perfectly silent. 'Time works wonders,' he said, at last. 'You wanted to see him, I suppose, and you risked his recognizing you?'

'See him!' said Mrs Silcote. 'I wanted to touch him, I wanted to kiss him; but I cannot do that. Do you remember, one day in your garden, pointing out to me that it would be a drawback to the boy if his low parentage was known?'

'I do. God forgive me if I did wrong.'

'You did right: even speaking from what you knew then. I know you, Silcote, as a good and kind man, though you have tried hard to sell yourself to the evil one. And so I tell you this: that I have doubts, in my utter ignorance, whether the world would take my marriage to be a legal one; and, therefore, I have remained unknown to the boy.'

'Where, and how, were you married?'

'In Scotland.' And she told him the particulars.

'Bless the woman!' he exclaimed. 'You are as much my daughter-in-law as if you had been married in St George's, Hanover Square, with eighteen bridesmaids. I wish I had known this. Once more, will you tell me the whole story ?'

'Not tonight.'

'There is no reason against your letting the boy know who you are.'

'Let it be—let it be. The father is outlawed, and the mother's claim cannot be quite proved. It would be a disadvantage to the boy. And hear me, you Dark Squire, with your bloodhounds. The boy has got to love me again, with a new fresh love overlying the mere old love which lives in his memory. He has been painting my face, and the new love showed itself in his eyes a hundred times.'

'Was there no recognition ?'

'A dim stirring of memory only, which made him more strangely beautiful than ever. Once or twice there was such a fixed stare in his glorious eyes that I thought I was betrayed. But I was not. It was only the old love of memory wedding itself to the new love of respect and admiration. Would you be loved better than that ?'

'Confound the woman!' said the Squire to himself, and then sat quite silent,—she going on mending shirts.

At last he said, 'The boy wants to go to Italy and study art. I have had bother enough with Italy, but I won't stand in his way. I recognize him as my grandson, and I like the boy. But is there any promise in these drawings of his ? We must not make a fool of the lad. I have seen nothing of his as yet.'

Mrs Silcote rose, and brought from a bureau a small canvass with a head, painted in oils, upon it. It was the likeness of herself which James had done. She said—

'Will that do ?'

'Do!' said Silcote, 'I should think it would. There is genius in every line of it.'

'So I thought, thinking at the same time that I might be blinded by my love. Let him go, Silcote. Did you ever know what it was to love, Silcote?—not to love with the old love and the new love with which my boy and I love one another; but to love blindly and foolishly, from an instinct more powerful than reason ? I loved so once, and believed myself loved still more deeply in return; and one fine day, I found that I had never been loved at all, and had only been tricked and deceived by words sweet as angels, falser than devils. I found that out one day, Silcote, and my heart withered utterly up within me. And I was desperate and mad, and only saved from the river by a gentle brother, who believed me lost —in one sense of the word. And he and I went back to the fields and the fallows, and fought nature for bread together, as we had been used to do when we were children together, and when mine was only a child's beauty.'

A very long silence, during which she sat as calm as Memnon. When she found her voice again, she went on—

'Do you begin to understand me? Are you capable of understanding the case of one who would have given up everything in this world, ay, and God forgive me if I blaspheme—would have given up all hopes in the next, for the love of one being, and then found that that love never existed at all?—that she had been a dupe and a fool from the first, and that, even while his hand was in her hair, he was laughing at her? *I* went through this, and did not die. Could you dare to warrant the same for yourself?'

A very long pause here. Buttons stitched on shirts, and shirts dextrously folded and placed away, Silcote sitting with his hands before his eyes the whole time. At last he spoke.

'You speak of my son Thomas, whom I loved once. Do you love him still?'

'I cannot say,' she answered. 'Do you?'

'And I cannot say either,' replied Silcote.

'He is your son,' she urged.

'And he is the father of yours,' he replied.

'You have the quickness of your family in answer,' she said. 'Leave this question.'

'You have told me part of your story, and I will not ask for details to-night. You ask me if I know what it is to awake from a dream of love, and find that that love never existed. I do! May I tell you my story? I have gone through all that you speak of, and am still alive. Men with my frame and my brain don't die, or go mad. But I warn you solemnly that, if you allow me to tell you my story, you must prepare your nerves. It is so ghastly, so inconceivable, so unutterably horrible, that I can only hope that the telling of it to you will not kill me.'

'You have been abused, Squire. And, may I ask, have you never told it before? The High Church people, among whom I have been lately, and who have done me good—although I don't go with them,

SILCOTE OF SILCOTES

I will allow that—urge confession. It is capable of any amount of abuse, this confession: but, looking at it in the light of merely a confidential communication of a puzzling evil, it generally does good. You have, with your jealous reticence kept some great evil to yourself for many years, I fear. Why have you never told it before?'

'Why—Temper, I suppose. I seem like the Ancient Mariner. I can't tell my story to any one whose face does not invite me; and your face was the first one which ever did invite me.'

'Then, Silcote, let me hear this story of yours.'

And so Silcote told his story.

'I was, my dear Mrs Sugden, an ambitious, handsome, young fellow,—very popular; with an intention of enjoying life, and in every way fitted for enjoying it. I was sole heir to a very large fortune; and, beside that, came from a family of attorneys: another fortune. No part of my scheme was idleness or luxury. I believed myself to have (nay, I had) considerable talent, not a mean share of wit, and a ready tongue; and I determined—don't laugh at a shipwrecked man—to follow my career as a barrister until I sat upon the bench. My family connexions started me very quickly in a fine practice; but bless you, I could have made my fortune without *them*. Ask any of my contemporaries. I am only telling you the plain truth, I assure you. Who am *I* that I should boast?

'I suppose that at twenty-five I was one of the most fortunate men that ever lived. With my talents and knowledge of law, I would have booked myself for six or seven thousand a year by my practice at forty. I loved my profession intensely: I was a lawyer in my very blood, and all that fate asked of me was to go on and make a noble fortune by the pursuit I loved best in the whole world. And I must marry, too: and a young lady, beautiful, well-born, rich and highly educated, was ready to marry me. And she had ninety thousand pounds of her own.

'Did I love her or her money? No, I loved her, my dear madam, ever since she was a child. And she loved me at one time. Look at me.'

Mrs Thomas Silcote looked at him very steadily indeed.

'Do I look mad?'

'No,' she said very quietly; 'you look perfectly sane.'

'Hah!' said Silcote. 'And yet I sit here and tell you as a solemn truth, that I *know* that at one time she did love me.'

251

'I have no doubt she did. You had better go on,' said Mrs Thomas Silcote.

'I loved her when she was a child; more deeply yet when I was courting her; still more deeply as a bride; until my whole soul merged into hers as a wife. There never was a woman loved as that woman was by me.'

'Well?'

'My sister Mary, whom you know as the Princess, had been a great deal in Italy, principally at Venice, and a great deal also in Vienna; for, next to Italian life, she loved the free and easy life of South Germany. My wife had a son, Algernon, now a master in this very college, and was a long time in recovering her health afterwards. The doctor strongly recommended a change of air and scene.

'At this conjunction of circumstances, my sister came back to England from Italy or Austria (she was always travelling between the two), and, finding my wife in ill health, proposed to take her to Florence to spend the winter. I was loth to part with my darling, still more loth to let her go with my foolish sister. But the doctors were all for it, and old Miss Raylock (you know her) was going also, and so I consented. It was term time, and I could not follow them for six weeks. I let her go, against my better judgement.

'For I knew my sister well. She is one of the most foolish and silly women that ever walked the earth. And she is very untruthful withal: but probably her most remarkable quality is her perfectly donkeyish obstinacy. Like most weak and foolish women, she has a love of mystery and of mysterious power, and she had got herself, before this, mixed up in an infinity of Austro-Italian plots, having no idea of their merits, but getting herself made a fool of alternately by both parties. I had argued with her on this matter often, but you might as well have argued with the pump. She believed herself trusted by both parties, whereas the fact was that she was merely used as a disseminator of false intelligence.

'When term was over, I followed them to Italy. The state of things which I found there was deeply displeasing to me. I found a coterie of English living in a free and easy manner in one another's houses; the leading members of which were my sister, Miss Raylock, a certain Sir Godfrey Mallory, and my wife. My wife and Miss Raylock seemed to be the only people who were living in the least degree up to the English standard of propriety, as it went in those days. As for my sister, she had succeeded in surrounding the whole party with all the political scum of Europe, as it seemed to me. I never saw such a parcel of cut-throat villains, before or since, as we were gathered every evening in my sister's house: nay, not only in my sister's house, but in my wife's—that is, my own. I wondered how they dared assemble there, and expected a descent of police immediately. There were two people about my sister, however, to whom I took a stronger objection than to any other two. The one was a man at that time acting as her major-domo, a German, called Kriegsthurm; the other was my late brother-in-law, the Prince of Castelnuovo.

'How they were allowed to talk the rank sedition they did was a puzzle to me. I am, like most Englishmen, perfectly liberal, rather seditious about foreign politics, but they seemed to me to be going rather too far. I found the truth out though, one night when I had retired from their intolerable jargon, and was smoking my cigar at a *café*. A very gentlemanly and quiet young man drew his chair near mine, and entered into conversation. I took a great fancy to the man, and we exchanged names when we parted. What the deuce was it? A Roman name, I remember. Colonna?—Orsini?— No—but a Roman name.'

'Not Frangipanni?'

'The same. How strange!'

'He is our new Italian teacher: he comes down twice a week by rail if he can get a class. One of Bett's men, that is all. The ghosts are rising, Silcote.'

'So it seems. Well, this man and I entered into close conversation, and he told me the history of the state of society up at my sister's villa. It was a house watched by the police for political purposes,—the Dionysius' Ear of the police. The people who assembled there were either spies or fools, with two exceptions.

'I asked him for those two exceptions, and the man was frank and gentleman-like with me. The exceptions he named were, strange to say, the very two men to whom I had taken such a great dislike—the Prince of Castelnuovo, and that very queer German Kriegsthurm.

'He went on in French, "I put my liberty in your hands, Monsieur. Why? I cannot say. But I am a patriot, and those two men are faithful patriots. For me I never go to Miladi Silcote's house. I am on my good behaviour. I do not wish to be suspect. I receive the prince, and also Kriegsthurm, at my home, where my beautiful little wife, also a patriot, entertains. But go to Miladi Silcote's, no. To Miss Raylock's but little now. Their patriotism is advanced, but they are indiscreet. Sir Godfrey Mallory also is indiscreet, in my opinion. My wife does not receive Sir Godfrey. I do not allow my wife to receive him!"

'Daughter-in-law, that was the first bite of the serpent. I knew that my wife had had one proposal before mine, and that the proposer had been Sir Godfrey Mallory. I knew that.'

'And also that she had refused him,' said Mrs Thomas Silcote, cheerily.

'Certainly. But here he was again, and they were living so very fast and loose. All Leicester Square round them—and—and—I can't go on.'

'You must go on to the end,' said Mrs Thomas Silcote. 'Now?'

'I sulked with her,' went on Silcote in a low voice. 'Not in words about that man; though I was jealous, I did not dare to do that. Besides, I could not. I suppose I must tell. I took her home, but my sister and her precious major-domo, Kriegsthurm, came too. And Sir Godfrey Mallory followed us. And I sulked with her all the time: though I loved her—oh woman! woman! you can't dream of my intense devoted love for that wife of mine!'

There was a long pause. He could not go on, and she would not speak.

'We were never the same to one another after this. I loved her as deeply as ever, but the devil had come between us, and would not go. I thought she had been indiscreet, and could not forgive it. I sulked with her, and was persistently hard with her. If I begin thinking of the beautiful quiet little ways and actions by which she tried to win me back, I shall go out of my mind at last, after all these years. When you have heard all, you will think me a madman for solemnly declaring this: that even now, after all is over, I would give all my expectations on this side of the grave—ay, and on the other also—to have her back even as she was at the very last. I may have been unkind to her, God forgive me; but no man ever so wholly gave up his soul to a woman, as I did to her, until that fatal night at Exeter.'

'Your mind is diseased, Silcote,' said Mrs Thomas. 'You have been abused. My instinct tells me so.'

'I guessed at the same thing to-night, when I saw her son; but listen. My theory always has been till lately, that I tired out her patience—that I turned her into a fiend by my own temper. But I had proofs. I struck Sir Godfrey Mallory (for he and my sister had followed me there to Exeter again, two years or more after my suspicions had begun), and then sat down to my briefs. The last proof came next morning, but I went into court as gay as ever to defend a sailor boy for murder. And, when the excitement of it was over, I turned into the man I am now and ever shall be. Can you conceive this ? A love so deep, so wild, so strong, so jealous as mine, for one who is still, after all—ay, hear me here—dearer to me than all life ? Can you conceive this, and hear what follows ?'

'What proofs had you ? Proofs against your wife ? Against Sir Godfrey Mallory ?'

His face was livid as he spoke, but he found words to utter the terrible secret.

'Worse than that. I had a letter telling me where to look for poison; and I looked and found it. But I never told her what I knew. I took her back to Italy, and she died there in a year. She never knew it. I was as mute as a stone to her. I was never unkind to her; but I never spoke to her; and she tried every beautiful little winning way of hers,—each one of which now, when memory is aroused, scorches my heart like fire,—to win me back. And I was cold stone to her. And she died, and her last look at me was one of love and forgiveness, and puzzled wonder at our estrangement. And memory of it all was dying out under the influence of time, and I thought I was forgetting all about it, until to-night I saw her son, and knew that I loved her better than ever. So now, instead of oblivion, there comes a new-born remorse. Do you want more ?'

'Yes,' said Mrs Thomas Silcote, boldly. 'Where is this letter which condemned her ? Have you got it ?'

'Do not go too far with me. I keep it in a box in my bedroom, and every night a devil comes and dances on that box, and I watch him. Leave me alone, woman; I may get dangerous.'

'Not you. Is this all you have to tell me ?'

'Enough, surely, I should think.'

The tall grey figure rose on him in contempt and anger. 'Then this, sir, is the miserable and ridiculous lie, with which you have been maddening yourself for thirty years! Have you believed this for all that time, and not died? Shame on you! shame, Silcote! Is it on such grounds as these that you have killed a most unhappy and ill-used lady, by your wicked jealousy and suspicion? Listen to me, sir. You are getting old, and your life may be too short for the work; but don't dare to die, don't dare to face the judgement, until every word of this wicked lie is refuted; and this poor lady's memory is avenged. Don't argue with me. It is a falsehood, sir, from beginning to end. Do you not see it now?'

'If it is,' said Silcote, 'and I begin to believe so, what room is there for me on the earth or in heaven, or elsewhere?'

'Right it, and ask the question afterwards. Go!'

XXIX

Mademoiselle Mathilde
1868

*'What beautiful stories one could write if one was rich and had leisure,'
Henry sadly remarked in 1868. He had neither. 'The fearful expenses
of pulling a sick wife about the country, literally to save her life, and
setting up a new house, have superimposed an alarming financial
crisis, and left me without any money at all.' Both he and Sarah were
hospitable by nature, the house at Wargrave with its terraces and
roses was an attractive spot, Henry was an excellent talker: many
friends came to tax at once his leisure and his precarious income. 'I was
with a poet once, and a great one, and we were in a boat on a cold,
steel grey river,' Henry recalled. The poet was probably Swinburne, a
frequent visitor, or it may have been 'my dear old Matt Arnold'.
Charles Dodgson was another good friend.*

*Inevitably, the Kingsleys got into debt. Charles came to the rescue,
to Fanny's dismay; her Charles had all he could do and more to support
his growing family, often driving himself over the edge of collapse
through overwork. Fanny had very little time for Henry, whom she
thought over-fond of rum and water, not to mention French wines; in
her two-volume* Life *and* Letters *of her husband, Henry's names does
not appear. It was just as well that Sarah had no children, although
her husband did not think so. 'Another wretched disappointment,' he
wrote to Alexander Macmillan. 'I believe these miscarriages are
worse than confinements. . . . Do you think you can lend me £35 out of
your private pocket?'*

Despite these worries, the year 1868 saw the publication of
Mademoiselle Mathilde *which, with* Ravenshoe, *remained the
author's favourite among his novels. Of 'the old friends which I have
called up in this quaint trade, called the writing of fiction,' he wrote,
'only two remain with me: the peak-faced man, Charles Ravenshoe,
and the lame French girl, Mathilde.'*

In order to gather background material for a description of the battle

257

of Solferino which he worked into Silcote of Silcotes, *Henry went to France to watch the army manoeuvres. In French history and the French people he found a theme and setting for his next novel, following his contemporary, Dickens, into territory penetrated nine years earlier in* A Tale of Two Cities. *The story concerns a family of the French nobility whose head, separated from his termagant of a wife, lives with his two daughters in Dorset. A romantic web is spun between the two countries, to be shaken by the gathering storms of Revolution and finally disrupted by the Terror. The loyal Mathilde, dutifully obeying her tyrannical and obstinate father, M. D'Isigny, goes to the guillotine impersonating her sister, who is married to a condemned French aristocrat.*

In the first of the two extracts that follow, Mathilde's selfish, scatter-brained sister Adèle, while affianced to an English baronet, keeps an assignation with her French lover, and is saved from her father's wrath by her practical and unselfish sister. In the second Mathilde goes to her death from the Abbaye prison when a word from her own lips would have saved her, but to her sister's peril. William, nicknamed the Silent, is the faithful English manservant who has followed her into the French prison.

I

Down in the valley the meadows were deep in grass, across which the tall and thickly-crowded hedgerow elms, now in full leaf, threw dark shadows, which grew ever darker as day waned. The air was faint and rich with the scent of woodbine and meadowsweet, and the gentle air merely moved the flower-spangled grass for one moment, whispered to the leaves, and died into stillness.

The long glorious day succeeding the last of which we have spoken had blazed intself almost into twilight, and the valley was getting more peaceful every minute, when Adèle, quite alone, crossed a cornfield, and passed into a long, dark, and beautiful lane, which led towards an unfrequented ford in the river.

She glided along in her silent, bird-like way, but looked round steathily many times. She, as her sister Mathilde had remarked to herself when she saw her furtive start, was after no good whatever.

'She will get into the most fearful trouble,' thought poor Mathilde. 'She has had a letter in a French hand by the English post. I got close enough to it to see that. It is my firm belief and persuasion that André Desilles has come over, and that she is going to give him an interview. Adèle is really, of all people I ever saw, the least capable of guiding herself. There is an utter want of discretion, an extreme reckless *abandon* about her conduct, which is actually terrible. We shall be well out of this without a fatal duel.'

She followed her instantly.

'I can at all events screen her somewhat by walking home with her. I doubt I shall have to lie a deal over it. It is shameful of André to behave so. Yet it is so singularly unlike him. Poor dear André and I never were friends—at least, I never got on so well with him as I might have—but he was always the most discreet and honourable of mortals. It seems to me an inconceivable thing that he has left his regiment and come here after Adèle, after knowing of her engagement with Sir Lionel Somers. Besides, it never seemed to me that he cared anything for her. I should have thought that he liked me by far the best. Yet, according to Mr Bone, he has been in constant communication with her. I cannot make the matter out completely; only it is evident that Adèle is bent on making a fool of herself, and ruining herself, and must be saved.'

So she followed the unconscious Adèle two fields off. She was quite sure that her walk would end in a painful scene: that there was trouble before her that evening, the greater part of which was sure to fall, somehow or other, on her unlucky head. Yet she was one of those who, as far as they are personally concerned, live in the present mainly. She has a happy habit of making the most of the present, and of leaving the future and the past. Many exceedingly sensitive and conscientious natures have exactly the same habit. Consequently, with illimitable and unknown trouble before her, she improved the present, and, poor soul! to a certain extent, enjoyed herself.

For the early English summer glories had voices, sounds, and scents for her, as much as, nay more than, for the lighter, thinner nature of Adèle. Mathilde could love with a deeper love than Adèle, and she loved De Valognes as Adèle was incapable of loving him. There was not a whisper of the summer wind across the flowered grass, not a scent of rose or woodbine, not a rustle of air among the trees, but what spoke of him, and of her love for him. Her whole great soul was filled with a tender love for him; and as she walked

under the gathering shadows and thought of him, and of the honour
he had done her among all women, her noble face developed a
radiant and glorious beauty, to which that of Adèle was small and
commonplace. Sir Joshua Reynolds was right. She was a wonderfully beautiful woman.

Voices in the lane which led to the ford. She hesitated what to do.
'I had better listen,' she thought. 'I need not tell. I *will* listen,
and I will scold them afterwards. I will break suddenly in on them,
and denounce them. I can look through the hedge here and see
them. I consider myself justified in so doing.'

She looked through the hedge, and then sat quietly down among
the wild parsley, and the arums, and the budding clematis, and the
fading primroses and violets, and put her hand to her head.

They tell one the story of Ginevra, lost to human ken on her
marriage day. They tell us in our own times of a beautiful bride,
lightning-stricken and dead under a sheltering crag. Dead these
two, leaving sorrow to the living. Mathilde lived on.

She had seen Adèle in the arms of De Valognes; she had heard
them interchanging that foolish lovers' babble—indescribable, not
to be translated—of which all of us have had, or shall have,
experience. She saw in an instant that she had been shamefully
deceived, and she sat down, in the lush growth of the English
hedgrow, with her hand upon her forehead.

If it had come to her by degrees; if she had been able to get a
suspicion of the state of affairs, it would have been easier for her to
bear it. But in the full flush of her gentle, honest love for him, she
had found him false, and herself a dreaming fool. Coarse hinds
have a horrible habit of knocking their wives and kicking them on
the head. In all England or in all Ireland no woman was worse
served that day than was Mathilde by the gentle and thoroughly
noble De Valognes.

The two lovers walked away towards the ford: but Mathilde sat
still behind the hedge with her hand on her forehead. 'It is so hard
to die like this, ma'mselle,' said William the Silent to her once.
'Bless you, I have died before this,' she replied; 'it is nothing when
you are accustomed to it. The details may be made more or less
agonizing, but it is only a matter of time, and the result is the same.'

Mathilde had died one of her deaths; and when she arose from
her seat in the hedgerow she felt giddy and ill. Her *self* had hitherto

been her self in relation to De Valognes, and that self was dead; so her own self, being now worthless, dead, and a thing of nought, she began to think more particularly about others.

What would be the first effect of Adèle's indiscretion? To Mathilde, with her ideas of propriety, the indiscretion was something absolutely monstrous and unheard-of; it was immeasurable. She had deceived her—that was nothing; but she had deceived her father, and had most shamefully deceived Sir Lionel Somers. What on earth was to be done? Discovery was almost certain, and then—

She determined most positively at once that she would lend herself no longer to the systematic deceit which was being practised on Sir Lionel. 'I never heard anything so monstrous in my life,' she said; 'Adèle's conduct transcends human belief. I will not lend myself to this deceit any longer; it must end. Yet I must save her somehow.'

Adèle rarely or never walked out by herself. Others beside Mathilde must have seen the way she went, and it was growing from twilight to dark. She would be missed and followed. Suppose her father should follow her. Which came first—the idea in her brain, or the sight of M. D'Isigny approaching in a leisurely manner three fields off? They came so quick one on the other, that she never could decide. Others beside herself had watched Adèle, and had given M. D'Isigny the route. He was not far off now, straight on the track.

Supposed she were to lie perfectly still now. Would it not serve them right? How would it end? De Valognes would be reprimanded furiously, and would most likely rebel, and Adèle would be sent to a nunnery. She could well revenge herself on them now by merely remaining quiet; but she had no spirit. She wanted spirit sadly in one way; and there were her father's broad shoulders advancing steadily and inexorably through the standing corn.

So she went through a gap in the hedge and confronted them. They were not in the least degree surprised or taken aback. No one cared for old Mathilde: she was nobody. De Valognes held out both his hands towards her, and when she was near enough took her in his arms and kissed her. She submitted quite quietly. Was he not her cousin?

'You must fly, Louis,' she said quietly and earnestly. 'My father is at the end of that field, and is coming straight towards us.'

'Now we are all undone together,' cried Adèle, pulling her beautiful hair in sheer desperation. 'Now, I *do* wish I was dead. Now, I wish I had never been born. Now, I wish that I was with my mother at Dinan. Now we are all undone together. My father will kill Louis, and I shall be sent to a nunnery and be *ennuyée* to death; and it is all thy fault, thou false and cruel sister. Thou has followed me, and by doing so hast given our father the route.'

Mathilde took no notice of her. She turned to Louis De Valognes. 'Time is very short,' she said; 'my father approaches. You must fly and hide. What do your eyes say, then—that you scorn it? You can add nothing to your deep dishonour, not if you were to hide under the manger in a stable. Your honour is gone, yet I believe that you love *her*. Think of the consequences to her if you remain here one instant longer.'

Louis de Valognes went at once. He was taken by surprise at her appearance, at her words, and at the voice of his own conscience. Three minutes afterwards M. D'Isigny entered the lane, and approaching the ford, saw his two daughters.

Adèle was sitting on the bank, weaving a garland of clematis round her hat. Mathilde had got off her shoes and stockings, and was washing her feet in the river. His steady persistent bullying made them as false as this.

M. D'Isigny found it necessary to account for his situation. He had no right to follow and watch his daughters, and he felt it now. His daughters, I regret to say, did not help him out of his difficulty. Adèle invoked the archangel St Michael, in her surprise, quite vaguely, as the first saint, and, of course, the most entirely un-appropriate one, who happened to come into her giddy head. Mathilde, with a vague impression of being near a ford, somewhat more logically invoked St Christopher, and began putting on her stockings. Between them both M. D'Isigny was thoroughly puzzled.

And he deceived them on his part. He affected a pleasant surprise at meeting them, and asked for their company home, which was most willingly accorded. So those three walked home together through the gloaming, each of them feeling very guilty towards the other, and all extremely afraid of one another. Under the circumstances, I need hardly say, that they were most ostenta-tiously agreeable and affectionate. Adèle was in a state of fairy-like airy gaiety and innocence; Mathilde, with her aching heart, walked beside her father, and talked with her usual calm sensible logic about the new-born revolution, about politics generally, about religion. As for M. D'Isigny, he surpassed himself. He was dignified and conciliatory; he was mildly dictatorial, yet tolerant. He opened up the storehouse of his mind, and displayed its treasures to Mathilde. There was not much to see there, but he showed it off well. He discoursed beautifully about the beauties of nature, which were spread about their path in every direction; pointing them out with his walking-stick. He pointed out to Mathilde that Nature was now in her creative mood, but in a few months more would pass into her destructive mood; from which he deduced the beautiful moral that life was short, and that you should cull the blossoms while they grew; with a great deal more nonsense, equally original and important. Mathilde pretended to listen to this balderdash with rapt attention, while Adèle danced on before them, and strewed their path with wild flowers, plucked in the innocent gaiety of her heart. It would have been uncommonly nice if either of the three had believed in it.

As it was, three self-convicted and self-conscious humbugs arrived at the door of Sheepsden together, and parted—Adèle to her bower, with a worn, old, ay, cruel and vindictive look in her beautiful face, wondering what Mathilde would do, or what she would say; M. D'Isigny to his reading-lamp, to ponder over what could possibly have taken his daughters to the ford, and what trick they were serving him; Mathilde to Father Martin's room, to lay the whole truth before him, in sheer desperation.

2

William the Silent, with his rat-catching cunning, caught a little mouse, which in its hunger he tamed, and gave to the bright-headed beauty. And it pleased her, and she lay on the stone bench, with her head now on her sister's lap, now on Mathilde's, playing with her little mouse, until Paris was in white hot wrath, and Brunswick over the frontiers.

The weather was as white and hot, and fierce as were the Parisians, and the smell which Mr Dickens, in his 'Tale of Two Cities', calls 'the smell of imprisoned sleep,' was hot and heavy. Yet there came no change. The elder sister sewed, and the younger sister played with her mouse. The Comtesse D'Aurilliac sat and glowered with her hands on her stomach, from time to time patiently taking up the stitches in her sister's knitting. The men of the imprisoned party were as polite, and the main part of the women as frivolous as ever; but there was no sign of a change.

Prisoners behind narrow-barred windows in a street have little opportunity for seeing the thunderstorm, which is to crash into their prison and burst their bonds, thrust up its cumulus above the horizon.

These poor people in the Abbaye did not really *believe* that anything violent or sudden would happen. They certainly said all day that their lives were in danger, and that they would lay them down at any moment; but few of them actually believed it. I should fancy (who can know ?) that the only man in the Abbaye who knew the danger, was Journiac de St Meard, who had looked on the Revolution, and had wept in his French way over the stark body of André Desilles.

Then came a day as all days come—a day which makes itself a day for a whole life. The boat goes down the river, and a dripping, frightened man comes back and tells of the disaster. The horse goes out, and there comes back a terrified groom. The carriage goes out, and the footman comes back white with horror. These supreme days come in the midst of the most carefully-tended luxuriousness, in accidents, in paralytic strokes, and such matters. Death marches in, triumphant over Luxury at all times.

If in times of perfect luxury and perfect peace such days come on us suddenly and swiftly, ruining and altering the current of lives, it is not to be thought violent or extraordinary that such a day should come upon our three watchers in prison, in a time of Revolution.

There are, I think, few of our readers who have not seen such a day: a day when death or extreme danger comes to the door, and when it is necessary not only to think but to act. The supreme day came to Journiac de St Meard, to Mathilde, and to William, in this manner.

At twelve o'clock Mathilde was sitting in the little room which she possessed with the two sisters, when Journiac de St Meard, with

William the Silent, came to the door and called her out. When she went out to them they motioned to her and shut the door behind her. When she looked on their faces she saw danger if not disaster. She was used to men, and she knew the look which comes on the face of brave men when there is danger abroad. They were both, Frenchman and Englishman, perfectly calm, but very pale. St Meard had his hand on the shoulder of the English groom, and was the spokesman.

'Mademoiselle Mathilde, there is serious trouble.'

'I read that in your faces. Can you trust me with the extent of it?'

'Can you trust yourself to our guidance?'

'Most heartily,' said Mathilde. 'I always want guidance, you know.'

'Then come with us,' said St Meard. And Mathilde went quietly and willingly.

They took her up a corridor to a bench at the end; and they all three sat down in a row.

'Well,' said Mathilde, 'I am going to be perfectly obedient, and perfectly submissive, for I know you two, and you are good. How much are you going to tell me?'

'Not much. This much, however. There is being made a partition of prisoners, and there should be no confusion.'

'You mean, I see, that the two sisters are to be removed; and that you think that I had better not take leave of them.'

'That is the case exactly,' said St Meard. 'Do not trouble yourself to take leave of them. They are going to liberty. Do not take leave of them.'

'Why?' said Mathilde.

Of all the whys ever uttered, this must have been one of the most difficult to answer. St Meard only said—

'You will meet them again; and your seeing them now would give rise to complications.'

And Mathilde said—

'I am content, as I always was. I trust you two.'

And after that she sat on the stone bench and talked, first only *causeries*. 'I hope that that foolish and fat old Comtesse d'Aurilliac will be put in the same prison with her good sister. That old woman of the cloister, her sister, would die if she were separated from her now. I hope, also, that they will not separate my two sisters, for they are as necessary to one another as are those two old women. For me, with my secret kept, *I* am safe. I hold but one life in my hands, for Lionel will mourn, but will not die.'

William went away, and she was left alone, sitting wearily on the stone bench, with Journiac de St Meard walking up and down before her.

'St Meard,' she said, boldly, 'I see two things very plainly.'

'And what are those, Mademoiselle ?'

'I see first,' said she, 'that you admire me—that you love me!'

'It is true.'

'I love you also. I love you very deeply. But that part of a woman's heart which is given to sentimental love will never be yours. It is given to an Englishman, Sir Lionel Somers, quite beyond recall.'

He bowed and said.

'I always supposed this. I was prepared for it. Yet I may minister to you ?'

She said only, 'Yes.'

'May I ask,' said St Meard, 'what is the second thing which you have seen in my face ?'

'Death!' she said. 'I have looked on death more than once, and I saw it in your eyes when you brought me here to this stone bench: and I saw it in the eyes of my poor old groom, William. Tell me, are my pretty sisters killed ?'

Such a dreadfully downright woman, this Mathilde of ours, forcing even Journiac to lie: for he said—

'I suspect that they have been ordered to the *Conciergerie*.'

William came back, and told her that she could go to her room again now. And she went to her room; but the sisters were not there.

William and St Meard had been, with a crowd of other prisoners, looking out of the window at the often described September assassinations: about which we will say as little as possible. I would not have wished to come to them, but the St Malo story brings me here, and I must go on. These two strangely-contrasted men—the dandy brave French soldier and the stolid English groom—had been watching this horrible affair from the same window.

The women had been kept from that window; but the men had crowded round it, and had watched one fall after another. There had been a strange discussion among them as to how they should act when their turn came. It was agreed, after the witnessing of many examples, that the difficulty of dying was only increased by trying to defend your head, and that the best way was to walk slowly, and put your hands behind your back.

'You see Bardot, down there?' said St Meard.

William saw him, and saw something else also. Saw, for instance, that the assassins, backed by a very slight crowd, were mainly on the right of the door; and that on the left of the door there were comparatively few of them. He saw also that the door was in the extreme left of the building, and that from time to time people came round the corner of the building, under the pepper-box turret, and either ran swiftly across the street, or turned back with shrieks (perhaps Dr Moore was one of them). He pointed this out to St Meard, and asked him if there was a 'right of way' round the corner.

When St Meard understood him he answered, 'Yes'. That he knew the place well. It was the *Allée des pas perdus*, and at the end were two turnings; to the right you found yourself in the *cul-de-sac* of the *Allee d'Enfer*, to the left you went straight into the *Rue de la Bonne Garde*. Which William remembered.

This young man also remembered about a certain rowing or scolding which he had got from D'Isigny one time. There had been a prize-fight in the Stour Valley, and that good-for-nothing old Martin, the poacher, had tempted William from his allegiance to go and see it. This prize fight had ended suddenly and fatally by a blow on the jugular vein; at which D'Isigny had rejoiced, because it had not only enabled him to point his moral against William more venomously, but had enabled him to bully Mathilde as an open encourager of assassins, instancing old Martin and Marat as two cases in point. This prize-fight came into William's head now; but he said nothing.

After a time they went back to Mathilde's door. They knocked; she told them in a calm, clear voice to come in. She had just risen from her knees, and had Lady Somers' missal before her.

'My dear friends,' she said, 'will they come for me to-night? Do you think I might go to bed?'

St Meard, seeing her noble and beautiful face set so coolly and so calmly, took a sudden resolution, like a Frenchman.

'Mademoiselle, no!'

'May I know what is happening?'

'Mademoiselle, yes. They are assassinating the prisoners. I have some dim hopes that I can plead successfully for my life, in consequence of my behaviour at Nanci when your cousin, André Desilles, was killed. This young man, from his absolute innocence, may escape; but it is doubtful. You, in your assumed character as Marquise de Valognes, must inevitably die.'

'I promised my father that I would die mute, and I will die mute,' said Mathilde.

'Mademoiselle, listen to me again. I am Provençal, and one of the jailors is my friend, for I speak his language. I know more than another. I know this. Danton and the secret Committee of the Commune have, through Marat, been removing prisoners to save them from this danger. You have not been removed, because Marat thinks that you are your sister: Marat has saved many on his own responsibility, and even now, if you declare yourself, he could save you.* You are provided with witnesses to your identity. This young man, myself, and my Provençal, who would swear, if I told him, that the devil went to mass and drunk nothing stronger than holy water. We would answer for the fact that you are not the Marquise de Valognes, who is suspected of being carrier-pigeon between Brittany and Coblentz, but her innocent sister, who has been living quietly in England.'

'That is all very well,' said Mathilde; 'but you do not consider my sister.'

'She is perfectly safe,' said St Meard.

'Indeed, she is not. I came here to France to fulfil a promise to my father, and I shall fulfil it.'

St Meard knelt at her feet.

'I implore you, Mademoiselle, to listen to reason.'

'You have no right to kneel to me, M. St Meard. I am *fiancée* to Sir Lionel Somers.'

'I will betray you,' said St Meard, rising furiously.

'You will not do so. In the first place, you gave me your honour as a gentleman that you would do nothing of the kind: in the second place, no one would believe you.'

* This mercy of Marat's individually rests, as far as I am concerned, on the authority of Lamartine. I believe in it myself.

He argued again and again, and William in his way argued also. But she said, first and last, 'You weary me, you two. I promised my father.' And so after a time they sat still, and saw her pray.

At last she said, 'Here they come'; and they came. The door was partly open, and the first person who entered was a large dog, who went to the water pitcher and lapped. Then came four men in slouched hats (like broad-leaved wideawakes), and then a neat man in breeches and a cutaway coat, and the cocked hat with which we are all familiar in the pictures of Napoleon.

'The woman calling herself the Marquise de Valognes?' said the well-dressed man.

'I am she,' said old Mathilde.

'Follow.'

And she followed, and St Meard and William followed also, but on the stairs there was a difficulty. Mathilde turned to St Meard.

'This missal,' she said; 'may he have it, to give to my sister?'

'It is a case for the tribunal,' said the well-dressed man; 'we know of no missals.'

The night was late when they got downstairs into the main passage or hall which led to the street. What need is there to describe it here? You may see the scene for yourselves in many books, among others in Knight's *Popular History of England*. A table with ruffians, guards with pikes, brandy-bottles on the side-table. The president, the awful 'man in grey', who strangely turns out to be no other than our old acquaintance 'Huissier' Maillard, interrogated her.

'You are the *soi-disante* Marquise de Valognes?'

'I am the *soi-disante* Marquise de Valognes,' she answered, firmly; and thought, 'I shall not die with a lie on my lips, after all.'

'You are accused of plotting at that hell on earth, Montauban, against the nation. You are accused of carrying news from Brittany to Coblentz. There is enough against you to destroy a hundred, for the nation is angry. It is accused against you that your lover, the Englishman there, and that she-wolf, your mother, have been conspiring with *émigrés* at Coblentz. What have you to say?'

'That you lie,' said Mathilde, pale with fury and scorn.

They told her to stand back, and she turned towards William, and slightly shivered, for William had done a strange thing, to her inexplicable. I beg your pardon for telling you these things, but I have begun, and must perforce finish.

William stood before her, with nothing on him but his breeches, his stockings, and his shirt. A loose-mouthed patriot, Jean Bon, who had once guided her father to Marat, remarked—

'Le citoyen se dérobe.'

'Malbrook s'en va-t-en guerre,' said Mathilde, which did her no good.

'William,' she said, 'why have you taken off your clothes?'

'It is so hard to die like this.'

'I have died before now,' she said, and turned to the table, for they called her.

'A La Force!'

'I am the friend of the people: I am the friend of Marat; but I cannot make my case good, and so—see, you men, I forgive you all.'

'I will compromise you by no messages,' said Mathilde to St Meard; 'but if you live to see any one whom I loved, tell them I love them still.'

So she went down the steps, carrying her missal, and entering the dark passage was lost to sight.

XXX

1869–70

'*My most industrious brother*,' *Charles once wrote of Henry; and no wonder. Driven by financial need, he followed* Mademoiselle Mathilde *with two books in 1869, neither a success. 'Illness and worry are not pleasant companions for the desk.'* Stratton, *set in Shropshire, displayed a feeble plot and stilted dialogue. In* Tales of Old Travel *he retold a number of adventure stories, ranging from Marco Polo's sojourn at the court of Kublai Khan to lesser known exploits such as those of Peter Carder, one of Drake's seamen; D'Ermenonville, botanist to Louis XVI, who took cochineal from Mexico to St Domingo; Robert Everard, a cabin boy marooned in Madagascar naked and defenceless who survived for three years as an outcast; Alvaro Nunez, the first European to see the Mississippi after captivity among Seminole Indians; and seven Dutch seamen who perished miserably from scurvy and starvation on the Arctic island of Jan Mayen in 1633. Henry was harsh to these unfortunate men. Recording their hopeless attempts to doctor themselves for scurvy he remarks: 'When folks in difficult situations begin thinking about their health and talking about their insides, it is all up with them. The United States were not founded, India was not conquered, nor Australia settled, by such men as these.'*

At this low ebb in his fortunes, Henry was lucky to be appointed editor of the Daily Review, *organ of the Free Church party in Edinburgh. In 1869 he sold his much-loved house at Wargrave and moved north. Contemporaries did not, apparently, consider him a good editor. An anonymous critic judged his leaders 'dictatorial, self-complacent, egotistical and ungrammatical'. He was by nature a lone observer and reporter, not the master of a pack. In 1870 the Franco-Prussian war gave him a fresh opportunity. He appointed himself war correspondent, and for a brief eight weeks sent back a stream of vivid, first-hand and even poetic despatches. 'The dead men look so pretty from a little distance; they group themselves as they fall.' (They wore their brilliant blue and scarlet uniforms.*) '*When glory is reduced to a handsome young Frenchman screaming himself to death in bed, Glory looks uncommonly small.*' '*I laid myself down amidst the grass on the hill to look at Metz and to examine Thionville. . . . There came a whispering wind through the grass: but it was not what I had come to hear; there came a wandering bee, but he knew naught of war and flew away again; there was perfect silence for an hour, and then the church bells began to ring, just as if there was no devil's game ready in sight of any of their steeples.*' On 1 September, 1870, he saw the fall of Sedan and was the first correspondent, with a colleague from The Times, to enter the town—'*through an open sewer with our bodies bent and our hats off.*' The French defeat moved him deeply. '*I am reading the end of a very old tale; here is the beginning of the end of poor old France, dear to us still in spite of all her crimes and follies.*'

XXXI

The Boy in Grey
Valentin
1871-2

On his return to Edinburgh Henry cast his impressions into a more permanent form, first in the story Malmaison *printed in a collection called* The Boy in Grey, *and then in a tale for boys called* Valentin, *published in 1872. According to his niece Mary, Henry was an excellent water-colour artist who 'looked at the beauty of the external world with the eye of a worshipper'; but unlike his brother he wrote little verse. The following lyric, interpolated into the story* The Boy in Grey, *suggests that had he done so he might at least have equalled, and perhaps excelled, his brother.*

The Blackbird's Song

Magdalen at Michael's Gate
  Tirled at the pin;
On Joseph's thorn sang the blackbird
  'Let her in! Let her in!'

'Hast thou seen the wounds?' said Michael,
  'Know'st thou thy sin?'
'It is evening, evening,' sang the blackbird.
  'Let her in! Let her in!'

'Yes, I heve seen the wounds
  And I know my sin.'
'She knows it well, well, well,' sang the blackbird.
  'Let her in! Let her in!'

'Thou bring'st no offerings ?' said Michael,
   'Naught save sin ?'
And the blackbird sang 'She is sorry, sorry, sorry;
   Let her in! Let her in!'

When he had sung himself to sleep
   And the night did begin,
One came and opened Michael's Gate,
   And Magdalen went in.

Valentin relates the adventures, told in the first person, of the son of a rich merchant of Sedan who is sent by his father through the Ardennes into Luxembourg, some two years before the outbreak of the Franco-Prussian war, to discover the intentions and dispositions of the Prussian army. After a series of fantastic and, indeed, absurd adventures, involving the Carbonari of the forest, wolves, spying, and even a conversation with the king of Prussia, Moltke and Bismarck, Valentin returns to his father, who removes his entire fortune to Germany, foreseeing the French defeat. Valentin, a Frenchman to the core, distinguishes himself at the École Militaire, marries his sweetheart and is commissioned into a regiment of Hussars, all by the age of eighteen. After more fantastic adventures he wins glory on the field of Sedan and, severely wounded and a prisoner, is nursed back to health by his wife, who reaches the battlefield disguised as a drummer-boy and shortly afterwards gives birth to a son. Freed by the king of Prussia, Valentin returns to his father's house just in time to save his family, aided by the last-minute arrival of a detachment of Prussians, from being obliterated by a rabble of Carbonari; and so the story ends.

Whether this farrago really appealed to young British readers it is impossible to say, but by means of its curious mixture of short, jerky sentences and long discursive asides on the complexities of European politics, Henry endeavoured to present the French spirit, French bitterness in defeat and French patriotism in a French idiom; his purpose transcended that of entertaining boys. It was written with strong feeling but evidently in a hurry and is full of wild improbabilities and loose ends. By this time Henry had lost his editorship—'the paper is not paying and they want a cheaper editor'—and retreated south to London where he rented a house at 24 Bernard Street, near Russell Square, for two years, and tried to live by his pen. His energies did not

*slacken, but his work deteriorated and his health began to give way. In
1871, besides* The Boy in Grey, *he published* Old Margaret, *a fantasy
in some respects anticipating* Peter Pan, *and a slight tale* Hetty. *The
following year saw* The Harveys *as well as* Valentin.

I

You can put your horse at a gallop over those lovely cultivated
downs in Lorraine and Champagne, and ride as straight as an eagle
flies. We know that to our ruin. The subdivision of land has made
every inch of ground valuable, and so we have no hedges at all. I
should like to see a German army advancing through the county
of Kent, just for curiosity's sake, before the volunteers of three
counties. I am under the impression that I would back the volunteers if they were properly handled.

Give them proper organization and proper recognition, and they
would play very heavy mischief with an invading army till your
regular army was ready (which it seldom is). As for your regular
army, they were made to conquer, and they always have conquered.
You English have scarcely a disaster to show out of America. I can
only remember two, both in Holland.

I had a fancy that the air of Champagne made the wine, for as I
rode (by the compass) the air was blowing from the pearly blue
hills of Champagne, far to the right, and I felt as though I had
drank a bottle of Moet or Veuve Cliquot. My horse was a splendid
beast, French bred, for he had the blood of his sire Monarque in his
veins, and his granddam was Blink Bonny. He had been crossed
into the grand Norman blood, and was heavier than a race-horse,
but had possibly more terrible powers of endurance.

I think that in your Life Guards the horses are a little too small
for the men, though they are unsurpassed as cavalry horses. It is
not that the horses are too small, but the men are too large.

This horse of mine, Rataplan, could carry me as a racehorse
carries a jockey. I was only ten stone as I rode, your Life Guards
ride fifteen; and Rataplan (to use your calculation) stood nearly
eighteen hands. I should have ridden straight through the Chasseurs
d'Afrique, with their pretty, weedy little Arabs.

I rode very hard, and towards evening I came to a little solitary farm, a rare thing in those parts, where the farmers live in the large villages; and so, in case of an invasion, put, to speak in a military sense, all their eggs in one basket. There was a very pretty maiden watering the cows, and as I am very fond of all maidens, pretty or otherwise (as I hope you are), I determined to alight here and get my horse fed.

She was very glad to see a French uniform. It was the first she had seen for twelve hours.

This seemed very ominous.

'You see,' she said, as I was taking the saddle off, 'that the good Emperor is tempting these dogs of Prussians on in order to destroy them; so I suppose that we shall have them here.'

'Are you afraid of them?'

'I! Not I. I was in Trèves, for a year, and was always among them. They are barbarians, and talk a savage language which I never could learn; but they are kind dogs enough. The people at St Privat and Ste Marie are afraid of them. Not I. Possibly one of them may try to give me a beery kiss, in which case I should slap his face, just as I should yours, if you offered to do it, and we should part friends.'

I said, 'I should accept that challenge if I were not married.'

'It is impossible; yet I think it must be true; young as monsieur looks, or he would have given me reason to smack his face.'

We both laughed. She was such a very pretty, plucky girl that I felt anxious about her. When we were in the stable together feeding my horse, I urged her to fly.

She said,

'No. My grandmother and I keep this farm, the men have gone away, and I got my grandmother away this morning.'

'Do you mean to say that you are going to remain alone here?' I said, aghast.

'Most certainly,' she said. 'Am I not a Frenchwoman? And you mistake the Germans. They will not hurt me, I know, the sentimental fools.'

'They are plundering in every direction,' I said.

'That is very likely,' she replied, coolly. 'I have heard of the French, nay, even of the saintly English doing the same thing. If they plunder me they will not get very rich; for if they can find my grandmother's gold (of which there is a good deal), it is more than

I can. I know that she has hidden it in the house, but where, I have not the least idea. Come in and eat while your horse is eating.'

She gave me cheese and wine. While I was eating, I said,—

'Did your grandmother desert you?'

'No; she is a very clever old woman. She, as an old Alsation, knew the Germans, and I knew that I was a better guard for the house than twenty hot-headed men. If our two men had stayed (which they did not) we should have had a fracas, and might have had the house burnt down. My grandmother would not tell me where the gold was, lest some riotous men of our own nation should force me to tell. Eat fast, the Uhlans cannot be far off. Pierre Leroy saw them ten miles off at one o'clock. I will go and saddle your horse for you.'

'Mais, mademoiselle?'

'Yes. Be tranquil. You must rest. Where are you going?'

'To Ste Marie aux Chênes.'

'You must ride hard. If you have despatches, read them and burn them here and now.'

'I carry no despatches on paper, I have them in my head.'

'*Bon.* Look out at the door, and let me serve France by saddling your horse.'

'I cannot bear it.'

'Please let me serve France, monsieur,' she said.

How could I help it? She would do it, and Bayard himself could not have resisted her. She brought my horse round, and then she made me hold him while she rolled up my cloak with the red side outwards.

She then put it over my right shoulder and under my left arm, and then she tied the ends with a piece of string under my left arm. I saw that my left arm and my right arm were quite free, and that the thick rolled cloak covered my heart.

'I learnt that at Trèves,' she said, laughing. 'By heavens! here they are. Take this kiss to madame your wife, and go for the sake of her.'

I kissed her, but I would not leave her until she urged me in such a way that I could not refuse. Then I left her.

There were those two black specks on the hill before us, which I knew well to be the terrible Uhlans. I rode straight towards them, and when I was within pistol shot of them I waved a white handkerchief. They both trotted towards me at once. I wheeled and covered them with my Deane and Adam's revolver, knowing perfectly well that I could bring down both their horses. I cried out, 'Ein, Ein!'

One fellow, a very nice young fellow indeed, came forward towards me. I talked to him in German. I told him that our pickets were close by (as indeed they were, though I did not know it), but that I was very anxious about the farm in the valley below, as it was held by a solitary young lady. I hoped that they would respect her splendid courage.

The young man said frankly that they did not make war against women, and that I might be well assured.

I nodded to him and sped away.

But I must tell you the end of this episode. Affairs had not heated themselves at that time, and there was much chivalry among outposts. As for German chivalry towards women, I think that has never been disputed. But among the soldiers there was but little anger at this time.

As I heard afterwards, within an hour after I rode away towards Ste Marie aux Chênes, two squadrons of cavalry rode up to and surrounded this young French girl's farm. The officer in command drew up bareheaded in the entrance to the farmyard, and called on the owner to come out.

The pretty solitary girl came out and confronted him.

'I am all alone, monsieur,' she said.

'So we have been given to understand,' said the German. 'In consequence of the necessity of war we must spend the night here.'

'All is yours.'

'Mademoiselle exaggerates with the politeness of her nation. Nothing is ours. Will mademoiselle point out to us the apartments which she desires to keep? If there is a battle I cannot insure mademoiselle; until that happens I can. If any of my soldiers offer rudeness to you, will you please mention it to *me*?'

There were three hundred and twenty men quartered in her house that night, and not one would stay covered as she passed in and out. All the chivalry of their nature was aroused by her fearless courage and trust in the German respect for women and children. They hurrahed to her as they went away, and the officer, who stayed last and had calculated the cost, offered her the money for the things which they had bought of her. She burst into tears, and said, as she handed it back to him—

'Pour les pauvres prisonniers, monsieur. Pour les pauvres prisonniers de la France.'

The house was held sacred after that. No battle was fought there: but it passed from battalion to battalion of the Germans. That one heroic girl had stayed behind in the farm when all the men had fled. She was a herione among the Germans.

Strong feeling was manifested against her by the French. She was accused of being a German spy, and of more things than I dare write. A Bavarian sergeant, it is said, won her heart while he was lying wounded at Briey. I know not how true that may be, but her end was very sad. She had to go to a violently French village not far from the Belgian frontier, on business for her grandmother. She was known there, and was insulted by several young men. She had to go out to a house outside the village after dark, but she never reached it. She was brutally murdered, it is supposed, from all that can be gathered, by a mob of revolutionists, for a German spy, and the end is too painful to tell.

2

They moved so suddenly and sharply that we were not ready for them. I could see the stars still when it began. The 17th were sleeping in the potato and onion field on the left off the road when I rode up. My horse, Rataplan, stepped gingerly among the sleeping bodies, and I found the Colonel of the 17th on horseback and smoking. I gave him General Ducrot's orders, and he read them.

'Lieutenant,' he said, 'my men are as tired as dogs; the Saxons also must be tired; you are well mounted; ride across those two fields, and see what you can. Bugler, sound réveille.'

My ride was never accomplished; I got to the little hedge above the cutting in the road just as the bugler blew, and I saw four young men, without their boots, rise from the straw in which they were lying, and look sleepily about them. The next instant the devil's game began.

Within two hundreds yards a terrible but not continuous volley of musketry poured in on us from the Saxons. The four men near me went down at once. I was not hit, strange to say, but of the four men sleeping in the *paille*, only one rose again. He was bareheaded and in his stockinged feet. He began to fire rapidly across the cutting, and I saw a tall Saxon, a nice-looking young gentleman, roll off his horse sideways, with his hands to his head. My instinct told me that he was dead, and I was sorry for him, for, after all, our quarrel was not with the Saxons, but with the Prussians. I fired as rapidly as I could with my revolver, with the solitary pair of red breeches before me; I knew my young man was badly wounded, and I called to him to come to the rear, but he would not. We were now partly protected by the little hedge, and I kept my horse's nose carefully against a poplar tree. My wounded young man also seemed to me to know what he was about, for he kept his head very carefully behind another poplar tree. How well I know those poplar trees now!

It was three minutes before the regiment was aroused. During that time the young man and I were simply fighting the whole of the 29th regiment of Saxons. It was no deed of heroism at all; they had nothing to fire at except us two, and as we were behind trees they could not hit us. I heard my young man laughing.

Then I saw the ghastly steel blue line of the Saxon rifles go to the shoulder, and so I knew that our 17th were in fighting order now. I gave one glance behind, only one, and I saw two or three strange things, as I was loading my revolver.

The 17th regiment was coming on in line, through the potato field. The Colonel was leading in the centre on a tall chestnut horse. The sun had scarcely risen, but the light of the morning was on their tired hungry faces.

Then I looked behind the Colonel, and I saw my own father's house.

Then I saw before me a German staff officer in blue, and I saw that men were coming with spades. 'Are they going to bring artillery to their centre?' I thought. Prussians would never do that. They were pitching the earth about, however. I fired six shots at the staff officer, but I could not hit him. I rode to the next tree where the young man was, and I said,

'Pick off that staff officer.'

'I can't hit him,' said the young man; 'he is covered.'

'Run out,' I said, 'to the next tree. I can't hit him with this

English revolver. Try that for old France; if it is suddenly done the chances are two hundred to one in your favour: you will cover him from the next tree.'

I rode with him from the one tree to the other, and gave him a hold of my stirrup. My horse was hit through the neck, but the young man, who kept his face averted from me, never reached the other tree, and never killed the Saxon officer. The horrible affray was well on between the two regiments now, and I saw my young man throw away his rifle, and hang heavily on to my stirrup.

Then, for the first time, he turned his face to mine, and fell dead.

Oh, heaven, send up pity in this wicked world! It was my brother Mark. Gained only to be lost!

XXXII

Finis

Henry's sales never recovered and life became a long struggle against poverty. He went on trying to borrow from Charles, and Sarah wrote what Fanny called 'money letters', and which she resented. Charles himself was no longer turning out best-sellers and, in Henry's words, 'the fount of willing aid dropped'. In 1873 he brought out Oakshott Castle, *a phantasmagoria involving mermen, mermaids and a great deal of nonsense; Henry himself admitted the plot to be 'a little startling'. 'It is life and death to me,' he wrote; but it fell flat. A mystery novel,* Reginald Hetherage, *followed, with no greater success.*

In 1874 the Henry Kingsleys moved to Kentish Town, then semi-rural and little better than a slum. Charles died, the fount dried up altogether and no help could be expected from Fanny, even if she had been able to afford it. As for George, he was nearly always abroad on his travels, leaving his wife and two young children to get along as best they could in their small house in Highgate with only one front window and a long strip of garden behind, where George's daughter Mary kept her fighting cocks. If you could penetrate into the interior, Mary recalled, 'you found in every room curiosities, from all manner of strange places, battling for space with the Transactions of half a dozen learned societies and books innumerable'; and in the attic it was 'probable you would have seen Henry Kingsley writing a novel; for he had sanctuary always in that house, and fled often to that upper chamber to escape from barrel organs and watercress women and divers disagreeable things that abounded to his distraction in Kentish Town; but, if the day was sunny, it is more probable still that Henry Kingsley would have been found enveloped in a blue haze of tobacco smoke, basking on the lawn, where he would have told you such tales of corroborees, black snakes, and bushrangers as would have made sleep a curse to you for a week to come.'

At last even this refuge failed. Cancer of the throat and tongue was

FINIS

diagnosed; the Kingsleys moved to a cottage at Cuckfield in Sussex to await Henry's death. Four more books appeared, the last posthumously. They made no mark and even less money; when he died on 24 May, 1876, aged forty-six, his estate was valued at £450. Sarah, an intelligent and perhaps unhappy woman—'her views', observed a contemporary, 'were certainly in advance of her time'—survived her husband by forty-six years.

PART THREE

GEORGE KINGSLEY
1826–92

XXXIII

George Kingsley

Notes on Sport and Travel

1899

The Rev. Charles Kingsley's fourth son, George, was born at Barnack rectory on 14 February, 1826. Two boys came between him and Charles the eldest: Herbert, born in 1820, who died of rheumatic fever when a fourteen-year-old schoolboy, and Gerald, born in 1821, who met a dreadful end at the age of twenty-three as a lieutenant in the Royal Navy. His ship, the gunboat Royalist, *was stationed in the Gulf of Carpentaria and completely ignored by the Admiralty for eighteen months, her crew 'roasting, rotting, and pining in her day after day', as Mary Kingsley wrote: and also dying, one by one. Gerald was the last of the officers to perish, and it was left to the boatswain to bring the leaking vessel into Singapore with her few survivors. The Admiralty's indifference extended to notifying next of kin; the news reached Gerald's father in the Chelsea public library, where he overheard a stranger remark: 'Dreadful bad business this about the* Royalist—*every single officer on board her dead—those who did not die of fever were eaten by cannibals.' The rector, who had adored his son, fainted away.*

A splendid career in medicine seemed open to George after his success as senior prizeman in anatomy at St George's Hospital in 1843 and when he qualified, still only twenty-one years old, at Edinburgh in 1847. He was a small man, five-foot-seven and lightly built: gay, goodlooking, versatile and able, 'the happiest of the three brothers', according to his daughter Mary. There was 'something wonderfully attractive even in the appearance of this lithe, square-shouldered man. His strong, mobile face was sunburnt and weather-beaten like the face of a sailor; his fearless, brilliant gray eyes looked right into the hearts of those who spoke with him; his whole form was alert and instinct with the warm, passionate spirit of life; and his conversation, ranging easily through every subject from philosophy to fishing, full of dry humour and flashing with brilliant wit and trenchant repartee, had a charm which was absolutely irresistible.' But she admitted that his 'awful temper' prompted him to hurl books at her head, and kept his family on tenterhooks during his brief and periodic sojourns in the small house in Highgate which he took after his marriage, in 1860, to Mary Bailey—'a lady', according to her daughter, of 'extraordinary benevolence' with a good head for business.

What their daughter Mary did not admit, but which the record makes plain, is that, for all his charm, he was very selfish. Rather than buckle to his chosen profession, heal the sick and keep company with his family, he gallivanted to every corner of the earth in attendance on one wealthy peer after another, enjoying himself to the hilt: sailing, shooting, fishing; surviving shipwrecks and grizzly bears, and narrowly escaping the tomahawks of Indian braves.

Three years after becoming a Doctor of Medicine, spent partly in further medical studies in Paris, he took service as private physician to the first Marquis of Aylesbury, and then performed the same office successively for the Duke of Norfolk, the Duke of Sutherland, the first and then the second Earl of Ellesmere. Enjoying the run of their libraries as well as of their deer forests and grouse moors, he accumulated a vast fund of knowledge, alike in natural history and in the byways of scholarship, which he was always intending to put to some use —a historical novel, translations from the German, a catalogue of Elizabethan dramas—but which somehow never got completed. There were too many temptations. 'I am here.' he wrote from Lairg in Sutherland to Alexander Macmillan, 'slaughtering salmon, stags, and fowl at a most fearful rate. I am either in the river or on the hill from six in the morning till nine at night, so you can readily imagine that I have not time left for mental work: indeed, I am so utterly insane about questions of wild Highland sport that I can produce, think, and dream of nothing else.'

Sport and a delight in nature remained his ruling passions. With true Kingsley enthusiasm he responded to the glory of skies and sunsets, the majesty of mountains, the drama of volcanoes and typhoons, but above all to the joys of killing as many as possible of the birds and beasts whose beauties he extolled. 'Scorning to finish the day' he wrote of a hunting expedition in the Alps 'without drawing blood from some-

GEORGE KINGSLEY

*thing beside ourselves', he shot a marmot whose cheeky facial expression
was 'perfectly delicious', followed by a brace of ptarmigan.*

*George Kingsley left a mass of notes, many letters, a few articles
and sketches, but never a book. After his death his daughter Mary
deciphered, with difficulty, a selection of the surviving letters, which
were nearly all undated, and incorporated them into a memoir which
Macmillan published, together with ten of the sketches, in 1899 under
the title* Notes on Sport and Travel. *Extracts follow from both the
sketches and the letters, arranged in chronological order as nearly as
this can be judged.*

XXXIV

From: Chamois-Hunting

(Published in Fraser's Magazine, August 1851)

In his vacations George made for Scotland or the wilder regions of Europe, and in the Tyrol took part in a chamois hunt. His companion, Joseph, was a 'fine, handsome jaunty fellow, with nut-brown hair curling round his open forehead, and a moustache for which a guardsman would have given his little finger'. They started from the village of Dumpfen, near Fend.

How intensely beautiful that dawn was with the pine woods steeped in the deepest purple, here and there a faint, gauzy mist, looking self-luminous, marking the course of some mountain brook through the forest! The gray cliffs stood dark and silent on the opposite side of the stream, and one far-off snow peak, just catching the faint reflected light of dawn, gleamed ghost-like and faint, like some spirit lingering on the forbidden confines of day. How intense was that silence, broken only by the harsh rattle of the torrent and the occasional faint tinkle of a cow-bell in the distance; or now and then by a spirit-like whispering sigh among the pines, that scarcely moved their long arms before the cold breath of the dying night!

*   *   *

Up, up, still up, across the little sparkling runlets, tumbling head over heels in their hurry to see what sort of a world the valley below might be! Up over masses of rock, ankle-deep in rich brown moss, bejewelled with strawberries and cowberries, garlanded with raspberries twisting and straggling out of their crevices, covered with rich ripe fruit! Up over bits of open turf, green as emeralds, set in pure white gravel sparkling like a thousand diamonds! Up through tangled masses of fallen pines, their bleaching stumps standing out like the masts of great wrecks,—terrible marks of the course of the avalanche wind! Up through one short bit more of pine

wood, over the split-fir fence and into the little mountain meadow
smiling in the level sunlight, with its bright stream tinkling merrily
through it, its scattered boulders and wooden *sennhutt*, with the
cows and goats clustered round it standing ready to be milked; one
of the latter, by-the-bye, instantly charges me, and has to be repelled
by my alpenstock, bayonet-fashion; while all around the sweet
breath of the cows mingles deliciously with the aromatic fragrance
of the pine forest, and the rich scent of the black orchis and wild
thyme!

Our path lay now, steep and rugged, along the edge of a ravine,
at the bottom of which we heard the torrent chafing and roaring
many a yard below us. There was a precipitous bank of rocks and
screes to our right, quite unclimbable, which seemed only to want
the will,—they certainly had the way—to topple us into the abyss.
Just as we were turning an abrupt angle very gingerly, with our
eyes fixed on our slippery path, and longing for an elephant's trunk
to try the sound bits from the rotten ones, we suddenly heard a
rushing sough, like the falling of a moist snow avalanche, and a
cloud passed across the sun. Glancing hastily upwards, I—yes I,
in the body at this present, inditing this faithful description of my
chase—saw, not a hundred paces from me, an enormous vulture!
Anything so fiercely, so terribly grand as this great bird saw I never
before, and can scarcely hope to see again. He was so near that we
could distinctly see the glare of his fierce eye, and the hard, bitter
grip of his clenched talons. The sweep of his vast wings was
enormous,—I dare not guess how broad from tip to tip; and their
rushing noise, as he beat the air in his first laboured strokes,
sounded strangely wild and spirit-like in the mountain stillness. A
dozen strong strokes, and then a wild swoop round to our right, and
away, like a cloud before the blast, till a neighbouring peak hid him
from our sight, followed by a wild shout of astonishment from
Joseph. I opened not my mouth, or if I did, left it open.

We were advancing along the base of the lowest tier of cliff,
which had a sort of step of snow running along it about half-way up
for some half-a-mile, bounded at one end by an immense mass of
screes and precipice, and at the other by a sudden turn of the rock,
when Joseph, suddenly dashing off his hat and throwing himself
prostrate behind a stone, dragged me down beside him with a vice-
like grasp that left its mark on my arm for many a day after. Utterly

taken aback at the suddenness of my prostration, I lay beside him, wondering at the change that had come over his face; he was as white as marble, his moustache worked with intense excitement, and his eyeballs seemed starting from their sockets as he glared at the cliff. Following his line of sight I glanced upwards, and my eye was instantly arrested by something. It moved—again—and again! With shaking hand I directed the telescope to the point, and there, at the end of it, hopping fearlessly on the shivered mountain-side, scratching its ear with its hind-foot, and nibbling daintily the scattered bits of *gemsenkraut* that sprang up between the stones, stood fearless and free—a chamois!

After watching him with intense interest for some moments we drew back, scarcely daring to breathe, and, sheltering ourselves behind a large stone, held a council of war. It was evidently impossible to approach him from where we were; we could not have moved ten steps towards him without the certainty of being discovered; our chance was to get above him and so cut him off from the higher ranges. Crawling backwards, we managed to place a low range of rock between ourselves and the cliffs, and then making a wide sweep, we reached their base at some distance from where the chamois was feeding.

After examining the precipice for some time, we found that the only mode of access to its summit, here some three or four hundred feet above us, was by a sort of ravine, what would be called in the Swiss Alps a *cheminée*, a species of fracture in the strata, the broken edges of which would give us some hold for foot and hand. At its upper termination we could see the end of a small glacier, slightly overhanging the cliff, from which a small stream leaped from ledge to ledge, only alive in the last hour or two of sun-warmth, giving promises, which certainly were faithfully fulfilled, of additional slipperyness and discomfort. But we had no choice. We had already spent nearly an hour in our cautious circuit: our scramble, wherever it took place, would cost us nearly another before we got above our expected prey; and if we hesitated much longer, he might take a fancy to march off altogether in search of the rest of the herd. So up we went, dragging ourselves and each other up the wet slippery rocks, getting a shivering 'swish' of ice-cold water in our faces every now and then, till we got about half-way up, when just as we were resting for a moment to take breath, we heard a tremendous roar, followed by a splintering crash just above our heads, and had the pleasure of seeing the fragments of some half a ton of ice, which had fallen from the glacier above, fly out from the shelf of rock under which we were resting, and spin down the rugged path we had just ascended. Thinking that this was quite near enough to be pleasant, and calculating that by every doctrine of chances the same thing would not happen twice in the same half-hour, we scrambled up as fast as we could before the next instalment became due, and at last reached safely the top of the precipice . . .

Trembling, partly with excitement and partly from the under-waistcoat of half-melted snow we had unconsciously assumed in our serpentine wrigglings, we lay and watched the graceful animal below us. He evidently had a presentiment that there was something 'no canny' about the mountain-side; some eddy had perhaps reached his delicate nostrils laden with the taint of an intruder. With his head high in the air, and his ears pointed forwards, he stood examining, as wiser brutes than he sometimes do, every point of the compass but the right. One foot was advanced; one moment more and he would have gone, when crack! close to my ear, just as I was screwing up my nerves for a long shot, went Joseph's heavy rifle. With a sinking heart I saw the brute take a tremendous bound, all four hoofs together, and then, like a rifle-ball glancing over the bosom of a calm lake, bound after bound carried him away and away over the snow-field and round the corner on our right, before I had recovered my senses sufficiently to take a desperate snap at him.

What we said, or felt, or how we got over the face of that cliff, I know not. A dim recollection of falling stones and dust showering round us,—pieces of treacherous rock giving way in our hands and under our feet, bruising slides, and one desperate jump over the chasm between the cliff and the snow,—and there we were, both standing pale and breathless, straining our eyes for some scarcely expected trace of blood to give us hope.

Nor a drop tinged the unsullied snow, at the place where he had made his first mad bound, nor at the second, nor at the third; but a few paces farther on one ruby-tinged hole showed where the hot blood had sunk through the melting snow.

Too excited to feel any uprising of envy, hatred, or malice against my more fortunate companion, I raced along the white incline, leaving him behind reloading his rifle (which was always a sort of solemn rite with him), and following without difficulty the deep indentations of the animal's hoofs, I came to where the cliffs receded into a sort of small bay, with its patch of snow on the same plane with the one I was on, but separated from it by a rugged promontory of cliff and broken rock. Cautiously I scrambled round the point, removing many a stone that seemed inclined to fall and give the alarm to the watchful chamois, and peeping cautiously round the last mass of rock that separated me from the snow-patch, I saw the poor brute standing not more than sixty yards from me, his hoofs drawn close together under him, ready for a desperate rush at the cliff at the first sound that reached him, his neck stretched out, and his muzzle nearly touching the snow, straining every sense to catch some inkling of the whereabouts of the mischief he felt was near him.

With my face glowing as if it had been freshly blistered, a dryness and lumping in my throat as if I had just escaped from an unsuccessful display of Mr Calcraft's professional powers, and my heart beating against my ribs at such a rate that I really thought the *gemse* must hear it in the stillness, I raised my carbine. Once, at the neck just behind the ear, I saw the brown hide clear at the end of the barrel, but I dared not risk such a chance; and so, stringing my nerves, I shifted my aim to just behind the shoulder, —one touch of the cold trigger, and as the thin gases streamed off rejoicing at their liberation, I saw the chamois shrink convulsively when the ball struck him, and then fall heavily on the snow, shot right through the heart. With a who-whoop! that might have been heard half-way to Innsbruck, I rushed up to him; one sweep of the knife,—the red blood bubbled out on the snow that shrunk and wasted before its hot touch as if it felt itself polluted,—and there lay, stretched out in all its beauty before me, the first *gemse* I ever killed, just as Joseph came up, panting, yelling, and *jödling*, and rejoicing at my success without a shade of envy in his honest heart.

Now I believe, in all, propriety, we ought to have been melancholy, and moralized over the slain. That rich, soft, black eye filming over with the frosty breath of death, and that last convulsive kick of the hind-legs ought perhaps to have made us feel that we had done rather a brutal and selfish thing; but they did not. This is a truthful narrative; and I must confess that our only feeling was one of unmixed rejoicing. I have occasionally moralized over a trout flopping about among the daisies and buttercups, and dying that horrible suffocation-death of my causing; but it was never, if I remember right, the *first* trout I had killed that day. My feelings always get finer as my pannier gets fuller, particularly if it be a warm afternoon, and I have lunched. But as for the unfortunate *gemse*, we rejoiced over him exceedingly; we shook hands over him; we sat beside him, and on him; we examined him carefully, minutely, scientifically, from stem to stern. I firmly believe that I could pick him out at this moment from the thousand ghosts that attend the silver-horned Gemsen König, if I had put the good luck to fall in with his majesty and his charmed suite. Joseph's ball had struck him high up on the neck, but had not inflicted anything like a severe wound. Had we fired on him from below he would have scaled the cliffs in a moment and been no more seen, at least by us; but as he knew that the mischief was above him, he dared not ascend,—to descend was impossible; and so, getting to a certain extent pounded, he gave me the rare chance of a second shot.

Long we sat and gazed at the chamois; and at the wild scene before us,—never shall I forget it,—shut in on three sides by steep and frowning cliffs, in front the precipice, and far, far down, the wild rocky valleys, divided by shivered ridges rising higher and higher till they mounted up into the calm pure snow-range set in the frame of the jutting promontories on each side of us,—looking the brighter and the holier from the comparative shade in which we were. Not a sound but the occasional faint 'swish' of the waterfall that drained from the snow-bed,—not a living thing *now* but our two selves standing side by side on the snow. We had killed the third, and there he lay stiffening between us!

XXXV

A Gossip on a Sutherland Hillside

(Published in Vacation Tourists and
Notes of Travel edited by Francis Galton, 1861)

From Lairg, in Sutherland, George set out early one autumn morning
with Donald the gillie over 'the great brown moor'.

How deliciously the fresh breeze sweeps round the corner, inflating
our lungs to their innermost cell, and how the waves lap and jump
under it! A wild night last night, judging from those piles of foam
along the shore; but those great straggling rifts are beginning to
show patches of the cold blue northern sky beyond. Nothing, after
all, but a sea-fog! Whether the weather be wet or dry, wet *we* shall
be on the hill, and those rifts will let light enough through to show
us deer, if the worst comes to the worst.

Trundle along, powney, through the stone-inclosed patches of
oats, trying to look ripe and failing most dismally in the attempt;
past little fields, half arable, half pasture, where the cow feeds
tended by the bit bareleggit lassie, wet through already, but caring
nothing for the wet now, whatever she may do when she finds herself a wrinkled crone at forty, bent double with rheumatism. Then
through the fresh sweet birch coppice, where the 'Ladies of the
wood' are tossing their lithe arms, and sprinkling sweet odours
and sparkling raindrop gems on every side; where the blackcock
whirrs up and sails away on his strong-beating wings, and the
daintily tripping roe crosses the road shyly, seeking her cosy lair,
among the sweet bog myrtle and warm tussock grass, after her
night's marauding among the oats. . . .

Something like the character of the people, serious and cheerful
at once, quiet and reserved in general tone, but with bright patches
of vivid green and bits of rarely-scented shrub here and there;
lighted up with little eyes of water moist and gleaming as those of a

296

girl, who has been crying for sheer happiness and breaks into a smile amidst her tears. Light and shade, rigid fanaticism and wild poetical fervour alternating in fitful gleams; the light at any rate predominating among those slim well-grown lassies and lither lads rattling on before us at a hand-gallop, going to gather in their marsh hay.

Neither Donald Dhu nor the collies being at home, we take the liberty of inspecting his habitation. The bothy is some twelve or fourteen feet long, and about four feet high in front, strongly built of stone, and nestled well under the bank, which almost touches the heather roof in the rear, making one speculate curiously as to how the summer thunderstorms treat his floor, and whether he goes out and sits on the roof for the sake of comparative dryness when the whole sheet of heather behind is running in a broad stream. There is a padlock on the door, but more for show than use, for the key is rusted tightly into it, and all power of locking has long since departed from the springs; still the thing looks well, and might, probably, prevent a particularly conscientious burglar from breaking in.

Bending low through the doorway, we see the secrets of Donald's domestic economy laid bare. A rude bed on one side, across which lay a pair of well-patched and well-soaked breeks; a table, consisting of a broad flat stone, miraculously balanced on divers bits of bogwood; a shelf, from which depends a worsted stocking with a needle sticking across a vast rent, Donald's last effort at mending himsel' given up in despair, with a stern determination to propose to the pretty lassie at Lairg next Sabbath; a tin plate, a fork stuck into the shelf to facilitate finding, a basin with a little dried porridge sticking about it, and a well-blacked crock, are all we discover in the semi-darkness until we stumble over something which proves to be a stump of bogwood with the roots whittled off to sufficient evenness to permit of your sitting upon it without being tilted into the fire, that is, if you understand it and are very careful. Window there is none; the hole in the roof, through which some of the smoke makes its exit when the fire is lighted, does double duty; and as we become accustomed to the twilight which fringes the perpendicular ray passing down it, we become aware of a few cast antlers, well gnawed by the hinds, a brown pan filled with water, in which lie soaking a couple of dozen split trout, red as salmon, twice as large as I can ever catch—confound that otter!—and in a particularly dark corner a couple of black bottles, which *ought* to contain whisky of the smallest still, but which on examination hold nothing but in the one case a dribblet of sour milk, and in the other, some tarry abomination used for doctoring the sheep. That little parcel wrapped up in a pocket-napkin is Donald's well-thumbed Bible; and many a tough bit of grace and free-will does Donald puzzle over when his work is done, lighted by those splinters of bogwood in the corner, which burn more brightly than wax—by-the-bye, the best-thumbed side of Donald's Bible is the Old Testament. If you have imagination enough to double the length of Donald's bothy without increasing its breadth or height, to turn the addition into a cow-house of the foulest description, to carefully avoid putting up any partition, as that would diminish the warmth both of yourself and the cow, and to make the whole affair ten times more filthy and uncomfortable then it is, placing a sea of liquid manure before the door, just high enough to permit every shower to wash a fair amount of it into the hut—you will get a very tolerable idea of a superior description of that happy home of the western Highlander, —the black hut—from which he has been so ruthlessly torn. If you doubt it, go and see for yourself, on the West coast and more particularly on the islands. Suppose a man and his wife, and half-a-dozen children, with in all probability, one, if not two, grandfathers and grandmothers, living in such a hovel, depending entirely on the miserable crops of oats or potatoes, without the remotest chance of a paid day's work from one year's end to the other, and you have the sort of existence Donald Dhu would have led in the good old times.

XXXVI

A Voyage to Algeria
1862

George was thirty-six before he set eyes on southern Europe and the Mediterranean. In 1862 the Captain of an old-fashioned wooden man-of-war, H.M.S. St George, took him on a cruise to Algiers by way of Lisbon and Gibraltar. During the voyage he kept a log from which the following extracts are taken.

Thursday—We are well round the corner, and in the Atlantic somewhere off Rochefort on the French coast. There must have been a gale from the eastward lately, for though we are far away from land, a number of shore-birds have come on board, poor little things! quite beaten. As they are all soft-billed birds I am afraid that they must die. I could only make out a redstart who tried pertinaciously to settle on the patent log line. Before we sailed we had a lovely little golden-crested wren on board for some time, and it was pretty and quaint to see the tiny thing peering and prying about the iron-tips of the mighty broadside guns. A sparrow-hawk also came on board, and oddly enough flew away in a direction opposite to the land. Jack is just like a great child, and goes skylarking and heaving his hat at the birds, and consequently overboard, to the diminution of his wages, till the Just Influence comes down on him like thunder and scatters him to the four winds of heaven. He is always in trouble is Jack, and likewise Bill the marine. Every morning there is a small row of the United Services, standing just abaft of the mainmast in charge of two marines with drawn bayonets. At twelve o'clock, I think, the hour when something wonderful happens to the ship, I see Jack the prisoner say to Bill his keeper, 'Off you go' in a low voice, and away they all troop to some mysterious place in the bowels of the ship. Likewise, every day after dinner, a long row of unfortunates are drawn up on each side of the quarterdeck, wombling and shambling and sniggering, each with a small white basin (with which he generally scratches his stern incessantly), soon after which the smell of rum pervades the ship, and I am told that the black-listers have had their grog, with a great deal more water in it than they like. We have a glass of sherry and a biscuit as soon as the sun is over the main-yards, which manoeuvre he somehow performs every day about twelve o'clock, and then there is an hour's smoking on the main-deck. This is mighty pleasant. But perhaps the cosiest part of the day is the smoking time after the wardroom dinner, when we sit on and about the two aftermost big guns on the main-deck, and listen to the band. It is quaint enough, the deck feebly lighted by the dips on the musicians' desks, and a lanthorn above us which is always distilling scalding tallow down somebody's back. The white beams above, with mysterious black arrows upon them for conveying fire, looking like enormous black beetles, and the handles of the cutlasses stored overhead, and the brass sights of the big black guns below glancing in the light, and in the background, which is forward, peering through the darkness a mass of wild strange faces, all wrapped in the most intense admiration of the music and drinking in every note. Mates, midshipmen, and all manner of officers, are waltzing and gallopading with each other hard all, occasionally as the ship gives an extra roll disappearing headlong into the darkness from which come sounds of lamentation, woe, and laughter. Nine o'clock—out lights between decks, stop smoking, and a book or a game of patience with the captain, or a game of whist in the wardroom, a long walk up and down the poop with the officer of the watch, and so to bed. A mighty pleasant life!

*　　　*　　　*

We shot several snipe in a garden of mighty pumpkins just under it, and as we did so the labourers issued forth for their afternoon's work. The men were dressed in white shirts and wide white drawers, red sashes, and enormously broad-brimmed hats; the women swathed in strange white garments, and their heads and part of their faces bound up in a white wrapper. Along the road, which was a little raised and about three feet broad, came ambling on a cock-tailed nag a smart-looking fellow with blue trousers, embroidered jacket, and scarlet sash, his wondrous saddle half concealing his pony, and with enormous wooden stirrups; by his side ran lightly and easily an attendant in light blue garments, who kept up with him with ease, and laughed and chattered as he ran. To us approached an enormous individual with a gun six feet long at least, whom we supposed to be a game-keeper; he discoursed long to us through his nose, but finding no results therefrom he went his way up to the mountains and we saw him no more.

It was wondrous pleasant, lying down to luncheon on the hot baking sand, with the air filled with the rich aromatic scent of the forest, and bright butterflies and gigantic grasshoppers fluttering and bouncing about us, to think of London the foggy, with its dirty, sloshy, melting snow, and cold, searching, rheumatizing winds. I am by no means sure, however, that one ought not to be frozen hard once a year; incessant sun mollifieth the particles and degenerates the pineal gland, wherein is the seat of the organs of activity according to the authors.

There are things, however, to which the sun gives additional force, as witness these grasshoppers, wondrous beasts with heads like horses, who jump four yards good at a leap, and smite one's midriff as a stone from a sling. See also the frogs, who are, though, a feeble, a numerous folk, and cover the marsh; I lost many a snipe from looking down at them. There was one smart young fellow with a stripe of the most vivid apple green down his back, who delighted me much. Why do they all, when they see me, put their hands over their heads, and after making believe to dive, sit down and look at me as much as to say 'You can't do that'? There are worse noises in the world than the cosy crooning conversation by day of well-bred frogs; they don't croak, they are only a little hoarse from sitting in the damp, like the member of the village choir when he had to sing a bass part,—a thought husky, as it were. At night it is another thing, and I question whether the frogs who croak at night are not another set,—a rowdy Haymarkety, in-office-all-day-and-out-for-a-lark sort of persons; but by day, and here, the frogs are aristocratic frogs and have manners corresponding. Bless me! if that delicate yellow thing with the spots was a dowager Portuguese princess, she could not look at me with more icy impertinence, or hold her chin higher in the air to show her yellow throat puffed up with windy importance. It seemed quite wrong to be snipe-shooting in the midst of all this life and sunshine, so unlike the cold steel-gray sky and rustling, lifeless, half-frozen sedges in which one kills friend Scape at home. Nevertheless we have killed them; put them out on the sand, pretty brutes,—how exquisitely marked are those feathers on the back, that tender creamy brown!

In Algiers, George went to an Arab banquet followed by a Dervish display.

There was then brought in and placed on the table a brazier of live charcoal. Three men squatted round it, active wiry fellows with long sinewy arms and bare throats, with the muscles standing out like cords. To each of them was given a mighty tambourine of the shape, make, and size of a corn-sieve, with parchment instead of perforations. These they took and thumbed and fingered and tapped, as a sort of tuning prelude; then, after a discussion as to their various states of tone, they were held over the brazier into which a little incense had been sprinkled and which glowered redly on their brown faces. This was done either to hallow them, which was probable, or to corrugate their tympanums into a proper state of exciting sharpness, which was still more so. After more thrummings and rappings and toastings, everything seemed right, and there was a moment's pause.

Swaying from side to side as they sat, they then began a monotonous nasal song, beating time to it on their tambourines. Gradually the song waxed wilder and louder, and the thumping and banging more and more energetic, though a rude time was always carefully kept; louder and louder till the whole place was filled with sound, and the faces of the performers flushed into a bright brick red and their eyes gleamed like live coals. Watching as carefully as I could for the infernal din, I saw one of the men cautiously take a pinch of something from his sleeve and cast it in the brazier. He then, as if accidently, waved the smoke backwards to the men sitting behind him, who soon began to show gorged faces and bloodshot eyes. One man evidently tried to avoid the fumes, he was wrestled with and held over the brazier, till I thought he would have had a fit. Suddenly, so suddenly as to startle one, two men bounced up from the floor with fearful yells, their faces, necks, and eyes engorged with blood, their lips working, and the thin foam appearing from between them in what, if wholly simulated, was the most perfectly imitated attack of sudden epileptic mania I ever saw. The moment they were on their legs they were laid hold of by the attendants behind, their skull-caps taken off, a long white garment slipped over their heads, and their long top-knots (and I was surprised to see what a quantity of hair these apparently shaven Moors carried under their fez) unwound and tossed in admired disorder about their necks and faces. Wrapped up as to their arms in the above-mentioned cloths, they looked like lunatics suffering from a severe relapse at the moment they were being shaved. They danced, they yelled, at first in cadence, and afterwards in short spasmodic howls; they jumped, they hopped, they kicked, they made as if they were going to plunge head foremost into the brazier; and at last began to spin their heads round and round upon their shoulders with a velocity that threatened to send them off into infinite space, with an initial velocity highly dangerous to the by-standers. Knavery or not, it was a really strange and wild scene. Whenever they seemed on the verge of doing themselves or the by-standers a mischief, watchful attendants started from the pillars against which they were leaning and caught them round the waist. One individual was very fond of casting himself suddenly and violently backwards against the wall; he was always caught just in time; but I was wicked enough to wish that his friend would 'miss his tip' for once, in order to see what effect the sharp contact of the marble would have upon him. The noise of the tambourines and the yells of the singers were absolutely deafening. There was not a moment's pause; it was one incessant throbbing, beating mass of sound. The faces of the two dancers became perfectly horrible; as their heads spun round and round, the white eyes glared from the tangled mass of hair, and the foam really and actually flew in flakes from their lips,—real epileptic foam tinged with blood. One of them had a mass of black hair, and the other still more of iron gray. The hair of both became perfectly matted with perspiration, and it was clear that human nature could not hold out much longer. Suddenly the gray-haired man yelled louder than ever and fell back, as if shot through the heart, into the arms of the attendants, who immediately bundled him up and carried him away into the outside darkness. The black-haired one freed his arms from their covering and made a dash at the lighted charcoal, biting and crunching it between his teeth as if it had been dry toast. Had he stopped there I should have been the more satisfied; but when he

laid a red-hot iron but on his white tongue till it frizzled, and
holding a piece between his teeth blew out till it blazed again,
lighting up his jaws like a lanthorn and sending a stream of sparks
like a firework, I began to think that I had seen the same sort of
thing before. He managed to upset the charcoal all over the floor,
which caused a slight commotion among the orchestra, but immediately danced it out with his bare feet, no very difficult feat for
a horny-hoofed Moor accustomed to walk barefooted over the
scalding stones of Algiers. Still the infernal roar continued, and
from the floor bounced up fresh dancers who danced themselves
into insanity and exhaustion; sometimes they reeled, panting and
groaning, to the feet of the sheik, who plucked them with the tips
of his fingers, kissed them on the forehead, and seemed to make
magical passes over them, they the while kissing and nuzzling over
his hand with apparent veneration. There was something very
striking about this; it gave one the idea that they believed in the
power of the sheik to comfort and relieve them under their self-
inflicted torments. Finally they were caught and carried out like
the first.

Meanwhile, my black-haired friend, refreshed by his supper of
live charcoal, was casting about for some other means of doing
himself a personal injury, and I was told by the dragoman that
something very horrible was coming. He howled his way to the
sheik, who put his fingers to his head in a mysterious manner like a
secret sign, and handed him an iron pin about a foot long, fairly
sharp at the end and about as thick as one's little finger; at one
end of this was a solid ball of iron, as large as a large orange and
with divers mysterious rings and bits of chain attached to it. On
getting tired of this charming plaything, the man howled ten times
worse than ever, and seemed very sorry indeed for himself, really
very sorry, as if he had to so something particularly unpleasant, but
which it was his duty to do. After several feints he advanced to the
centre of the court, and, throwing his head back, stuck the sharp
point of the spike into the inner corner of his right eye, holding it
perpendicularly there for a few seconds. Then with yells worse
than ever he began screwing it round and round, forcing the eye
farther and farther out, till I really began to be afraid that it would
part company with his head altogether. Humbug though it might
all be, the thing was really horrible; the unnatural round white eye

coming farther and farther out on to the gorged and purple cheek, the contortions of agony, simulated or not, while the creature's incessant ear-splitting yells and the unceasing *tum-tumming* of the tambourines, really almost made one's head spin. He had enough of it at last; his yells subsided into panting groans, and, holding his head forward, the spike with its heavy ball remained suspended from his eye for half a second and then tumbled with a bump and a jingle on the floor. At this moment a young Nubian, who was sitting close to me under a flaring tallow candle, jumped up with a yell and a bounce that made me start from its evident sincerity. I thought for a moment that he was stricken with insanity; but turning to the spluttering candle, and scrubbing himself back-handedly between the shoulders, he cursed it in set terms; and we discovered that a stream of scalding tallow had quietly dribbled between his shirt and himself, and given at least one individual a real sensation. Savagely he blew the candle out, and defiantly he squatted under it, bouncing up again with a fresh yell as he brought his blistered back into sharp contact with the wall. The black-haired maniac still continued the principal performer, and grew more and more mad; a tenth of the energy he used would have sufficed a navigator for a day's hard work. On the sheik handing him a sword he became dreadfully sorry for himself again, and howled in agony of spirit. At last, placing the pummel of the sword on the floor he cast himself upon the point, he being naked saving and excepting a very scanty pair of cotton drawers. I confess that the action did not seem as energetic and determined as that of Saul in the picture Bible; and his hands fumbled with the point in a manner which suggested the idea of his not wishing it to penetrate too deeply. He did the thing very well however, struggling with all his might apparently on the sword, gyrating round and round and yelling as furiously as ever. At last, raising himself upright, foaming and raging, he presented the disagreeable spectacle of the sword sticking in the navel standing straight out from the body. With this appendage he staggered once or twice round the court, and at last pulling out the sword, fell backwards, was caught and carried away, and we saw him no more.

Of course this is for the most part charlatanism, but I think that with it is mixed up a vast deal of real and possibly dangerous excitement. I am certain that most of the performers worked themselves into a state but little removed from mania, and, if I may believe what I am told, that many of them did it from a religious feeling. Much of this excitement is, I suspect, caused by burning stimulating narcotics in the incense; most probably some form of Indian hemp, *bhang* or *haschish*. The tremendous engorgement of the face and neck, and the state of the eyes, could hardly have been assumed at a moment's notice by a mere effort of the will. It would, I think, be far better without the tricks than with them; but there are those who think the liquefaction of the blood of St Januarius an edifying addition to the sacrifice of the Mass. The French do not like it at all, and the men are not allowed to go through the performance without the express permission of the Prefect of Police. If these fellows were to descend into the street and do their lunacies before an impressionable mob of Moors, I think there would very probably be a row; the thing is catching, and I myself had a horrible inclination to cast my 'tubular turban' into the arena and go raving mad with the rest.

The following year George went to Naples, where the Duke of St Albans picked him up and took him in the ducal yacht to Syracuse. He wrote to his wife:

We have had wonderful snipe shooting, and have killed nearly a hundred in the last three days. Only think of us, shooting snipe amidst magnificent tufts of papyrus and beds of the most exquisite wild narcissus—infinitely sweeter than the cultivated ones—and acres and acres of lovely sweet-scented purple iris, with the vultures soaring above us and the swallows skimming over our heads—and all this at Christmas time! Our best shooting was about the fountain of Cyane—now only a mass of rushes and great reeds. You cannot imagine how beautiful the papyrus is with its strong green stalks rising ten or twelve feet high, crowned with most graceful tufts of light green filaments a foot or two long. One corner of the river, where we were actually shut in on all sides by these lovely reeds, and they were reflected in the bright, clear water, was the most exquisite bit that I ever saw in my life.

A few days afterwards he wrote:

Surely this is one of the loveliest place in the world! Last night,

A VOYAGE TO ALGERIA

just at sunset, we ran through the Straits of Messina, and had the bright green tinted hills, with the beautiful crescent city at their feet, on the left hand; and, on the right, Reggio, backed by the tumbled masses of Calabria, ranging away, peak after peak, till they culminated in the wild Aspromonte hills, snow covered and storm swept; and around us was the blue sea, flecked with the white sails of the feluccas—a scene to be everlastingly remembered. We seemed to be in a great river, and neither the Rhine nor the Danube could show anything to be compared with it. We left Syracuse, the evening before last, in a diligence, and lumbered along all night to Catania, where we caught our steamer, and in her came on here. Half the day we spent sailing along under Mount Etna, which, half covered with snow, soared up into the blue, far above all. Every mile opened some lovely valley planted with lemon-trees on its sides, and with its floor covered with the débris brought down from the hills by the torrents which, in bad weather, fill it with a mass of raging water. We must have passed at least twenty ridges running down from the higher mountains to the sea, most of them terminating in an abrupt crag with a little town blinking white in the sunshine at its foot, and an old ruin standing on its summit; while, high up on the mountain side, hung other villages perched on the most fantastic crags. Inland, a wild, serried mass of broken peaks, sprinkled with fresh-fallen snow—which added immensely to their apparent height,—formed a background which was really grand. In fact, we had the three great requisites for a perfect landscape— snow mountains, beautiful, broken green foreground, and deep blue sea. This coast of Sicily is, indeed, immeasurably finer than anything I have ever yet seen or ever expect to see: every mile of it is picturesque. Etna was smoking away as usual, and the light, fleecy clouds threw most delicious soft, dove-coloured shadows on the bright, white snow . . .

This town of Messina has a bustle and a life about it which is quite refreshing after the silence and isolation of those wild marshes in which we have been lately. It is really a pleasure to hear the noise, to feel the pressure of a crowd about one, and the very air seems full of human sympathy. I am entertaining great hopes that I shall be able to make up a good book on the Balearics; they are quite unknown to the world, and are, I hear, full of wonders and beautiful scenery.

307

He was in Palma, in the Balearic Islands, when an invitation reached him from the Duke of Sutherland to visit Egypt as the guest of the Khedive. This potentate died before they got there, but George went on to Syria and the Aegean. In 1866 he was back again in Egypt in the suite of yet another Duke—Rutland this time—and then to Spain with Lady Herbert of Lea and her two sons. The following year her elder son, the Earl of Pembroke, took him to New Zealand and the South Seas, and here they travelled for the best part of three years, 'dropping down from one lovely island to another, seeing the strangest sights imaginable, and being treated like princes by the natives, who literally loaded us with presents'.

In the century between Captain Cook's great voyages and the Pembroke-Kingsley cruise, what Alan Moorehead calls 'the fatal impact' between white men and Pacific Islanders had transformed and degraded the Polynesian way of life. The erstwhile paradise of Tahiti had become a port of call for hard-bitten whalers and traders, while missionaries strove to enforce a wholly alien code of morals, and beachcombers made a mockery of the missionaries' code. Yet there was still much to be seen that struck the visitors as beautiful, carefree and fine. George wrote vividly, if not regularly, to his wife, and Lord Pembroke's account appeared in print as South Sea Bubbles, by the Earl and the Doctor, *published by Bentley in 1872. In his preface the Earl wrote 'This little work was composed originally of different sketches taken from my log and put into shape,' but Mary Kingsley states that her father wrote 'some of the chapters' for amusement during his periods of leisure.*

In New Zealand they passed their days, according to Mary, 'in a condition of almost monotonous bliss', fishing, shooting, swimming, and revelling in the scenery. In his notebook, quoted in Notes on Sport and Travel, *her father wrote:*

You can have no idea of what a glorious pleasure there is in fishing in a new sea in ignorance of what you are going to catch, more particularly if you have the slightest interest in ichthyology. Shall I ever forget the moment when I saw my first *Chimaera australis* handed into the boat! A fish which I had marvelled at from my boyhood upwards, and almost fancied to be the dream of some mad naturalist, so wild and weird was his delineation—not half so wild and weird, however, as his reality. At the moment when I held

up my first cavalli—apparently, like a dyer's hand, subdued to
what he lived in—to compare his shifting tints with the exquisite
bright sapphire blue of the sea before me, tints so delicate and dainty
that I knew not what to liken them to except a certain sheening,
shimmering, lissom silk robe, half green, half blue, and flecked
with gold, seen long ago—right through the world!

If you have the good luck to be in that most glorious of harbours
Port Abercrombie—Lord! to hear the air there ringing with the
notes of the bell-birds and tuis in the sweet, fresh, misty mornings
you will have sport which will make you forget for the moment
even the Tay itself. Mind! I don't for one moment mean to compare the sport which can be had out of a boat to that you get by
artfully casting your fly into pit swirls and runs,—that, I think,
would be absurd,—but for boat fishing it can hardly be beaten.
And some of this harling is carried on in the midst of scenery which
is indescribably lovely. The trees of New Zealand, particularly the
shore-growing trees, are very varied and of great beauty and richness of colour; but the monarch of them all is the pohutukawa,
whose foliage resembles somewhat that of a large-leafed species of
ilex, but whose picturesque limbs and glorious flowers are peculiar
to itself. The former stretch themselves right out over the sea in the
quiet bays; and to look on the magnificent scarlet blaze of the
stamens of the latter, setting the bright, still water below them
aflame, just about Christmas time, is worth the voyage to New
Zealand ten thousand times over. Really, I used sometimes to find
it difficult to realize that I was actually catching wild fish amid such
brilliant beauty; and a half-sort-of-suspicion that I am poaching
the gold-fish in Chatsworth Conservatory, and a wonderment
whether the old Scotch gardener would come and catch me, would
come over me, ever and anon, in spite of myself.

You catch all kinds of fish—snappers, rock-cod, and what not;
the spoon is a novelty, and they rush at it like women at a new
fashion in bonnets. But besides these,—the fish, not the women,—
you come across the kahawai, a fish which for beauty, pluck, and
everything but flavour, has a perfect right to consider himself the
worthy representative of *Salmo salar* himself in these seas.

The first rush of a kahawai is really splendid, and your reel
acknowledges his power by discoursing as sweet a music as it has
ever done by Shannon or Brora, and tough old twenty-foot-long

'Chevalier' bends his honest back to the very grips. Not only does he rush like *Salmo salar*, but he emulates him in the art of throwing himself clean out of the water, over and over again—a performance which always causes a most exquisite throb of mingled fear and admiration to pass through my bosom. The Maoris, who are—or were—a race of splendid fishermen, killed their kahawai by hundreds with a bait made out of the curved portion of a Venus'-ear shell, set into a backing of hardwood, and cunningly tied to a hook of bone (human bone for preference), and I have been told by experts that the best part of an inner tabernacle for this purpose is the front part of the shin—the tibia of the anatomist. I have caught many a kahawai with this apparatus, but I think that a slip of a sardine-box some three or four inches long, fastened to a piece of kauri wood, and deftly curved into a shape which will produce a judicious wobble (not a spin, that is to be avoided) when it is going through the water, is quite as good; and a sliver from the tail of the first fish which you catch is decidedly better than either, for with it you have a chance of catching fish who would not stir at the mere motion of a bait without the further attraction of smell— a sense which, I am convinced, is highly developed in most sea- fishes, if not in our English river ones. Taste is also developed in many fishes to a high degree. With what an expression of disgust will a fish blow a morsel from his mouth when he finds that it does not suit his palate! and what a way through the water he will send it!

In Auckland they bought and fitted out a little coasting schooner called the Albatross, *and in October 1869, set out for New Caledonia. Their first landfall was the Isles of Pines.*

We sailed away from New Zealand about a month ago, and went northward for a week without seeing anything but one sunfish. At last we saw something that looked like the masts of ships sticking up in the water; this, we thought, must be the Island of Pines, and so it turned out to be—a wonderful place encircled with coral reefs, through which we threaded out way to a quiet harbour, with the surf foaming and thundering on the reefs outside. This harbour was full of rocks, and creeks, and bays more marvellous than were ever imagined in a dream, and islands innumerable of quaint and fantastic shapes, some of them being so deeply cut round their bases by the action of the water that they presented the appearance of elegantly shaped flower-baskets fifteen or twenty feet high, the flowers being represented by candle-nut palms and Norfolk Island pines. The surface of these islands we found to be carved and worn into innumerable holes and crevices, separated from each other by knife-edges of rock which caused our boots to come to speedy grief; and in these holes we often found, huddled together, three, four, or five venomous water-snakes,[1] semi-comatose in the fervid tropical heat, so that we could drag them out by their flattened tails, and take them on board the yacht for examination. Real savages, with extraordinary bushy masses of hair on their heads, came off to us from the bright, sandy beaches; they knew nothing of money, and had to be paid in tobacco: the whole scene was just like a picture in Captain Cook. Going on shore, our wonder became even greater. To say nothing about strange trees and flowers, my shooting bag consisted of pigeons and flying-foxes, great fruit-eating bats which climb and scramble about the trees like monkeys, and fly as strong and as free as a pheasant. The pigeons were of three sorts. One large, almost as large as a hen pheasant, bronze and the most glorious purple; another, smaller, bright green with a yellow breast and tail, and a black and white ring round his neck; the third, smaller still, magenta and green— the loveliest little creature that I ever saw. The shells and fish were equally strange and beautiful; the latter were poisonous, and it was lucky for us that we found this out from the natives before we tried to eat them. But Lord! the coral reefs! It is of no use trying to describe their beauty. Look down through water, tenderest green, so transparent that the bottom can be seen at ten fathoms; look down on miles of the most exquisite corals and sea fans crimson, and mauve, and white, with fish cobalt blue, orange, purple, and emerald green, gliding and flashing in and out among them like great butterflies—and then—then you will fall far, far short of the reality. Oh, they are immeasurably more lovely than anything that I ever dreamt of!

We spent a fortnight at this wonderful Island of Pines, where the Norfolk Island pine grows side by side with the coco-nut tree; and then we went northward again till we came to a small island south

[1] *Hydrophis.* 'Every hole in which we found them had an easily ascendable talus on one side.'—Note to *The Field.*

of New Caledonia—a wild, bare mass of red and white volcanic rock with but very few trees on it, but what there were crowded with singing birds, some like the New Zealand tui, some like a small honey-bird. It was a desolate-looking place, but we had to stop there for water, so we got through the time as well as we could, scrambling about the coral-reef ridges and poking about for strange beasts and shells. I saw a sea anemone quite as large as my hat, and an innumerable variety of creatures that I had hard work even to give an approximate name to . . .

They reached Tahiti in August 1870, whence George wrote to his wife:

One of the canoe races was superb. Two huge, long canoes, in each forty or fifty men, twenty or more paddles a-side rising and falling in regular time, digging away for life, and in the bow a captain, dancing, yelling and stamping, and whirling his paddle round his head like a bedlamite drum-major. When it was all over, they lay under the stern of the French frigate, beating their paddles against the side of the canoes in time to the music of the band—a glorious row! But more glorious still was the singing of the 'Hymenès,' Hymns—forsooth! would that they sang such hymns in the little bethels—by the native choirs in the Governor's garden in the evening. It was a mixture of Usquikiah, sweet waters, and a Tyrolese singing meeting in the Jellah Thal: the perfect time, and the marvellous accuracy with which each individual took up his or her part, put me much in mind of the latter. It was a fairy scene: the hanging lanthorns of paper dotted about among the trees; the soft white of the graceful, clinging, unstarched dresses; the beautiful black hair, glossy and clean, of the women, encircled by wreath and coronets of bright yellow made of the dried leaves of the bananas, long strips of which many wore round their necks in the ancient manner. And then the music of 'the hymenès,' the perfect time, the perfect cadence, the strange humming bass (like the sound you hear when you 'listen' to a shell, magnified a thousand times), the wild high, long-drawn falsetto notes, the smiting together of hundreds of hands in perfect unison, all ending in a deep sigh! It was finer than all the songs of Arabs, than all the savage music that I've ever heard.

But I cannot tell you all the wonderful things we've seen—besides, some of them were not quite proper. The natives are happy, contented lotus-eaters. 'How do you Kanakers live?'—'Oh, we live in houses.' 'How do you get your living?'—'Oh, we play games.' They are far higher, far more beautiful, more graceful than the Maoris, and are bubbling over with life and good-humour and genuine kindliness. As you walk along, the great, strapping brown fellows will greet you with a smile and a cheerful 'Ya rana'='Good morning—God bless you. How I loves to see your 'andsome face.' They wear a loose white shirt, and a sort of kilt of blue or scarlet cotton wrapped round the loins, which is printed with all sorts of fantastic devices of their own imagining. They are as proud of their hair as the women, and wear it in much the same way. The women have long, loose muslin dresses reaching from the neck to the ankles, without any waist, and they arrange them in all sorts of coquettish manners as they walk, or rather trip along. Very pretty green and pink are the favourite colours, though pure white is very popular. Their hair, which is beautiful, glossy black, is carefully dressed with coco-nut oil, and they have head-dresses of bright yellow plantain or banana leaf, and sometimes a bunch of feathery stuff, which they get from the coco-nut palm, which is really prettier than any ostrich feathers I have ever seen. . . .

From Tahiti they proceeded to Eimeo, Tubuai with its innumerable terns and frigate-birds, and Samoa where they drank kava 'chewed by a beautiful princess' garlanded with crimson hibiscus flowers, and fished for palolo, a sea-worm which tasted like delicately dressed crab mixed with spinach. They made for Fiji, but disaster struck before they could reach port.

About nine o'clock Pembroke had gone to bed, and I was walking aft in the cabin when I felt the ship strike under my feet, the heaving with the blow. I called Pembroke, and we rushed on deck to see, but when we got there see we could not. The night was awful, the seas breaking over us, and when one bigger than usual came, it caught us up and threw us farther on the reef.

'We were, I must say, all of us as cool as cucumbers. We immediately lowered the boats, with much difficulty getting them over the side of the ship opposite to where the sea was breaking, where, though much knocked about, they were comparatively safe. Then there was nothing to do but to wait; and that waiting was not very pleasant, for we feared that we should be driven over the reef into deep water, where the ship would have gone down immediately. However, at last the sea seemed to lose its power, having driven us up as far as it could reach, and we went below. It was a miserable sight to see all our countless treasures hurling about in the cabin, and to hear the cracking and crashing of the poor old ship; but there was no help for it, and we did the best we could till daybreak. When that came we found that we had been thrown about one hundred and fifty yards over the reef, and that there were two small islands about a mile and a half from us. We soon landed on one, in no small fear of being eaten, but found that both of them were unhabited, though there were evident marks of past cannibal feasts. We rigged up a sail for a tent, lighted a fire, and did what we could, though the rain was coming down in absolute torrents. The boats went back to save what was left of the livestock and provisions, for we could find nothing eatable except one another; and then we rigged up more tents and took it easy. Here we had to stay for nine days. We were not quite sure where we were. The captain tried to take an observation when the sun gleamed out for a moment, but a great sea-bird settled suddenly on the top of his head. We were in constant dread of the natives, though, as it turned out afterwards, there was little fear of their disturbing us; but at last the weather moderated, and we took the boats, and after thirty hours, fortunately fell in with an English vessel which took us to Levuka. Coming down here, we ran on to another coral reef, and stuck there for twenty-four hours, but that was a mere picnic. It is a great pity losing our collections; they were really wonderful; but that cannot be helped, and we were lucky to escape with our lives. I certainly never expected to be playing Robinson Crusoe at my time of life, and believe me, my darling, it's much better fun in the book than it is in reality.

XXXVII

South Sea Bubbles

1872

The wreck of the Albatross *is described in greater detail by the Earl, whose impressions of the South Sea Islands were every bit as favourable as those of the Doctor; the only aspect he heartily condemned, apart from such annoyances as mosquitoes and biting ants, was the wreck of Polynesian gaiety and custom on the reef of missionary endeavour. He was even a bit equivocal about cannibalism, suggesting that it had been ended only by the introduction of pigs.*

Although the Earl and not the Doctor was the prime author of the book, some extracts follow which reinforce accounts of shared experiences, George no doubt added his own touches.

I can never forget the scene that burst upon my astonished and half-opened eyes as I turned out of bed one morning and found myself entering the port of Papiete. Great mountains, of every shade of blue, pink, grey, and purple, torn and broken into every conceivable fantastic shape, with deep, dark mysterious gorges, showing almost black by contrast with the surrounding brightness; precipitous peaks and pinnacles rising one above the other like giant sentinels, until they were lost in the heavy masses of cloud they had impaled; while below, stretching from the base of the mountains to the shore, a forest of tropical trees, with the huts and houses of the town peeping out between them.

The finest islands of the West Indies idealized, with a dash of Ceylon, is all I can compare it to. And the natives! How well they match the scene! The women, with their voluptuous figures,—their unique, free, graceful walk,—their nightgowns (for their dress is nothing but a long chemise, white, pale green, red, or red and white, according to the taste of the wearer, which is invariably good) floating loosely about in a cool refreshing manner,—their luxuriant black tresses, crowned with a gracefully plaited Araroot chaplet, and further ornamented by a great flowing bunch of white 'Reva-Reva,'—their delicious perfume of cocoa-nut oil (it is worth going to Tahiti for the smell alone),—and, above all, their smiling handsome faces, and singing, bubbling voices, full of soft cadences, —all this set off by the broken, scattered rays of green light shining through the shady avenues. Oh, that I were the artist that could paint it! What pleasant places those avenues are for a stroll in the evening, when the heat of the sun is beginning to die away. To meet the great, strapping, pleasant-looking men, in their clean white shirts and parti-coloured waistcloths, each greeting you, especially if you are English, with a ready smile and a hearty 'Ya rana!' which means all kinds of salutations and blessings; sometimes, even, if they like the look of you, stopping to shake hands, with no earthly object but kindly goodfellowship. I have seen even small piccaninnies stop in their infantine gambols, and toddling up with their little faces puckered into dimples, and their little puds held up to reach your fingers, pipe out a shrill 'How do you do?' And as for the young ladies! the most bashful and coy will never pass you without a greeting, a glance of the eyes, and a slight gathering in of her dress with her elbows to exhibit her buxom figure to full perfection. Or else perhaps she will come up coquettishly, and ask you for the loan of your cigar, take a few puffs at it, and hand it back again gracefully to the rather astonished owner; and then, with a parting compliment, which you most likely don't understand, let you go you way in peace—or *not*! I suppose it is a fault on the right side, but they are a trifle too amiable sometimes. The conduct of Mrs Potiphar would scarcely have excited a passing comment if she had been lucky enough to have lived in Tahiti.

The streets of Papiete at night are very pleasant and merry. The first night we arrived the doctor and I went for a stroll; and, following the run of the crowd, soon found ourselves in the principal grogshop street. There all was reckless jollity and good nature. Gangs of French sailors careering wildly to and fro, singing part-songs at the top of their voices, in capital time and tune, all the natives within hearing joining in; native men and girls sitting about doorsteps of the shops, or strolling up and down together, some romping, some spooney. By the bye, the proper way to walk with your lady-love in Tahiti is as follows. You put your arm round her neck, and she hers round your waist, and hangs on your breast in a limply affectionate manner. It is as much *selon les regles* was walking arm-in-arm, and is much prettier to look at. But the man should be tall, for to see a stumpy little French sailor clawed in this way by the big brown object of his affections is a thought ludicrous.

At last we came to a place where two streets crossed each other. Each corner house was a grogshop, where a lot of jolly Frenchmen were singing in chorus, a crowd of natives standing round and joining. Another knot was collected round the doctor, who was holding forth about European politics (the war between France and Prussia had just broken out) to a learned native, who translated all he said to the eager bystanders, while I was being addressed by a brown lady in her native language, which edified me exceedingly. Behind each bar the ideal French barman presided, with the sleeves of his dingy white shirt rolled up, brawny, bull-necked, black-haired, and shaven. Here and there an unmistakeable Yankee skipper might be seen amongst the mob, with an occasional English Jack, or Scotch storekeeper . . .

The lighted shops and stores surrounded by the beautiful trees, the gaily dressed girls, the rollicking sailors, the pleasant smell, the perfect cleanliness, the universal mirth, civility, and good nature of every one, the utter absence of quarrelling, jostling, or rudeness, made a very novel, picturesque, and pleasing night scene . . .

Things that would strike you anywhere else as wrong and degrading, seem somehow only natural and beautiful in those lovely islands . . .

By the way, those brutal flies are the only things that refuse to be Society Islandized. Under the most softening influences they still retain the tiresome energy and vulgar conceited obtrusiveness natural to their race. They are the Scotchmen amongst insects.

If you are wearied with the busy—I mean lazy—hum of men, you go out in a canoe on to the great coral reef that forms the harbour, and dabbling your hands and feet in the cool water, gaze dreamily down at the gorgeous sights beneath you: the beautiful coral, with its mysterious caves and fissures, from which you almost expect to see real water-babies appear; coral, some of it like great crimson fans woven from the most delicate twigs—some of a beautiful mauve or purple—some like miniature models of old gnarled trees—some like great round mounds of snow-white ivory, chased and carved with a superhuman delicacy—some like leaves and budding flowers—while all about are scattered magnificent holothuria and great red and yellow starfish, that look as if they were made of leather, with horn buttons stuck all along their feelers for ornament; and echini, with their dense profusion of long brown spikes, covering them so completely as to make an unlearned person like myself wonder how they can get at their food or mix in society. Still more beautiful when they are dead and their spikes are gone, and nothing remains but their round white skeletons, splendidly embossed in long lines with purple and pink knobs. Fish of every shape and colour swimming lazily in and out of the black-looking caves and fissures, or coasting round under the overhanging edges of the coral precipices. Some of the finest cobalt blue, some golden, some pink, some more like beautiful orange and purple butterflies than natives of the sea, with long white rat's rails, swimming or floating or floating frontways, sternways, sideways, with apparently equal ease and partiality. Some variegated like harlequins; many, not with their hues more or less blending into each other where they meet, like Christian fishes, but mathematically divided by regular distinct lines, as if they had paid for their colours, and had them laid on by the square inch . . .

When the nights are calm and dark, away go the natives to spear fish by torchlight. They use several kinds of weapons, according to the size of the prey they are hunting, but the ordinary spear is like a small metal broom, made of a lot of iron rods diverging outwards from the staff on which they are lashed, between which the little fish become jammed without being much injured. Silently your canoe glides over the coral reef through the clear shallow water, and you stand up with the torch in one hand and the spear in the other all ready for action. A blaze of light shines close to you and suddenly the figure of the bowman in some other craft becomes revealed like some splendid bronze statue, the torch lifted on high, the form bent slightly forward, the eyes intently fixed on the surface of the water, and the right arm raised to strike, while behind you dimly distinguish the black crouching figure of his comrade, noiselessly and almost without motion propelling and steering the long narrow piroque. Whish! Down drops the end of the torch—he's got one! So he has sure enough, for I hear the tap, tap of his spear against the side of the boat, and the squatter of the fish as he drops into the bottom of it. I see one! and make a desperate

lunge, whereby I lose my balance and topple over, luckily not overboard, dropping my spear into the water, on one side, and the
rather heavy reed torch on the other, which leaves us in utter darkness, in which I hear, not weeping and gnashing of teeth, but a
most unmistakeable gurgling and chuckling from my native companion usually the most polite and dignified of mortals ...

We strolled about the gardens all the evening, carefully stepping
over or picking our way between the numerous babies that were
scattered about the ground in such profusion as to make it very
difficult to walk without committing infanticide, receiving information from the civil naval men amongst whom we had already
an extensive acquaintance, and interchanging ready laughs and
symbolical compliments with the young ladies we were jammed
against in the crowd. They were so clean, graceful, good-humoured,
merry, that I would have defied the most sour-hearted Methodist
preacher to have kept up a cool dignity amongst them long. At one
time we were standing close to two of them, when one turned
round to the doctor with a smile, and asked him for his cigar. He
presented it with great civility, and the young lady, after a few
modest sucks, handed it back with the utmost grace. I grinned in
spite of myself, but the doctor made an elegant bow, and puffed
away coolly, saying that there was nothing like falling in with the
customs of the country. We soon got accustomed to this little
courtesy afterwards.

The Albatross *left Samoa on October 18, 1870, bound for Levrulra
in the Fiji Islands and then New Zealand. She approached Fiji in
deteriorating weather, and on October 21st she struck the reef.*

At about ten o'clock, as I was dozing off, I felt a sudden shock, a
terrible lurch, and long trembling grind. The doctor shouted to me
that we had struck, but it needed not that nor the cries on deck to
tell me what had happened. I rushed out of my cabin to get on deck,
when a heavier lurch and crash sent me slithering right across the
saloon under the table. I scrambled up again and made for the
companion, Mitchell appearing from his cabin with a hurried
'What's the matter?'

'You may say your prayers now' replied I with a ghastly grin,
'for the game's up with us.' We climbed on deck and found

ourselves in about as awe-inspiring a position as could well be imagined: the vessel lying almost on her beam-ends, the foam flying over her in a white cloud, every sea lifting her up and bringing her down again with a sickening crash, that made the cabin-floor heave like an earth-quake, and her whole frame tremble, the scream of wind sounding even above the roar of the surf, and all these horrors magnified by an intense darkness. The doctor and I said 'Good-bye;' indeed as that moment I don't think anybody but the skipper expected to live ten minutes.

Nor should we if the vessel had been deep laden, in which case she would have been crushed against the edge of the reef and sunk in deep water. As it was, every sea drove us further and further on to the coral.

The courage and steadiness shown by all hands was very striking. Braund (the master) behaved as he always does in times of danger, cheery voice ringing out above the infernal din, and his honest face lit up by a quiet smile whenever it became visible in the glare of the skylight. Tim Bougard (the mate) backed him up in a cool smart way, and the men did all that men could do. There was no confusion or unnecessary shouting; the boats were all got over to the leeside and made ready to be cut away at a moment's notice, a work of no small difficulty when the angle of the slippery decks and the perpetual jerks and plunges of the vessel are considered.

As far as my own feelings were concerned, I could not help being amused by noting that with all the awe of death, and wonder about what was to come was mixed a kind of sulky irritation at being turned out of my warm bed into the cold water, and a feeling of unutterable disgust at the destruction of all my knick-knacks and curiosities.

And when I succeeded in realizing the end that I thought was coming so soon, a host of old familiar faces from all parts of the world flitted swiftly before my mind, never so vividly remembered, and never perhaps better loved than at that moment, striking me with a sharp pang of sadness.

The skipper came up to us, and kindly and gently advised us to go below and get dry clothes while there was yet time. So down we went and sat talking at the foot of the companion, cheerfully enough all things considered, Mitchell and Warden (the steward) bustling about to the imminent danger of their bones to collect a few provisions and necessaries before everything was spoilt by the water that was fast filling the vessel.

Then an alarm came that we were being driven over the reef, and should sink on the other side, so we went on deck again, and waited, ready to take to the boats. Soon it was discovered that the water was quite shallow to leeward, so there was no fear of that particular danger. We went below again it being determined to stick to the vessel till daylight if possible, and felt quite cheery at the reprieve. It is wonderful how soon men *get accustomed* to being in danger, whether it is unconscious fatalism, or merely the natural carelessness of human nature I don't know. The saloon was now getting full of water, so we were obliged to cram outselves into Mitchell's little cabin up to windward, where we passed rather a terrible night, though we laughed and joked as much as we could to keep our spirits up.

Our prospects certainly were not pleasant; the ship could not hold together long, and we might have to go many miles in the strength of the gale in open boats before we could reach an island; and if we did happen to hit upon an inhabited one we should be nearly certain to be killed and eaten by the inhabitants.

It was a sad thing to hear the crashing and straining of an old ship, and the mournful toll of her bell overhead, and to see the decks opening and the bulk-heads breaking up inside her, with the chairs, books, clothes, mats, and a hundred odds and ends floating about the cabin. But every thing pathetic or tragical has a comical side to it, and I could not help laughing to see the steward scrambling about collecting various articles for preservation, and continually slipping up when a heavy jar came, and almost disappearing in the dirty water to leeward. To make it better he had my matches and their appurtenances, my pipes and tobacco in his pockets; their appearance when produced was rather 'mixed'.

Occasionally the skipper came down to report the state of affairs, or advise what should be provided, and though I know he was terribly cut up, he talked coolly and cheerily, and was very gentle and considerate. . . . Collecting provisions and necessaries, and longing for light, the weary hours passed away.

Oct. 22—At last the day broke, gloomy, wild, and wet, and we went on deck to find out our situation. About a mile to leeward of us on the same reef appeared a small island, and about half a mile from that a rather larger one; the vessel was lying about fifty yards inside the first break of the reef in about three feet of water.

The very heaviness of the sea had been our salvation, hurling us right up on to the coral ledge into comparative safety.

Then one by one the boats were sent off, laden with compasses, quadrants, guns, ammunition, provisions, blankets, &c. Joining company again clear of the breakers we made for the little island, thirteen men in all, and all ready to fight if necessary.

It was a little coral-sandy place about one hundred and fifty yards long, by 100 wide, with a steep beach, and a second step or terrace about thirty yards back, as if there had been a recent elevation.

We landed, and emptied the boats of their sodden and sloppy contents, and then by way of making things more thoroughly miserable, the rain came down in a black, hopeless, tropical torrent.

Depressed and exhausted as we were, it was certainly most wretched; we made a kind of shed out of the sail of the life-boat, and at last succeeded by means of a dead log and some tarred twine in making a fire, which improved matters a little; then every one except the doctor, Warden, Little Taff (cook's mate) and I, went off to the wreck to fetch the live stock, and save what they could. Meanwhile the doctor went exploring for water, which he didn't find, while I amused myself by trying to dry the blankets and clothes as they came ashore, rather a futile occupation. Taff got us some bacon and tea, which we ate ravenously.

As I lay down I seemed to feel the ground shaking and heaving under me. I thought it was an earthquake at first, so did the doctor, but we found it was nothing but imagination, produced by the continued jarring and shaking we had had all night.

I could also hear the voices of the men shouting above the roar of the surf, and several times the illusion was so strong that I went down to the beach, fancying the boats had come back from the wreck. At last they all returned, very tired, having brought ashore the livestock, sails, preserved meats, pots and pans, mattresses, meats, &c. After they had had some food, they rigged up two capital tents, a big one with the vessel's square sail, and a smaller one for the doctor and me, out of the topsail.

Louey, an ingenious little Noresman, chopped himself some sticks and made a splendacious bedstead to sling his mat to.

I have succeeded in saving my manuscripts, though they are rather damaged. 'Whatever anybody may say of your poems, none can call them *dry*,' remarked the doctor, with a grin.

Close to our camp is an old native 'Marai,' or place of sacrifice, formed of big flat coral-stones. A kind of rough line, about three feet wide, runs down the middle of it towards the sea, terminating in a *cul de sac*. The height of the chained posts on each side of it tells very plainly what has been hung to cook there. A most villainous looking hole! And a nice place for a lot of shipwrecked mariners to have within twenty yards of their camp; something like skulls and bones that the old hermits used to keep about them, to remind them of their end.

We can make out two islands in a west by south direction; one a low clump of trees, like the one we are on, and the other a high mountain, some thirty miles off.

Though we do not know yet exactly where we are, as no place in the chart answers exactly to the bearing of this island, there is no doubt that we are somewhere in the Ringgold islands, the most cannibalistic part of the Pacific. So we may think ourselves very lucky to have hit on an uninhabited place.

Great reefs stretch away in several directions as far as we can see; more dangerous water for navigation cannot be imagined.

It came on to pour again, but the skipper and his men rigged mats and boatsails round the bottom of our tent, and made us pretty snug. Nothing could be kinder and nicer than they all have been, and we are more grateful than we can say.

Made a capital dinner on chicken-slop, and soon turned in. Rained hard all night.

Oct. 23 Everyone discovered this morning that they were very much bruised and knocked about, a fact that they were quite unconscious of yesterday.

At low water most of the party went off again to the wreck, and brought off more things.

The skipper tried to get an observation, but was put out at the critical moment by a bird settling on his head. The only reef resembling this on the chart is a place called Nukumbasanga, in the extreme north-east of the Ringgold islands.

The poor old ship is breaking up, her lee side being raised two feet or more, and all the butts open enough to put your hand between.

Our plan at present is to wait for fine weather, determine our position, and run right away in the boats for Sevulsa, some one hundred and fifty miles; for if we are compelled to stop anywhere, we shall have to fight to avoid being eaten. We have got five guns, two axes, two revolvers, and five tomahawks, and I think all of us intend to take 'utu', as the Maories call it, for ourselves before knocking under ...

Oct. 24 It cleared a little in the morning, and the camp soon presented the appearance of a great washing establishment, every wettable article being hung out to dry. I went to get a dip in the sea when I met old Nelson, rushing violently through the bush in pursuit of an imaginary turkey (we have turned all out live stock loose on the island). Mitchell afterwards went out on the same quest, armed with a gun, wounded the turkey, and a pig in the nose, who disappeared squeaking, whereon Mitchell came back disgusted.

His appearance is rather wild; he has been working like a brick for the last three days, and has worn his knees sore with the friction of his wet breeches. So he sports a pair of 'pajamas' which he tucks up above his knees, and which, combined with a flannel shirt and a pair of Davy's boots unlaced, and about three sizes too large, give him an appearance of a cross between Robinson Crusoe and a brigand in a play.

Tim went off in the dingey and saved some more miscellaneous articles.

The captain got an observation today that makes him pretty sure we are on the Nukumbasanga reef, though it is quite misplaced on the chart.

Most of the company are rigged in my socks, which I should think would want tying up at the toes to make them fit.

In the afternoon a regular hunt after live stock, the skipper managing to shoot a pig. Killing the fowls for dinner is great fun: we go after them through the bush with long sticks, driving them towards each other, and making long sweeps at them whenever we get a chance, but the trees generally get in the way of the stick and the fowl scuttles away into the bush triumphantly, till at last some one makes a lucky shot and bowls him over.

At four o'clock it came on to pour heavily again.

This is miserable weather.

After dinner we went down to the big tent and had a talk. It would have made a splendid sketch in the flickering candlelight—the two long rows of men on each side, lying on their mats or bedding in every kind of position; some dozing, some smoking, talking, or reading old scraps of newspapers that had been saved by some chance, while in the centre were heaped up cases, guns, clothes, and all kinds of odds and ends.

There we turned in for the night; the skipper, who could not take more care of us if we were his own children, looking in to see that we were all right . . .

I feel as if I had been months in this place, and, strange to say, am getting quite contented with the life. I get up at day-break, and bathe; then, if it is not raining hard, pick up shells and so on till breakfast. After that smoke pipes, read Shelley, write up my log, help to hang up the clothes to dry, and take them in again drenched half an hour after; then luncheon; then more pipes, and a stroll round the beach to study the habits of terns, or throw stones at them; then dinner, and cards or a chat in the big tent. When I want exercise I go and chop down a tree. But where's the romance of this kind of thing? Unless you call it romantic to hear the terns screaming on the other side of the island in the middle of a dark wet night, and to creep through the bush towards the place where they are crying, expecting to find a canoe full of hungry, murderous savages, just landed, with the head chief serving out sherry and bitters to give them an appetite for supper.

Well, there is a certain grim pleasure, certainly, on such occasions, in grasping a tomahawk or a revolver, and thinking of the life you will take as payment before you give up your own. But that is a selfish, avaricious feeling, not worthy of the name of romance.

It strikes me more and more forcibly every day, how strangely cool and fearless men get when they have been placed for a while in a desperate situation. We all of us know, I suppose, what we have got to go through in making our escape—fatigue, exposure, misery and danger, for thirty or forty hours on end at the shortest, and an indefinite time if the wind comes ahead, besides the prospect of certain death if it comes on to blow hard. And yet no one seems funky, and we are all longing to make this attempt. The main reason for this is the almost superstitious confidence we have got in the courage and resources of the skipper, who is one of those men created especially to lead others. We all feel that he will bring us safe through if it is possible, and if not, we can but die once . . .

By three o'clock the boats were all loaded and ready for a start. The men very naturally wanted to save all their things; the consequence of which was that the fish-fag and lifeboat were filled with lumber even above the thwarts, and, with their crew of five men each, were almost down to the water's edge at every little lurch, by no means a proper trim to go one hundred and fifty miles through open sea, tide rips and perhaps breakers.

However, we didn't like to throw away anything till it was absolutely necessary; so as soon as the dingey, that had been used to bring off the cargoes of the other boats from the shore, was ready, the sails were set, anchors weighed, and with the lifeboat as commodore leading the way, we crossed the reef and bid farewell to Nukumbasanga . . .

An awful night it was! hour after hour pulling and baling in a rough broken sea, wet to the skin and tired to death. Listening nervously for the roar of the surf, watching the black masses of water as they charged our bows and shut out the dim horizon, and gazing up anxiously at each cloud as it rose and hid the stars.

'What a precious scrape we are in!' I kept thinking. 'I wonder if we shall be living still two days hence? I always used to complain that I never met with any adventures in my travels, but this business will set me up in that line for some time if I get out of it alive.' And then again a ghostly procession of old faces and places passed before me, with an intense vividness and reality in their perfect love and happiness, that seemed like some bitter devilish mockery.

A feeling of want of sympathy is the mainspring of human misery. In joy and in sorrow the stars twinkle, the wind blows, and the sea moans alike. And then from the depths of a man's soul rises the cry that has been the origin of so many great religions: 'Oh, God! give me a sign that I may know that I am not utterly lonely and forsaken' . . .

At last the day began to break, and as soon as it was light we got the other boats alongside, and served out their biscuits, brandy, and water. Such a pale woe-begone set of wretches as we looked in the morning light I never saw. Fashionable young ladies after a heavy ball at the end of the season were nothing to it. I believe we would all have sold our birthrights for a cup of hot tea.

We found that we were literally on the reefs, the water being quite shallow, but it did not break anywhere as far as we could see: this accounted for the nasty short sea we had noticed all night . . .

The little boat made capital weather of it, and the Fish-fag did pretty well; but the lifeboat was so heavily loaded that she could scarcely rise to the sea, and took it first over the weather quarter and then over the lee gunwale, in a most unpleasant style.

The doctor, who had had his spell at the oar, went fast asleep, in spite of the continual sluices of cold water, which were scarcely enough to keep me awake, as I was steering, though I had done no pulling in the night.

We passed right over the long chain of reefs, there being no actual break on them that we could see, but soon got into a very nasty tide-rip that we were very glad to get out of again, with the boats in such a trim.

In about five hours we had run pretty close to Kamai, and then, being assured of our position, we made all sail before the wind for the north point of Tavinni, whose great heavy-clouded mountains began to grow distinct. There we managed to get something to eat and drink, and though the chicken was strongly flavoured by the various articles it was jammed against in the locker, and the biscuits were steamy and inhabited by cockroaches, we felt much more lively after it . . .

Another sip of brandy, to give us a gallop for the land, for our troubles were nearly over. And then away we went, and a precious pull we had: the tide was against us strong, and the deep laden boats seemed as heavy as lead to our weary muscles. When, at last, we got alongside, and found ourselves on the deck of the vessel, I could scarcely stand from cramp and fatigue. The passengers looked curiously over the bulwarks at the strange boat procession, each laden with such an extraordinary cargo of nations. And well they might stare, for we certainly were not pretty to look at.

Our clothes had been dirty and drenched with salt and fresh water for nine days on end: our arms and faces were of the colour of a boiled lobster, with the skin peeling off them—my nose, in particular, being literally raw;—our eyes fearfully bloodshot, our lips cracked and bleeding—altogether, an imaginative man might have taken us for a gang of over-worked firemen, from the infernal regions, coming up to get fresh air. However, they were all very obliging and kind, one old gentleman in particular, who provided us with blankets, &c. to sleep on.

The sun was just setting as we reached the vessel, and we soon sat down to a capital tea, with butter and real bread! My word!— as they say in the colonies. Oh, the pleasure I experienced that night in hearing the pouring rain, and knowing it could not get at me.

And so this unpleasant adventure came to a happy conclusion.

XXXVIII

Sport in North America
1870-5

Between 1870 and 1875 George accompanied the Earl of Dunraven, who like Lord Pembroke became a close friend, on several sporting expeditions to northern Canada and the United States, in the course of which, according to his daughter, 'they shot not only moose in the forests of Acadia, but also every kind of living thing that is regarded on the Western Continent as being legitimately shootable, with the solitary exception of their fellow men'. As usual he kept no journal, but in occasional letters to his wife, and in almost illegible notes found by his daughter, recorded some of his experiences.

First, a moose hunt in northern Canada.

The ground is carpeted in such a manner as to throw the delicately designed carpets of the East into almost blatant vulgarity. A little farther on groups of stunted pines, decked with greenish gray pendant Spanish moss, waving weirdly in the evening breeze, backed by still loftier conifers, interspersed with the white skeletons of dead forest monarchs, victims of the bush fires, standing out against the gold and crimson and pink and purple of the evening sky with a sharpness and a clearness unknown in more southern climes. Press through the swamp, where grows the strange Indian cup and divers things which seem more suited to a tropical than to a sub-arctic flora; crush through the interlacing fir branches as you follow the narrow, devious moose track, and out on to the inexpressibly lovely carpentry of the barren, with its unending wealth of lichens and mosses, into which your moccasined feet press ankle deep; cross the swamp again, where the greenery rises, thick as air, on every side, and out on to 'the hard wood ridge,' where the tall, slender birches show their ash gray stems in endless colonnades, and the 'windows' cut by the fierce, narrow blasts are as sharply defined as though made by the stroke of some vast civilized missile, and you are in the loved home of the giant moose, the grandest of all the bone-horned creatures.

There are some moose bulls who do not utterly refuse to listen to the voice of the charmer, but who take as little notice of its as suits their purpose, and, oddly enough, these are usually young moose bulls. It is your old moose bull who comes up bravely to the tootlings of a dirty rogue of an Indian and gets himself shot, poor fellow, for his pains—the older the fool, the bigger the fool, if indeed it be folly. My last moose was one of these wise youths, and we called him, from our little clump of bushes at the edge of the forest 'barren', from dewy eve all through the moonlit hours till dawn, and called him, but in vain. My Micmac friend (a gluttonous villain who had only killed two people in cold blood, and wore strings on his pantaloons where buttons should have been) discoursed the sweetest music that ever was heard in moosedom. He climbed up a little tree, and sat there 'wouking' as gently as any sucking dove; he climbed down his little tree and shoved his nose into the bushes close to the ground and 'wouked' 'an't were any nightingale'; he 'roused the night out with a catch,' and the night revenged himself by uttering a demoniacal yell that nearly sent the heart of me through the soles of my moccasins; he was yearning, he was reproachful, he was coaxing, he languished in despair, but that wily young moose bull would not face the open. We could hear him, away there in the dark forest, dashing his horns against the branches, swaggering around, rampaging, and 'raising h-ll generally,' as they say 'out West,' but he would *not* take the open; and at last we got bored of uttering our blandishments, and in the earliest morning— how cold it was sitting there like a hot-house flower in a florist's window! the night is coldest, not darkest, before the dawn—we determined to challenge him to mortal combat. Choking with rage, we uttered the most defiant snorts, drew our fragile birch-bark trumpet across the stem of a dead pine to simulated the sharpening of mighty antlers, and smashing twigs to impress him with an adequate idea of our matchless force and prowess, to show him that we were a rival worthy of his horn—but he came not . . .

As neither love not war suited our friend, our hand was played out, and, reckless of the consequences, we lighted a little fire, so small that you might have put it into a breakfast cup, and heated a little drop of tea, and then wended our way campward, cold, stiff, and disconsolate, in the dawning. What a cowardly brute a bull moose must feel to be afraid of a doctor, not even in his professional capacity, and a dirty rogue of an Indian with strings on his pantaloons where the buttons ought to be!

'Wh-e-ww!' What a soft, low, thrush-like whistle to the left of me! Trained so well long ago in dear old Sutherland to drop to the faintest whisper, I settle down silently into the bog, which receives with a clammy, chill embrace, and gently, ever so gently, turn my head to catch the direction of Noel Glode's extended finger. Through the haze I peer across the 'barren,' and, saints and snakes! there, two hundred yards away, black as midnight, gigantic as all outside, just sneaking out as 't were from the dense growth of young pines, is the great bull moose, slowly turning his ponderous head, with its massive, palmated, whitish brown horns and 'prehensible muzzle,' to right, to left, as he warily gazes around him. Aha! my artful one, if you had come out in the moonlight I might have missed you for want of light. If you had charged me in the bush I might have missed you from—Two hundred, Noel? Crack! Missed! Nose thrown up. A moment's pause. Crack! Slap! Habet! and he's gone! The wall of greenery hath devoured him! Gone, and shut the door after him, it seems, so utterly is all trace of his passage instantly erased by the closing branches. After him we go! Noel points at a black mass under the birches. I fire, hit it, and am none the better for expending a bullet on a rotten log. But the shot awakens the echoes, and something more. What a plunging and a crashing to the right! Our moose, in a temper or dying. 'Let us sit and wait a bit while he bleeds and cools and stiffens'—bless us! how brutal it looks on paper—say I. 'No!' squawks the Indian. 'We lose him in the hardwood!' Against my will, I advance into the thicket. What a stamping and a floundering! And what a rush as we near the noise! Away he goes! Away to the *Ewigkeit*! Adieu, my moose! My Indian! 'I told you so, most miserable of Micmacs. There goes eight hundred pounds of moose meat to rot in some horrible swamp—a useless death . . .'

Try, and try hard we must, for the ridges are stony, and swamps are 'poached' by innumerable crossings and recrossings of tracks, more or less recent, of wandering cows and bulls. What a difficult piece to puzzle out is this, where the gray limestone crops out from the soft green bog, with only a moss-filled cranny here and there, or a bit of Capettarie, with its dainty pink stems broken and its dark green leaves crushed, to show where the sharp-edged hoof has passed. Is that blood? No, not moose blood, at least, only the blood of Adonis, wept for by apricot-cheeked Syrian women long ago and far away, staining the anemone leaves. On, on, squelching through the oozy morasses, scrambling over the smooth, damp rocks, through the dense thickets, over the slippery logs, hopelessly hoping on. No large drop on stone or twig smeared off from the wound as the mighty beast passed by. No sign of hope, except that the position of the rare hoof-marks shows that our quarry is walking slowly, not going at his natural swinging trot, careless in his strength, scattering the black peat over the green moss as he goes, but that he is walking slowly perforce. And see now! how widespread the prints of those giant hoofs, expanding under the weight of the dying mass, which the faltering legs strive to the last to support, like the failing knees and ankles of that dying gladiator, the real not the false one, at Naples. Indians are the most marvellous trackers in the world. Are they? I would rather have an Australian black fellow with me now than the keenest-sighted Rouge that ever wore moccasins. Still on, I watching the bushes for a glimpse of the great head, Noel watching the track; and he touches me with one hand, and almost touches the dead moose with the other.

Poor fellow! there he lies, so quiet, so calm, perfectly composed in every limb, almost graceful now just as the warm life died out of him, without spasm or struggle. What a strange look of ironical, sarcastic resignation there is in those deep cup lips, drawn up at the corners by the last thought that passed through the subtle brain!

From Fort William, a Hudson's Bay Company post, they crossed part of Lake Superior to reach the mouth of the Mackenzie river. Already caribou were getting scarce, and the trout fishing proved disappointing; but the lakes and forests were magnificent. Travelling by wagon and canoe they proceeded to Lake Katchibone, Lac-de-Mille Lacs, Lac-la-Croix 'bright with birch trees', Racing Lake where they saw 'a great pow-wow of Indians', to Fort Frances, Lake of the Woods and so to Fort Gary, with 'a wooden town, Winnipeg, growing up round it'.

In the infant Chicago, Lord Dunraven saw a splendid Wapiti head, and could scarcely wait to bag a better one. Off he went with George to Nebraska, where the American garrison at Fort MacPherson supplied them with a guard to protect them from Indians while they hunted up the Platte river, killing 'elk, white-tail and black-tail deer, antelope, swans, immense geese, ducks, and small game without count'. To his wife he wrote in November, year unknown:

This elk running is perfectly magnificent. We ride among the wild sand hills till we find a herd, and then gallop after them like maniacs, cutting them off, till we get in the midst of them, when we shoot all that we can. Our chief hunter is a very famous man out West, one Buffalo Bill. To see his face flush, and his eyes 'shoot out courage'—as his friend and admirer Texas Jack says—*is* a sight to see, and he cheers us on till he makes us as mad as himself. One day he and I had seven elk on the ground at once, of which number he credited me with three, not bad for a beginner. These elk are really the great Wapiti which you and the children have seen so often at the zoo. The herd out of which we got our greatest number contained quite a hundred and thirty, a most splendid sight. A few days later we saw another herd of at least twice that number. It is absolutely impossible to describe the grandeur of their rush as they go thundering along. Despite the great hardships and the very rough work the sport has quite repaid me. We four, Lord Dunraven, Buffalo Bill, Texas Jack, and I, killed fifteen elk on this trip. We also saw wild horses, but, of course, did not hunt them. Soon after our return we fitted out again and went south for buffalo. We only found two, both of which we killed, Lord Dunraven one, I the other.

November 16th—The gale has blown itself out and the day is lovely, though intensely cold, but with plenty of blankets we shall do very well, though soldier's tents are hardly the sort of thing for this climate. I suppose that people would be considered mad at home were they to leave their houses in the coldest mid-winter and betake themselves to tents for a fortnight together; but here, where every man is a soldier or a hunter, no one thinks anything about it. We have a quaint sort of stove which keeps us warm as long as it is in, but as we have to turn out of our blankets into the cold half a dozen times a night to keep it going, it is a question whether it is a great advantage. We are up long before daybreak and in bed at

333

seven. One comfort is, that this cold will keep the Indians quiet, but next spring they expect a big war, particularly about the North Pacific Railroad, which runs right through their hunting grounds. After all, one cannot be surprised at the poor wretches fighting; they depend wholly on the buffalo for food, and the railway and its consequent settlers will soon drive them away for ever. Quite lately these grand rolling plains were black with buffalo, and the Indians lived in abundance, now we are considered lucky to have killed two . . .

In notes jotted down at the time he described Buffalo Bill (William Cody), with one or two others of his kidney 'the only men who can cope with the nimble, quick-witted Indian . . . who know every double turn of his subtle, twisty and turny mind, and hunt him as a nobler species of game, in whose killing there is infinite credit'.

Buffalo Bill, as to face and feature, is a noble Vandyke stepped from its frame. Oh! that I had the pen of a lady-novelist to describe his manly charms! Half hidden by their long black fringes, his large, lustrous eyes so full of slumbering fire, which flashes into flame in moments of excitement—Jack says that you can 'see the courage shooting out of 'em,' when he's charging Indians—his firm sensitive mouth, his delicately moulded chin, covered, yet not concealed by a pointed beard of silky brown untouched by scissors, his pale morbidezza complexion, and glory of glories, his magnificent hair, sweeping in natural curves over his strong, square shoulders, on which the marble column of his neck is poised with the grace of an Antinous—aha! that's the man I think! . . . one of the handsomest and the best built men I have ever seen. As for his manners, they are as perfect as those of the Vandyke would have been. I have never met with a more thorough gentleman, quiet, calm, and self-possessed, full of memories of strange adventures, yet never thrusting them too prominently forward, but telling them with a quiet earnestness which gives to them a far greater reality than any highly-wrought description could possibly give. No wonder he has become a western hero. Sudden he is, I fear, and quick in quarrel, and when aroused he shoots straight, as the nearest town can testify, but what then? His life or theirs! . . .

Buffalo Bill has two styles of dress: the first, which is the one which he usually wears in the Settlements, is of beautifully dressed buckskin, decorated with fringes and lappets innumerable, and gorgeous beyond description, but, as he well knows, worse than useless in the plains; then he being a member of the House of Representatives of his State, thinks fit to assume, at times, a civilian and civilized garb—short black jacket, black pants, and thin kid side-spring boots, which makes him look like the aforesaid Vandyke nobleman trying to disguise himself as a steamboat steward. For some inscrutable reason he delighteth to hunt in this peculiar rig, adding thereto, however, a white Texan sombrero, which, when the leaves thereof are tied tightly down by a handkerchief knotted under his chin, assumes a prudish and poke-bonnet-like appearance which entirely unprepares you for the noble face and flashing eyes which suddenly appear at the end of its tunnel when he turns the apparatus end on towards you. By the way, the first time that I met Bill and Texas Jack—they had just been burnt off the prairies and were thirsty—they were both attired in fringed buckskin trousers and black velveteen shooting jackets of the real old keeper cut—I often wondered what became of those said jackets, I never saw them again. Were they taken off in a little difficulty and 'smushed' by the gentlemanly barman, or how? Do tell!—Of the many marvellous deeds done by Buffalo Bill, it is not for me to write; are they not all related, more or less badly, in the dime novels beloved by western men? I have only to say that he got his title when killing buffalo for the Kansas Pacific Railroad, when it was his custom to bring in a buffalo's tongue for every cartridge which he took out with him . . .

Indian hunting is, in fact, the real profession of both Jack and Bill, they being retained as trackers, aye, as fighters too, in the case of horses being run from the neighbourhood of the Fort; though, from time to time, they are put in charge of a band to see that it does not exceed the limits of its Reservation, and to lead it out to the hunt as a shepherd leadeth his flock to the pasture. They have the strangest feelings about Indians, these two. Though, when on the war path, they would no more hesitate to shoot down an Indian off his Reservation, than they would hesitate to throw a stone at a felonious chipmunk, they have a sympathy and a tenderness towards them infinitely greater than you will find among the greedy, pushing settlers, who regard them as mere vermin who must be destroyed for the sake of the ground on which depends their very existence. But these men know the Indian and his almost incredible wrongs, and the causes which have turned him into the ruthless savage that he is, and often have I heard men of their class say that, before God, the Indian was in the right, and was only doing what any American citizen would do in his place. It is not so much that the intentions of the U.S. Government are not good, as it is that the manner in which they are carried out is extremely evil. The men who are told off as Indian agents are notorious for their wholesale peculations, and for the riches which they amass; and the wretched native, driven to desperation, and knowing that death is certain, chooses to meet it in his own way, and make it as sweet as he can with revenge. Buffalo Bill and Texas Jack have the same feelings for Indians that the true sportsman has for game, 'they love them, and they slay them.' They admit that in many respects they resemble human beings, but hold that they are badly finished, their faces looking as if they had been chopped out of red-wood blocks with a hatchet, and say that they must never be trusted, friendly or unfriendly, and that they must be shot if they will steal horses. I remember once shooting a swan, the leader of a party of five, two old and three young ones, and sending one of the men to recover it. He came back to me in quite a melancholy state, and told me that the cry of its mate had made him feel so sad, 'the poor thing was a-mourning so.' Yet this good fellow would describe his shootings of Indians as coolly as if he were describing a shot at a rabbit, and would have heard the death shrieks of squaw and warrior with equanimity, if not with pleasurable excitement . . .

George and his companions returned several times to the Western plains and the Rocky Mountains. His letters, nearly all undated, continued sporadically to reach the small, and perhaps at times forlorn, house in Highgate, telling of arduous adventures, narrow escapes and stoic endurances. George was undoubtedly the most muscular, if the least Christian, of the three brothers.

FORT MACPHERSON, 9th November

We have had a long hunt, at least thirty days in the saddle, which has brought me down as fine as a stax and as strong as wire. Our hunting was not so good as last year, however, as the prairie fires have swept the whole country. Where then we found beautiful grass and tall trees is now a black, arid wilderness; desert is not the right word for it, the desert is infinitely varied and beautiful in comparison to a burnt prairie. We had to ride one day at a hard-gallop to get through; the wind blew half a gale, and whirled the burnt grass and sand about to such an extent as to make it almost impossible to face it . . .

Tell the learned one that rattlesnakes have been quite plentiful this year; in fact, we have been obliged to be very careful in our deer-stalking on foot. They 'whizz' quite sharply, but more slowly, not up and down, but in lateral coils, turning the head first one way and then another, not raised more than an inch or two above the ground, watching for an opportunity to strike. But they are slow, stupid brutes and do not strike at any distance. When on horseback, one can put them down with the butt of the rifle and pull the rattle off the tail with one's free hand. The last rattle near the body is always black, as if filled with coagulated blood. The rattles have evidently nothing to do with the spine, but are altered scales, just as the rhinoceros horn is altered hair . . .

The country is indescribably black and dreary; under the moon-light—we started at four in the morning yesterday—the effect was strange and artificial to a degree, looking more like some queer, exaggerated stage effect than a natural reality. A year of two more of this burning and hunting will be done in this part of the world. Good-bye, I am dead tired, we were in the saddle at four in the morning and only reached here at four in the afternoon.

In Salt Lake City they were 'snowed up among the Mormons' in December but, after hunting in the Rockies under conditions of extreme cold, found one of America's best cooks, and best wine cellars, in a hotel in Denver. 'I hope that we have done with Indians now,' wrote George. 'I really fear that they will have to be wiped out if they will not settle and be civilized—and they won't ! . . . poor brutes, they are great ruffians, but the majority of whites with whom they come in contact are quite as bad, so they improve one another.'

In 1874 they were on the Yellowstone hunting bears but 'though we have been in a country swarming with grizzly bears we have only killed one'. In October he wrote from Wyoming:

THE KINGSLEYS

We only reached the railroad last night after a most toilsome journey of nearly a thousand miles, principally on horseback; and very glad I am to get a few days' quiet, the first I have had for two months, and the last I am likely to have for some time, for soon, I suppose, we shall be off again, away to the mountains, now covered with snow and ice, to sleep in buffalo robes and endure all manner of hardships. We saw the geysers, but they are so very marvellous that it is hard to describe them . . .

I can't tell you all that we've done since I wrote last. We have been reduced to trout more than once; and though they are very fine and beautiful to look at, the trout in these parts are precious poor eating . . .

We talk of going straight east to Quebec to hunt caribou in snow shoes; as we have neither of us had a pair on in our lives, and know as much about them as we do about the astrolabe, I don't see very well how this is to be accomplished, but I suppose we shall try. If we can walk on snow shoes we can, if we can't walk on snow shoes we can't.

Good-bye, I am pretty well tired, having only reached this place at five in the morning after travelling, night and day, across an awful country.

In the depths of winter they hunted wild sheep in the snow-deep Rockies and fished for trout by first cutting through two feet of ice.

. . . we crouched just like so many big frogs, each one over his own hole, with a short stick and a bit of string, bobbing for the trout, who came up and stared at us, and gasped, and blew bubbles at us in the funniest manner. We caught scores; but it was horribly cold, the trout froze stiff as soon as they were pulled out, and the lines were covered with ice every few minutes, so that we had to roll them under our feet to break it off. It was too cold for bears; there were lots of them in the mountains, but they don't like the cold any more than I do.

But summer came, with glorious wildflowers and a temperature of 90 degrees in the shade. They were still hunting 'big horn' at an altitude that made George 'quite sick and giddy, but we got our sheep'.

In Denver, Colorado, in 1874, he unexpectedly encountered his

338

brother *Charles*, and treated him for pleurisy. After several years spent wandering about the West in conditions that must have proved taxing to a man of fifty or so, the two companions made their way south. In Florida, George caught sawfish and wrote a letter to The Field in praise of their family affections. In Louisiana he shot snipe, 'that sweetest of all singing birds. What are all the bubbling and the gugglings of any number of nightingales in the almond blossomed thickets of Arbana to his melodious 'Skape! scape! scape!"?' And the 'beautiful, sharp-tailed, creamy willow grouse' among the cedars— 'how red and bright his blood looks on the frozen snow!'

And so 'I wander, always did, and always will as long as there is a new bit of world to see'—and he might have added, another animal to stay. Lord Dunraven went home, but George continued to Newfoundland, then was heard of in Cape Colony, went round the world again revisiting Australia and New Zealand, and looked in on Japan; but 'none of these things', observed his daughter, 'was considered by him to be more than a mere stroll . . . He enjoyed them all, in a way, just as he enjoyed most things that did not involve life in a town, or noise; these he hated with a great cordiality.'

XXXIX

Finis

When he returned to his base at Highgate he found his wife in poor health, and the house noisy; try as she would, his daughter could not keep her fighting cocks from crowing under his study window, and their one and only servant, 'old Mrs Barrett', tried just as vainly to avoid falling downstairs with her dustpan, pail and brushes. To cap it all, Mary possessed herself of a tin of gunpowder her father was keeping in his study and, 'desirous of seeing how military mines worked', blew up a tub of liquid manure over the 'great spring blanket-wash' hanging on the line.

In the hope of improving Mrs Kingsley's health, in 1879 they moved to Bexley Heath in Kent. These hopes were disappointed and they moved again to Cambridge, where Mary's brother Charles was reading law at the University. Although Mary adored her father, even worshipped him, she was convinced that it was his long absences, his deliberate seeking-out of danger, and all the anxieties suffered over the years, that caused her mother's ill-health. 'Her mind was kept in one long nervous strain which robbed her of all pleasure in life outside the sphere of her home duty and the companionship of books.'

In the house in Mortimer Road, Cambridge, George Kingsley assembled his vast collection of notes, books, specimens and manuscripts: enough, Mary said, to fill volumes on a wide range of topics such as early English literature, Semitic tradition and 'the idea involved in sacrificial rites', concerning which Mary had for many years been collecting information and translating from the German. 'He did not consider it sufficiently complete for publication' and Mary did not care to 'make him responsible for it' in its incomplete form after his death.

Now at last his wanderings seemed to be over. Rheumatism troubled him. He took to watching cricket. His brilliant conversation, a mind that was 'a perfect treasure-house of learning', attracted many friends. Then a winter spent in Suffolk to look after the patient of an old friend and fellow-doctor brought on an attack of rheumatic fever which damaged his heart. Nursed back to health by his wife, to the detriment of her own, and by his daughter, he spent his convalescence once more going round the world. But the therapeutic magic of wandering had gone. On the morning of February 5, 1892, Mary Kingsley, who had been sitting up all night with her mother 'as usual', found her father dead in bed. She was thankful that he had been spared pain or prolonged illness; he had gone to bed 'rather better than usual, making plans to visit Lord Sandwich next day'. Six weeks later, Mrs Kingsley died.

At his death there passed away, Mary wrote, 'a strangely fascinating man, gifted with insight and sympathy'; a man whose mind, 'tolerant, scholarly and humourous', was stored with facts that might never again be assembled; a man who all his life, in the face of great temptations, 'never did a mean act or thought a mean thought, and never felt fear'. Of all the notes and manuscripts, the esoteric knowledge, nothing remains but a single volume of sketches and part-letters; his transient immortality lay in the memories of the many friends who loved and survived him. The Puritan conscience which drove his brothers to constant toil, the ambition which spurred them, seems in George to have been wholly lacking; content to enjoy life in his own peculiar way, to enjoy above all the beauties of the earth where man had not sullied them, evidently made him, as his daughter opined, the happiest of the three brothers.

INDEX

INDEX

INDEX